GENDER AND ELECTIONS, SECOND EDITION

This new edition describes the role of gender in the American electoral process through the 2008 elections. Tailored for courses on women and politics, elections, and gender politics, it strikes a balance between highlighting the most important developments for women as voters and candidates in the 2008 elections and providing a deeper analysis of the ways that gender has helped shape electoral politics in the United States. Individual chapters demonstrate the importance of gender in understanding presidential elections, voter participation and turnout, voting choices, the participation of African American women, congressional elections, the support of political parties and women's organizations, candidate communications with voters, and state elections. This updated volume also includes new chapters that analyze the roles of Latinas in U.S. politics and chronicle the candidacies of Hillary Clinton and Sarah Palin.

Susan J. Carroll is professor of political science and women's and gender studies at Rutgers University and senior scholar at the Center for American Women and Politics of the Eagleton Institute of Politics. She is author of *Women as Candidates in American Politics* (2nd ed., 1994) and editor of *The Impact of Women in Public Office* (2001) and *Women and American Politics: New Questions, New Directions* (2003).

Richard L. Fox is associate professor of political science at Loyola Marymount University. His research examines how gender affects voting behavior, state executive elections, congressional elections, and political ambition. He is the author of *Gender Dynamics in Congressional Elections* (1997) and coauthor of *Tabloid Justice: The Criminal Justice System in the Age of Media Frenzy* (2nd ed., 2007). He is also coauthor, with Jennifer Lawless, of *It Takes a Candidate: Why Women Don't Run for Office* (Cambridge University Press, 2nd ed., 2010).

Gender and Elections

SHAPING THE FUTURE OF AMERICAN POLITICS

Second Edition

Edited by

Susan J. Carroll
Rutgers University

Richard L. Fox
Loyola Marymount University

DAMAGED

CAMBRIDGE
UNIVERSITY PRESS

CAMBRIDGE UNIVERSITY PRESS
Cambridge, New York, Melbourne, Madrid, Cape Town, Singapore,
São Paulo, Delhi, Dubai, Tokyo

Cambridge University Press
32 Avenue of the Americas, New York, NY 10013-2473, USA

www.cambridge.org
Information on this title: www.cambridge.org/9780521734479

First published 2006
Second edition published 2010

Printed in the United States of America

A catalog record for this publication is available from the British Library.

Library of Congress Cataloging in Publication data

Gender and elections : shaping the future of American politics / edited
by Susan J. Carroll, Richard L. Fox. – 2nd ed.
    p.   cm.
Includes bibliographical references and index.
ISBN 978-0-521-51820-8 (hardback) – ISBN 978-0-521-73447-9 (pbk.)
1. Women in politics – United States.   2. Elections – United States.
3. Voting – United States.   4. Women political candidates – United
States.   5. Sex role – Political aspects – United States.   I. Carroll, Susan
J., 1950–   II. Fox, Richard Logan.   III. Title.
HQ1236.5.U6G444   2010
320.082 – dc22   2009025165

ISBN 978-0-521-51820-8 Hardback
ISBN 978-0-521-73447-9 Paperback

Contents

List of Figures, Text Boxes, and Photos

Figures

Text Boxes

Photos

List of Tables

Acknowledgments

This volume had its origins in a series of three roundtable panels at professional meetings in 2002 and 2003 focusing on how women fared in the 2002 elections. Most of the contributors to this book were participants on those roundtables. As we gathered at these professional meetings, we began to talk among ourselves about a major frustration we faced in teaching courses on women and politics, campaigns and elections, and American politics. We all had difficulty finding suitable, up-to-date materials on women candidates, the gender gap, and other facets of women's involvement in elections, and certainly, none of us had been able to find a text focused specifically on gender and elections that we could use. We felt the literature was in great need of a recurring and reliable source that would first be published immediately following a presidential election and then updated every four years so that it remained current.

At some point in our discussions, we all looked at one another and collectively asked, "As the academic experts in this field, aren't we the ones to take on this project? Why don't we produce a volume suitable for classroom use that would also be a resource for scholars, journalists, and practitioners?" In that moment *Gender and Elections* was born. We are enormously grateful to Barbara Burrell for organizing the first of our roundtable panels and thus identifying and pulling together the initial core of contributors to this volume.

We produced the first volume of *Gender and Elections* in the immediate aftermath of the 2004 presidential election. Gratified by the positive response, we are pleased to provide this updated and expanded version that includes information through the 2008 elections. We hope to continue to revise and publish new editions following future presidential elections.

We have added two new chapters to this edition, reflecting important developments in American electoral politics. In recognition of the growing significance of Latinos in U.S. politics, a chapter on the political role of Latinas seemed a necessary addition, and we were delighted when Christine Marie Sierra agreed to write a chapter on the political engagement and contributions of Latinas to electoral politics. History was made in the 2008 elections not only by the election of the first African American as president but also by the campaigns of Hillary Clinton for the Democratic presidential nomination and Sarah Palin for the vice presidency on the Republican ticket. Although several chapters in this volume deal in one way or another with the campaigns of Clinton and Palin, the historic and unprecedented nature of the candidacies of these two women seemed to merit a more in-depth examination, leading to the addition of another new chapter by Susan J. Carroll and Kelly Dittmar.

The second edition of this book would not have been possible without the assistance of the Center for American Women and Politics (CAWP) at Rutgers University. Debbie Walsh, director of CAWP, has embraced and encouraged this project and been supportive in numerous ways, especially in making CAWP staff available to assist on the project. Gilda Morales, who is in charge of information services at CAWP, continues to be an invaluable source of knowledge about women and politics, and several contributors relied on her expertise as well as the data she has compiled over the years for CAWP. We also would like to thank Jessica Rowan who offered technical and logistical support.

While everyone at CAWP was helpful, we want to single out Kathy Kleeman, a senior program associate at CAWP, for assistance above and beyond what we ever could have expected. Kathy, for both editions, has spent numerous hours making each volume much better than it otherwise would have been. She brought a third set of critical eyes to the reading of every chapter, and as an extremely skilled writer, she helped to make all of our chapters more readable, accessible, and polished. We are especially indebted to her.

Finally, we also would like to thank Cambridge University Press and our editor, Ed Parsons, in particular, for unwavering enthusiasm and patience. We have both thoroughly enjoyed working with Ed and hope to continue the partnership through future election cycles.

Contributors

Barbara Burrell is a professor in the political science department at Northern Illinois University and the director of graduate studies for the political science department. She is the author of *A Woman's Place Is in the House: Campaigning for Congress in the Feminist Era* (1994) and *Public Opinion, the First Ladyship and Hillary Rodham Clinton* (2001). Burrell also has published numerous articles on how gender interacts with the electoral process.

Dianne Bystrom is the director of the Carrie Chapman Catt Center for Women and Politics at Iowa State University. A frequent commentator on political and women's issues for state and national media, she is a coauthor, coeditor, and contributor to fourteen books – most recently *Legislative Women: Getting Elected, Getting Ahead* (2008); *Communicating Politics: Engaging the Public in Democratic Life* (2005); *Gender and Candidate Communication* (2004); and *Anticipating Madam President* (2003) – and has written several journal articles. Her current research focuses on the styles and strategies that female and male political candidates use in their television advertising and their news coverage by the media.

Susan J. Carroll is a professor of political science and women's and gender studies at Rutgers University and senior scholar at the Center for American Women and Politics (CAWP) of the Eagleton Institute of Politics. She is the author of *Women as Candidates in American Politics* (2nd ed., 1994) and editor of *The Impact of Women in Public Office* (2001) and *Women and American Politics: New Questions, New Directions* (2003). Carroll has published numerous journal articles and book chapters focusing on women candidates, voters, elected officials, and political appointees.

Kelly Dittmar is a Ph.D. candidate in political science at Rutgers University. Her current research focuses on the role of gender within political institutions and the gender dynamics of U.S. campaigns and elections. Dittmar's dissertation explores gender considerations in campaign strategy.

Georgia Duerst-Lahti is a professor of political science and department chair at Beloit College. She regularly provides analysis and commentary for state and national news coverage of U.S. politics, especially on gender and elections. She also works as a senior specialist on women's leadership and empowerment for the U.S. State Department. Her most recent coauthored book, *Creating Gender: The Sexual Politics of Welfare Policy* (2007), develops a theory of gender ideology in policy making. She has also coauthored, with Rita Mae Kelly, *Gender Power, Leadership, and Governance* (1995). Her articles have appeared in journals such as *PS, Sex Roles,* and *Public Administration Review.* She continues to explore masculinity and masculinism in politics, especially the U.S. presidency.

Richard L. Fox is an associate professor of political science at Loyola Marymount University in Los Angeles. He is the author of *Gender Dynamics in Congressional Elections* (1997) and coauthor of *Tabloid Justice: The Criminal Justice System in the Age of Media Frenzy* (2nd ed., 2007). More recently, he coauthored, with Jennifer Lawless, *It Takes a Candidate: Why Women Don't Run for Office* (Cambridge University Press, 2nd ed., 2001). His articles have appeared in *Journal of Politics, American Journal of Political Science, Political Psychology, PS, Women & Politics, Political Research Quarterly,* and *Public Administration Review.* His research focuses on the manner in which gender affects voting behavior, state executive elections, congressional elections, and political ambition.

Susan A. MacManus is Distinguished University Professor of Public Administration and Political Science in the department of government and international affairs at the University of South Florida. She is the author of *Young v. Old: Generational Combat in the 21st Century* (1996) and *Targeting Senior Voters: Campaign Outreach to Elders and Others with Special Needs* (2000); editor of *Reapportionment and Representation in Florida: A Historical Collection* (1991) and *Mapping Florida's Political Landscape: The Changing Art and Politics of Reapportionment and Redistricting* (2002); coeditor, with Kevin Hill and Dario Moreno, of *Florida's Politics: Ten Media Markets, One Powerful State* (2004); and coauthor, with Thomas R. Dye, of *Politics in*

States and Communities (11th ed., 2003). Her research on women candidates, officeholders, activists, and voters has been published in *Social Science Quarterly*, *Public Administration Review*, *Journal of Politics*, *Women & Politics*, *Urban Affairs Quarterly*, *National Civic Review*, and *The Municipal Year Book*, among others.

Kira Sanbonmatsu is an associate professor of political science and senior scholar at the Center for American Women and Politics at Rutgers University. She is the author of *Where Women Run: Gender and Party in the American States* (2006) and *Democrats, Republicans, and the Politics of Women's Place* (2002). Sanbonmatsu studies gender, race, parties, elections, public opinion, and state politics. Her most recent articles have appeared in *Politics & Gender* and *American Politics Research*. Her current research concerns the backgrounds and recruitment experiences of men and women state legislators.

Christine Marie Sierra is professor of political science at the University of New Mexico. She teaches and researches in the field of American politics with a focus on race, ethnicity, and gender. She publishes on Latino electoral politics, Hispanics in New Mexico, Latino activism on immigration policy, and Latina women in the United States. Sierra is the principal investigator of the Gender and Multicultural Leadership Project, a national study of elected officials of color in the United States (www.gmcl.org).

Wendy G. Smooth is an assistant professor of public policy in the departments of women's studies and political science at the Ohio State University and a faculty affiliate with the Kirwan Institute for the Study of Race and Ethnicity. Before joining the faculty at Ohio State, she served as an assistant professor of political science at the University of Nebraska–Lincoln. Her research focuses on the impact of gender and race in state legislatures. Smooth's research on women of color in American politics appears in journals such as *Politics & Gender* and *Journal of Women, Politics and Policy*. Currently, she is completing a manuscript titled *Perceptions of Power and Influence: The Impact of Race and Gender on Legislative Influence*.

SUSAN J. CARROLL AND RICHARD L. FOX

Introduction

Gender and Electoral Politics in the Early Twenty-First Century

The 2008 elections in the United States will surely be remembered most for the historic election of Barack Obama as the first African American president. In a hotly contested and intensely watched presidential campaign, Senator Obama defeated Republican Senator John McCain and won a higher percentage of votes than any Democratic presidential candidate since Lyndon Johnson in 1964.

Nevertheless, throughout the 2008 presidential election process, gender played a more direct and prominent role than at any time in history. In one election cycle, the country experienced perhaps the two highest-profile candidacies of women in U.S. history. Senator Hillary Clinton emerged as the early front-runner for the Democratic nomination for president, ultimately winning twenty-three state primaries and caucuses in the longest and most competitive presidential nomination process in the modern era. Although Obama ultimately edged out Clinton to become the Democratic nominee, Clinton is the first woman ever to have come close to winning a major party's presidential nomination.

After Barack Obama chose Senator Joe Biden rather than Hillary Clinton as his running mate, Republican John McCain surprised the country and chose a woman, Alaska Governor Sarah Palin, as his vice presidential nominee. As the first female Republican candidate for vice president, Palin joined Democrat Geraldine Ferraro, who was Walter Mondale's vice presidential running mate in 1984, as the only women to have ever run on a national ticket.

The candidacies of Hillary Clinton and Sarah Palin were major breakthroughs for women, but even before the historic 2008 election, the traditionally masculine face of top leadership in national politics had begun to change. Most notably, in 2007 Congresswoman Nancy Pelosi was elected

1

Speaker of the House after Democrats recaptured a majority of seats in both houses of Congress in the 2006 elections.

Women clearly have been making great strides in the political life of our nation, and gender has been playing an increasingly visible and important role in elections. This volume analyzes various aspects of electoral politics, showing how underlying gender dynamics are critical to shaping the contours and the outcomes of elections in the United States. No interpretation of American elections can be complete without an understanding of the increasing role of women as political actors and the multiple ways that gender enters into and affects contemporary electoral politics.

THE GENDERED NATURE OF ELECTIONS

Elections in the United States are deeply gendered in several different ways. Most obviously, men dominate the electoral playing field. Eighteen of the nineteen major candidates who vied for the Democratic and Republican nominations for president in 2008 were men. Similarly, men constituted the vast majority of candidates for governor and Congress in 2008. Most behind-the-scenes campaign strategists and consultants – the pollsters, media experts, fund-raising advisers, and those who develop campaign messages – are also men. Further, most of the best-known network news reporters and anchors, charged with telling the story of the 2008 election and previous elections (such as Charlie Gibson, Brian Williams, and Brit Hume), were men. The most visible exception was Katie Couric, anchor of *CBS Evening News*. A 2007 Media Matters study of cable television news (such as Fox News, CNN, and MSNBC) found that more than 80 percent of program hosts were men. Also, more than 75 percent of political newspaper columnists and editorial writers across the country are men.[1] The leading voices in political talk radio, to whom millions of Americans listen every week, are men, such as Rush Limbaugh and Sean Hannity. And the majority of those contributing the largest sums of money to candidates and parties, perhaps the most essential ingredient in American politics, are, of course, men.[2]

Beyond the continued dominance of men in politics, gendered language permeates our political landscape. Politics and elections are most often described in terms of analogies and metaphors drawn from the traditionally masculine domains of war and sports. Contests for office are often referred to by reporters and political pundits as battles requiring the necessary strategy to harm, damage, or even destroy the opponent.

The headquarters of presidential campaigns are called war rooms. Candidates attack their opponents. They raise money for their war chests. The greatest amount of attention in presidential races is focused on critical battleground states. In the post-9/11 environment of recent elections, candidates across the country have touted their toughness in wanting to hunt down and kill terrorists.

Along with the language of war, sports language is also prevalent in campaigns and in media coverage of campaigns. Considerable attention is devoted to discussion of which candidate is ahead or behind in the horse race. Similarly, commentators talk about how campaigns are rounding the bend, entering the stretch drive, or in the final lap. Although language drawn from the racetrack is common, so, too, is language drawn from boxing, baseball, football, and other sports. Coverage of political debates often focuses on whether one of the candidates has scored a knockout punch. When a candidate becomes aggressive, he or she is described as taking the gloves off. A popular political cable television talk show is named *Hardball with Chris Matthews*. Candidates running for elective office frequently talk about making a comeback, scoring a victory, or being in the early innings of a campaign. When a campaign is in trouble, the candidate may need to throw a Hail Mary pass. If something unexpected occurs, commentators report that a candidate has been thrown a curve ball.

The language of war and sports, two of the most traditionally masculine domains in American society, is so prevalent in our political discourse that it is even used by those who wish to increase women's political involvement. For example, to provide more opportunities for women to enter politics, advocates frequently argue that we need to level the playing field.

As the language used to analyze politics suggests, our expectations about the qualities, appearance, and behavior of candidates also are highly gendered. We want our leaders to be tough, dominant, and assertive – qualities much more associated with masculinity than femininity in American culture. In the post-9/11 environment, a military background, especially with combat experience, is a very desirable quality for a candidate, but military credentials remain almost exclusively the domain of male candidates. A military background is particularly desirable for a presidential candidate, who, if elected, will assume the responsibilities of commander in chief. However, because the American public has seen very few women among generals or top military officials, the idea of a female commander in chief still seems an oxymoron to many.

Americans even have gendered expectations about how candidates and political leaders should dress. While women politicians are no longer expected to wear only neutral-colored, tailored business suits, jogging attire or blue jeans still are not nearly as acceptable for women as for men. Americans have grown accustomed to seeing their male political leaders in casual attire. During the 1990s, we frequently saw pictures of Bill Clinton jogging in shorts, accompanied by members of the Secret Service. More recently, we saw images of President George W. Bush on his ranch in jeans and cowboy boots. To counter criticisms that the McCain campaign had spent an extravagant amount on designer clothes for her and her family, Sarah Palin made a few campaign appearances in 2008 in her blue jeans – a first for a high-profile woman candidate! However, she was careful to pair her jeans with professional-looking jackets and nice jewelry, thus appearing casually dressed only from the waist down. Although Palin broke new ground in 2008 by wearing jeans in public, she is still the exception to the rule. We have yet to see a picture of Nancy Pelosi or Hillary Clinton outfitted in jogging shorts or blue jeans and cowboy boots.

Finally, elections in the United States are gendered in the strategies that candidates employ in reaching out to women and men in the general public. Candidates, both men and women, strategize about how to present themselves to voters of the same and opposite sexes. Pollsters and campaign consultants routinely try to figure out what issues or themes will appeal specifically to women or to men. Increasingly, candidates and their strategists are designing different messages to be delivered to voters on the basis of their gender and other demographics. Specially devised appeals are directed at young women, working-class men, senior women, single women, married women, suburban women, white men, and women of color, to name only some of the targeted groups.

In short, when we look at the people, the language, the expectations, and the strategies of contemporary politics, we see that gender plays an important role in elections in the United States. Even when gender is not explicitly acknowledged, it often operates in the background, affecting our assumptions about who legitimate political actors are and how they should behave.

This is not to say, however, that the role of gender has been constant over time. Rather, we regard gender as malleable, manifesting itself differently at various times and in different contexts in the electoral process. In women's candidacies for elective office, for example, there has been obvious change. As recently as twenty years ago, a woman seeking high-level office almost anywhere in the United States was an anomaly and might have faced overt hostility. Clearly, the electoral environment is more hospitable now. Over the years, slowly but steadily, more and more women have entered the electoral arena at all levels. In 2008 Hillary Clinton was for many months the front-runner to become the Democratic Party's presidential nominee. And as we begin to look forward to the 2012 presidential elections, Sarah Palin is frequently touted as a possible contender in the Republican Party.

POLITICAL REPRESENTATION AND SIMPLE JUSTICE: WHY GENDER MATTERS IN ELECTORAL POLITICS

In addition to the reality that gender is an underlying factor that shapes the contours of contemporary elections, examining and monitoring the role of gender in the electoral process are important because of concerns over justice and the quality of political representation. The United States lags far behind many other nations in the number of women serving in its national legislature. Following the 2008 elections, the United States ranked number 84 among countries throughout the world in the proportion of women serving in their national parliaments or legislatures; only 16.8 percent of all members of Congress were women. In mid 2009, women served as governors in only six of the fifty states, and only 24.3 percent of all state legislators across the country were women according to the Center for American Women and Politics.[3]

Despite the relatively low proportion of women in positions of political leadership, women constitute a majority of the voters who elect these leaders. In the 2008 elections, for example, 70.4 million women reported voting, compared with 60.7 million men, according to U.S. Census figures. Thus, 9.7 million more women than men voted in those elections.[4] As a matter of simple justice, something seems fundamentally wrong with a democratic system that has a majority of women among its voters but leaves women so dramatically underrepresented among its elected political leaders. As Sue Thomas has explained, "A government that is democratically organized cannot be truly legitimate if all its citizens from … both sexes do not have a potential interest in and opportunity for serving their community and nation."[5] The fact that women constitute a majority of the electorate but only a small minority of public officials would seem a sufficient reason, in and of itself, to pay attention to the underlying gender dynamics of U.S. politics.

Beyond the issue of simple justice, however, are significant concerns over the quality of political representation in the United States. Beginning with a series of studies supported by the Center for American Women and Politics in the 1980s, a great deal of empirical research indicates that women and men support and devote attention to somewhat different issues as public officials.[6] At both the national level and the state level, male and female legislators have been found to have different policy priorities and preferences. Studies of members of the U.S. House of Representatives, for example, have found that women are more likely than men to support policies favoring gender equity, day-care programs, flextime in the workplace, legal and accessible abortion, minimum wage increases, and the extension of the food stamp program.[7] Further, both Democratic and moderate Republican women in Congress are more likely than men to use their bill sponsorship and cosponsorship activity to focus on issues of particular concern to women.[8] Similarly, several studies have found that women serving in legislatures at the state level give priority to, introduce, and work on legislation related to women's rights, health care, education, and the welfare of families and children more often than men do.[9] When women are not present in sufficient numbers among public officials, their distinctive perspectives are underrepresented.

In addition to having priorities and voting records that differ from those of men, women public officials exhibit leadership styles and ways of conducting business that differ from those of their male colleagues. A study of mayors found that women tend to adopt an approach to governing that emphasizes congeniality and cooperation, whereas men tend to emphasize hierarchy.[10] Research on state legislators has also uncovered significant differences in the manner in which female and male committee chairs conduct themselves at hearings; women are more likely to act as facilitators, whereas men tend to use their power to control the direction of the hearings.[11] Other research has found that majorities of female legislators and somewhat smaller majorities or sizable minorities of male legislators believe that the increased presence of women has made a difference in the access that the economically disadvantaged have to the legislature, the extent to which the legislature is sympathetic to the concerns of racial and ethnic minorities, and the degree to which legislative business is conducted in public view rather than behind closed doors.[12] Women officials' propensity to conduct business in a manner that is more cooperative, communicative, inclusive, public, and based on coalition building may well lead to policy outcomes that represent the input of a wider range of people and a greater diversity of perspectives.[13]

The presence of women among elected officials also helps to empower other women. Barbara Burrell captures this idea well:

> Women in public office stand as symbols for other women, both enhancing their identification with the system and their ability to have influence within it. This subjective sense of being involved and heard for women, in general, alone makes the election of women to public office important.[14]

Women officials are committed to ensuring that other women follow in their footsteps, and large majorities mentor other women and encourage them to run for office.[15]

Thus, attention to the role of gender in the electoral process, and more specifically to the presence of women among elected officials, is critically important because it has implications for improving the quality of political representation. The election of more women to office would likely lead to more legislation and policies that reflect the greater priority women give to women's rights, the welfare of children and families, health care, and education. Further, the election of more women might well lead to policies based on the input of a wider range of people and a greater diversity of perspectives. Finally, electing more women would most likely lead to enhanced political empowerment for other women.

ORGANIZATION OF THE BOOK

This volume applies a gendered lens to aid in the interpretation and understanding of contemporary elections in the United States. Contributors examine the ways that gender enters into, helps to shape, and affects elections for offices ranging from president to state legislature across the United States. As several chapters in this volume demonstrate, gender dynamics are important to the conduct and outcomes of presidential elections even though, to date, a woman has not won a major party's nomination for president. Gender also shapes the ways candidates appeal to voters as well as the ways voters respond to candidates. Many women have run for Congress and for offices in state government, and this volume analyzes the support they have received, the problems they have confronted, and why there are not more women candidates. Women of color face additional and distinctive challenges in electoral politics because of the interaction of their race or ethnicity and gender, and this volume also contributes to an understanding of the status of and electoral circumstances confronted by women of color, particularly African American women and Latinas.

In Chapter 1, Georgia Duerst-Lahti discusses the gender dynamics of the presidential election process. She examines the meaning of the phrase "presidential timber" to demonstrate how masculinity has shaped ideas of suitable presidential candidates. Duerst-Lahti argues that embedded in presidential elections and the traditions that accompany them are implicit assumptions that make presidential elections masculine space, including the test of executive toughness, a preference for military heroes, and the sports-related metaphors employed in describing presidential debates. Americans have carefully sought the right *man* for the job of single great leader and commander in chief of "the greatest nation on earth." She demonstrates how this construction of the presidency leads to struggles over different forms of masculinity and has implications for women as candidates and citizens.

In Chapter 2, Susan J. Carroll and Kelly Dittmar examine the 2008 candidacies of Hillary Clinton for president and Sarah Palin for vice president, focusing on the ways that various gender stereotypes influenced the strategies employed by their campaigns, the media's coverage of their campaigns, and public reactions to the candidates. Carroll and Dittmar review the history of women's efforts to run for president and vice president, focusing largely on major party candidates. They then provide short overviews of the backgrounds and accomplishments of both Clinton and Palin before turning their attention to gender stereotypes. Despite their different ideologies and personas, Hillary Clinton and Sarah Palin both had to deal with gender stereotypes that their male competitors did not face. Carroll and Dittmar assess the specific ways in which gender stereotypes related to experience, toughness, the role of commander in chief, children and spouses, and sexuality affected the campaigns of both women.

In Chapter 3, Susan A. MacManus focuses on the changing dynamics of gender and political participation, particularly on the techniques that political parties and women's groups used to bolster female registration, turnout, and candidate selection in the 2008 election. She chronicles the historic fight for women's suffrage and examines changes over time in registration and turnout rates. MacManus details the razor-sharp targeting of women through the use of various advertising and mobilization tools, and she provides examples of direct-mail ads that were used in the 2008 election to persuade women voters and to boost their turnout rates. MacManus devotes particular attention to the use of female star power and woman-to-woman mobilization efforts. Many high-profile women played key roles in convincing women to vote and to support one presidential candidate over the other in 2008.

In Chapter 4, Susan J. Carroll examines voting differences between women and men in recent elections. A gender gap in voting, with women usually more likely than men to support the Democratic candidate, has been evident in every presidential election since 1980 and in majorities of races at other levels of office. Carroll traces the history of the gender gap and documents its breadth and persistence. She examines the complicated question of what happens to the gender gap when one of the candidates in a race is a woman. Carroll reviews different explanations for the gender gap and identifies what we do and do not know about why women and men in the aggregate differ in their voting choices. She also analyzes the different strategies that candidates and campaigns have employed for dealing with the gender gap and appealing to women voters.

In Chapter 5, Christine Sierra focuses on the role of Latinas in U.S. politics. She assesses the evolving nature of the Latino electorate and describes the political and voting behavior of Latinas. Sierra also examines Latina officeholders and the roads they have traveled. She devotes particular attention to the role Latina voters played in 2008 in the battle for the Democratic nomination, at the national conventions, and in the general election. Her detailed analysis of the 2008 presidential race examines how the Democratic and Republican campaigns tried to reach out to the Latina electorate.

In Chapter 6, Wendy G. Smooth traces African American women's participation in electoral politics from Democrat Shirley Chisholm's historic 1972 campaign for president of the United States to former senator Carol Moseley Braun's 2004 campaign for the Democratic nomination to the lower-profile, third-party presidential bid of Cynthia McKinney in 2008. The chapter provides a historical overview of African American women's political participation as candidates in American politics. Following the passage of the Voting Rights Act of 1965, African Americans made unprecedented strides in electoral politics. Since the passage of that legislation, the number of African American elected officials serving at every level of government has soared. Smooth chronicles the successes of African American women in politics, the continued barriers they face as they seek greater inclusion in the American political system, and their activism in overcoming those barriers.

In Chapter 7, Richard L. Fox analyzes the historical evolution of women running for seats in the U.S. Congress. The fundamental question he addresses is why women continue to be so underrepresented in the congressional ranks. Fox examines the experiences of female and male candidates for Congress by comparing fund-raising totals and vote totals. His analysis also explores the subtler ways that gender dynamics manifest in the electoral arena, examining regional variation in the performance of women and men running for Congress, the difficulty of change in light of the incumbency advantage, and gender differences in political ambition to serve in the House or Senate. The chapter concludes with an assessment of the degree to which gender still plays an important role in congressional elections and the prospects for gender parity in the future.

In Chapter 8, Barbara Burrell examines the roles played by political parties and women's organizations in promoting and facilitating the election of women to public office. The conventional view has been that parties primarily have recruited women in "hopeless" races and as sacrificial candidates in contests where the party had little prospect of winning. Over time, political parties have become somewhat more supportive of women's candidacies even as the role of parties in campaigns has been challenged by other groups, such as women's political action committees. Burrell describes the increasing involvement of women in the party organizations and the evolving focus on electing women to public office as a means to achieve equality. The role of national party organizations and women's groups in increasing the numbers of women running for and elected to Congress is examined, with particular attention to the financial support such organizations have provided for women candidates.

In Chapter 9, Dianne Bystrom examines the impact of the media on candidates' campaigns for political office. Studies have shown that newspapers often cover women less than their male opponents, focus on image attributes over issue stances, and raise questions about the women's viability. Consequently, candidate-mediated messages – television advertising and Web sites – are particularly important to women candidates as they attempt to present their issues and images directly to voters during a political campaign. The chapter reviews the state of knowledge about women candidates, their media coverage, television commercials, and Web sites, and it provides examples of how women candidates may be able to capitalize on their controlled communication channels to influence their media coverage and create a positive, integrated message that connects with voters.

Finally, in Chapter 10, Kira Sanbonmatsu turns to the often-overlooked subject of gender in state elections. She addresses two central questions: How many women ran for state legislative and statewide offices in 2008? How did the performance of women candidates in 2008 compare with previous elections? Sanbonmatsu analyzes the cross-state variation in the presence of women candidates, including the role of political parties in shaping women's candidacies. She also considers the reasons for the variation across states in women's presence in statewide executive office. Understanding why women are more likely to run for and hold office in some states and not others is critical to understanding women's status in electoral politics today, as well as their prospects for achieving higher office in the future.

Collectively, the chapters provide an overview of the major ways that gender affects the contours and outcomes of contemporary elections. Our hope is that this volume will leave its readers with a better understanding of how underlying gender dynamics shape the electoral process in the United States.

NOTES

1 Locked Out: The Lack of Gender and Ethnic Diversity on Cable News Continues. Media Matters for America. May 7, 2007. <http://mediamatters.org/items/200705070003?f=h_report> April 29, 2009.

2 Donor Demographic: Gender. Center for Responsive Politics. 2008. <http://www.opensecrets.org/pres08/donordemCID_compare.php?cycle=2008> April 29, 2009.

3 Center for American Women and Politics. 2009. Women in Elective Office. Fact Sheet. New Brunswick, NJ: Center for American Women and Politics.

4 Center for American Women and Politics. 2009. Gender Differences in Voter Turnout. New Brunswick, NJ: Center for American Women and Politics.

5 Sue Thomas. 1998. Introduction: Women and Elective Office: Past, Present, and Future. In *Women and Elective Office: Past, Present, and Future*, eds. Sue Thomas and Clyde Wilcox. New York: Oxford University Press, 1–14, quote at 1.

6 Debra Dodson, ed. 1991. *Gender and Policymaking: Studies of Women in Office*. New Brunswick, NJ: Center for American Women and Politics.

7 Most recently, see Michele Swers. 2002. *The Difference Women Make: The Policy Impact of Women in Congress*. Chicago: University of Chicago Press.

8 Swers, *The Difference Women Make*, 2002.

9 For examples, see Susan J. Carroll. 2001. Representing Women: Women State Legislators as Agents of Policy-Related Change. In *The Impact of Women in Public Office*, ed. Susan J. Carroll. Bloomington: Indiana University Press, 3–21; Sue Thomas. 1994. *How Women Legislate*. New York: Oxford University Press; Michael B. Berkman and Robert E. O'Connor. 1993. Women State Legislators Matter: Female Legislators and State Abortion Policy. *American Politics Quarterly* 21(1): 102–24; and Lyn Kathlene. 1989. Uncovering the Political

Impacts of Gender: An Exploratory Study. *Western Political Quarterly* 42: 397–421.

10 Sue Tolleson Rinehart. 2001. Do Women Leaders Make a Difference? Substance, Style, and Perceptions. In *The Impact of Women in Public Office*, ed. Susan J. Carroll. Bloomington: Indiana University Press, 149–65.

11 Lyn Kathlene. 1995. Alternative Views of Crime: Legislative Policy-Making in Gendered Terms. *Journal of Politics* 57: 696–723.

12 Impact on the Legislative Process. 2001. In *Women in State Legislatures: Past, Present, Future.* Fact Sheet Kit. New Brunswick, NJ: Center for American Women and Politics.

13 See, most recently, Cindy Simon Rosenthal. 1998. *How Women Lead.* New York: Oxford University Press.

14 Barbara Burrell. 1996. *A Woman's Place Is in the House.* Ann Arbor: University of Michigan Press, 151.

15 Debra L. Dodson and Susan J. Carroll. 1991. *Reshaping the Agenda: Women in State Legislatures.* New Brunswick, NJ: Center for the American Woman and Politics.

1 Presidential Elections

Gendered Space and the Case of 2008

The presidential election of 2008 began November 3, 2004, the day after the 2004 election. Shortly thereafter, a tongue-in-cheek Associated Press (AP) article led with the following: "Wanted: a former altar boy from the Southwest who speaks Spanish, married into a rich Republican family from Ohio and revolutionized the Internet after working as a volunteer firefighter in Florida. Position: president of the United States."[1] Using findings from exit polls to construct the profile of the perfect presidential candidate for 2008, the article went on to propose that he

- Be "a Medal of Honor winner" with combat experience who helped normalize relations with Vietnam
- Love outdoor sports and drop his *g*'s "when talkin' about huntin' and fishin' and car racin'"
- Be a former quarterback for the University of Michigan Rose Bowl team
- Be a "trained economist who taught in Minnesota, where he met his wife, a nurse," whose father is a former governor
- Be "a volunteer fireman" who "drove his pickup truck to help out the World Trade Center site"
- Be "a billionaire in his own right who developed software"

Although not fitting this profile, five prominent men and Hillary Rodham Clinton were mentioned in this article as potential candidates. It closed with, "Mr. Perfect might be a Mrs. – the first woman to head a majority party ticket. But it would be a lonely job, what with her husband fighting in Iraq."

For presidential candidacies, the press serves as the great mentioner, without whose attention no candidate can be seen as viable. The power of mentioning, or not, has implications beyond individual candidates.

13

What the press assumes, and the way it frames its coverage of presidential elections and candidacies, has consequences for what readers think about and, to a lesser extent, how they think about it.

The AP article described here focuses on the next election and the candidate characteristics needed to win. Distributed on November 6, 2004, it is among the first articles to frame elements of the 2008 presidential election. Importantly, the article's framing is highly gendered (see Text Box 1.1), and one suspects that neither the author nor the readers thought much about this fact. As a result, its assumptions about masculinity as an implicit criterion for the presidency – combat experience, huntin', quarterback, fireman – go unexamined.

Yet, the article's headline, "Finding Mr. or Mrs. Right for a run in 2008," and closing paragraph both assume that a woman can be president. In other words, they cue the reader to think about a woman as the right or perfect presidential candidate in 2008. This cuing is no small matter. Because only men have ever been president, and because certain functions of the presidency, such as commander in chief, are particularly associated with masculinity, the assumption that a woman could be the "Mrs. Right candidate" represents a major shift in cultural understandings of both women and the institution of the presidency. So potent is the association between masculinity and the presidency that an organization called the White House Project has been established with a core purpose of shifting this cultural link.[2] One of its primary strategies, in fact, is to have the media treat a woman in the presidency as normal, much as the AP article seems to do.

However, most of the characteristics ascribed to the ideal candidate in this AP article suggest a profile consistent with men rather than women in U.S. society. Taking note of this fact helps to reveal how presidential elections are gendered space.

- Although a woman could easily be from the Southwest, speak Spanish, and have married into a rich Republican family, the Catholic Church only allowed altar boys, not altar girls, at the time current presidential candidates were growing up.
- Firefighters remain overwhelmingly men, especially in volunteer corps.
- Until recently, women have been barred from combat duty, so few have been positioned to win the Medal of Honor. However, a woman might well have negotiated with the Vietnamese: women have long been associated with peace, more are in the diplomatic corps, and three of the last four secretaries of state have been women.

TEXT BOX 1.1: A gender primer: Basic concepts for gender analysis

To undertake gender analysis of presidential elections, some basic concepts and definitions are needed. *Gender* can be defined as the culturally constructed meaning of biological sex differences. Males and females share far more physiologically than differ, yet in culture, we largely divide gender roles and expectations into masculine and feminine, even though biologically and culturally more than two genders exist. Importantly, in contrast to sex, gender is not necessarily tied to a human body.

Gender is assigned as follows:

- An attribute or property of an individual, entity, institution, etc.

  She's a wise woman.
  Men dominate physics.

- Ways of doing things – practices or performance

  He throws like a girl.
  She fights like a man.

- Normative stances toward appropriate and proper ways of behaving, allocating resources, exercising power, and so on

  Men shouldn't cry.
  Fathers must provide and mothers give care.
  A woman's place is in the home.

The process of assigning gender is known as "to gender" or "gendering."

- To gender or gendering is to establish a gender association.

  Metrosexuality describes Yuppie urban men with a softer side.
  The field of nursing is highly feminized.

- To regender or regendering is to change from one gender to another gender.

  Before typewriters, secretaries were men.
  Girls now outperform boys in school.

- To transgender or transgendering is to cross gender boundaries, weakening gender norms and associations, and it is open to both men and women.

  Half of medical students now are women, so medicine is changing.

Gender ethos is defined as the characteristic spirit or essential and ideal attributes that correspond to gender expectations.

  Football is among the most manly of all U.S. sports.
  A Madonna with child quintessentially expresses femininity.
  The military is imbued with masculinity.

Source: Compiled by author.

- No woman has yet played quarterback for a Big Ten school or any major college team. In 1999–2000, a female placekicker on the Colorado State University football team encountered extreme sexual harassment. (Interestingly, Condoleezza Rice may have benefitted from an association with football simply because she claims that her dream job is someday to be National Football League commissioner.)
- While economics has the smallest proportion of female Ph.D.'s in the social sciences, women have entered the field in growing numbers, so a woman might have strong economic credentials. However, only about 10 percent of nurses are male, so she probably would not have one as her husband.
- Finally, if a woman became president, she might well be lonely, as is the first woman to serve in any position. However, no commander in chief has ever faced the challenge of leading a nation in war with a spouse on the battlefront, because the wives of presidents have always functioned as helpmates, regardless of their other career interests and professional credentials. Certainly, many people expressed concerns about the role Bill Clinton might play were Hillary Clinton to win, but not because he would either be a helpmate or be on the battlefront. Similarly, Sarah Palin's son went to Iraq, but not her husband, Todd.

In other words, while a widely distributed AP article mentioning that a woman could be a viable candidate may help to normalize the idea of a woman as president, much more needs to happen. We cannot simply "add and stir" in a woman without changing the elements associated with masculinity. Such "equal" treatment ignores important differences and (dis)advantages. Because so much that is perceived as contributing to presidential capacity is strongly associated with men and masculinity, presidential capacity is gendered toward the masculine; as such, women who dream of a presidency must negotiate masculinity, a feat much more difficult for them than for any man.

Text Box 1.2 rewrites the AP article to approximate a perfect candidate based on culturally feminine roles and associations to illustrate the central claim of this chapter: that presidential elections are gendered space, that much of what happens in a presidential election becomes a contest about masculinity that is integrally intertwined with understandings of what makes a candidate suited for this masculinized office and institution. Neither Hillary Clinton nor Sarah Palin approximated this profile of Mrs. President. The woman within the presidential pool (governor, senator, vice president, military leader) who most closely fits the profile is

TEXT BOX 1.2: Finding Mrs. Right for a run in 2008: Not the same as Mr. Right

The November 6, 2004, article "Exit Polls Can Lead the Way in Finding Mr. & Mrs. Right for a Run in 2008," by the Associated Press's Ron Fournier, used exit polls to "build a perfect candidate for 2008." Despite suggesting that Mrs. Right could fit the bill equally well as Mr. Right, the article concentrated on aspects consistent with masculinity. Given the considerable difference in life experiences between women and men, what factors known from exit polls and other sources in 2004 could be used to create an ideal female candidate for 2008?

- A fifth-generation Latin American woman from Arizona, she comes from a long line of Democrats, including political officeholders from New Mexico.

- As a child she considered becoming a nun, which endeared her to a favorite uncle, a Catholic bishop in Florida who has close ties to the Cuban community. They share a love of the outdoors, gardening, camping, and fly-fishing.

- She took first place in the individual medley on the U.S. national swim team, missing the Olympics only because of an injury.

- As an army nurse, she served in the waning days of the Vietnam War. She received a medal of commendation for helping evacuate mixed-race children.

- She married an Anglo army officer who specialized in military intelligence. He retired as a general in 1992. He speaks Arabic fluently, and President George H. W. Bush recognized him for outstanding service during the Persian Gulf War.

- She founded a company that placed temporary nurses, becoming a multimillionaire when she franchised the business. She has helped many women start their own businesses as a result.

- Throughout this time, she raised four children and transformed the public education system in her city as a volunteer activist. She interrupted her career to care for her son for three months when he suffered life-threatening injuries caused by a drunk driver. She sits on the national board of Mothers against Drunk Driving.

- Her company created software, now used nationwide, that digitized and standardized patient medical records and enabled patients to access them twenty-four hours a day, seven days a week. She made even more money from the software than from the nursing business.

- She became governor of Michigan and is in her second term. Her husband intends to campaign hard on her behalf, as he has done in the past.

arguably former Kansas Governor Kathleen Sebelius, whose name floated
for a while as a potential Democratic vice presidential pick; ultimately, she
became cabinet secretary for the Department of Health and Human Services in the Obama administration. She is the daughter of former Ohio
governor John Gilligan. She has chaired the Democratic Governors Association but has spent her life in public service, not in the private sec-
tor making millions. Her husband, K. Gary Sebelius, is a federal magis-
trate judge and the son of a former Republican U.S. representative. They
have two grown sons. Rather than huntin' and fishin' – hobbies Sarah
Palin claimed, to great fanfare – Sebelius is active in many environmental
causes. As governor, she has worked closely with first responders but was
not one herself. She is a Catholic, but her archbishop imposed a "pas-
toral action" on her, demanding that she no longer receive the Eucharist
because she is pro-choice. Although Sebelius is a governor, many consider the state of Kansas insignificant in presidential politics. Indeed, she
has connections to Michigan, but only through her vacation homes. In
other words, the female candidate with the best profile comes up short of
the masculinized characteristics highlighted in polls.

   This chapter's primary purpose is to show ways that gender, especially
masculinity, manifests in campaigns. I attempt to raise awareness of this
implicit dynamic and to counteract some of the potency that masculinity
gains from simply being "ordinary." This chapter also touches on the process of opening, or regendering, presidential election space for women, a
process that moved some distance with the strong primary race of Hillary
Clinton and the Republican pick of Sarah Palin as the vice presidential
candidate.

   As the chapter by Carroll and Dittmar in this volume shows clearly,
women find a contest about masculinity a distinct hurdle compared to
male candidates, but men who run for the presidency must also negotiate
masculinity. Masculinity takes many forms, each competing to be considered hegemonic – that is, the controlling, best, and most valued version.[3]
Drawing on work by R. W. Connell, this chapter looks into masculinity
more carefully and explores the gendering of presidential timber – an ill-
defined but commonly employed concept about suitability for the presidency. I examine overt references to masculinity as well as the ongoing
struggle for hegemony between two forms of masculinity in the United
States, dominance masculinity and technical expert masculinity. I do so
to make explicit the implicit masculine qualities of the presidency deemed
essential in a successful presidential candidate.

   This chapter explores presidential elections through the concept of
gendered space rather than just discuss elections. While elections – with

their aspects of candidate recruitment and winnowing, formal prima
and general elections, caucuses, conventions, debates, and the like – ce₁-
tainly are part of election space, so is much more. For example, the presidency as an institution occupies a place in history inside the U.S. government system, in relationship to Congress, other national institutions,
and political parties. Each of these places is part of presidential election
space. So is the entire environment of those elections, with their places
in the public mind, the news and opinion media, American culture, and
all the people – present and past – who help to create and sustain presidential elections. These people include the candidates, the elite political gatekeepers, pollsters, campaign consultants, campaign workers, voters, even apathetic citizens. Each occupies a place in presidential election
space. This large and somewhat amorphous space that includes everything related to presidential elections is the locus of analysis.

Ironically, the "space invaders" Hillary Clinton and Sarah Palin did not
so much highlight masculinity as shift the gaze away from it, making the
masculine nature of the presidency even harder to see. Hence, I focus on
presidential selection processes to demonstrate ways that they are themselves implicitly imbued with masculinity and therefore foster conscious
beliefs that masculine persons should be president. To do so, the chapter
tackles

> a recurring paradox. The categories of men and masculinity are fre-
> quently central to analyses, yet they remain taken for granted, hid-
> den and unexamined.... [They are] both talked about and ignored,
> rendered simultaneously explicit and implicit...at the centre of the
> discourse but they are rarely the focus of the interrogation.[4]

As will become clear, some media coverage – especially from op-ed
pages – explicitly deals with men and masculinity in the presidential election. More often, however, as in the AP article examined at the beginning of this chapter, coverage treats masculinity paradoxically by ignoring its central place in presidential elections even while highlighting it. In
the process, it ignores ways in which presidential elections are gendered,
thereby perpetuating men's greater potential to be seen as presidential, to
the detriment of female candidates.

STAGES OF PRESIDENTIAL ELECTIONS:
PARTS OF GENDERED SPACE

The early stages of any presidential election are an insider's game, with
party elites and elected officials talking to the press about potential

candidates and the press reporting on them. Year 1 begins the day after the previous campaign – November 3, 2004, for the 2008 election. For the press to mention a candidate regularly is exceptionally important: no press mention, no candidacy. The press covers candidates who undertake testing-the-water activities and can create potential candidates simply by mentioning that some individuals could be candidates.

Years 1 and 2 of any election cycle focus on factors that provide candidates strategic advantages to win the next election. Chief among these factors is whether the race includes an incumbent president or is an open seat. In 2004, George W. Bush ran as an incumbent president, and he was assumed to be running for reelection as of the day he was declared the winner in 2000. The 2008 election proved to be unusual in that no incumbent or former president or vice president stepped forward as a candidate, a situation seen for the first time since 1928.

Another relevant factor is the influence of the recent elections, reflected in such elements as the margin of victory, big mistakes made by a candidate or a campaign, and strategies that worked particularly well. The 2004 election taught Democrats to employ a fifty-state strategy as used effectively by Republicans and to be prepared at the polls for voter suppression tactics. Further, it taught them to prepare for smear tactics relatively early in the cycle, such as those undertaken in 2004 by the outside group Swift Boat Veterans for Truth. Finally, Democratic success in sweeping both houses of Congress in 2006 pulled momentum away from Republicans, generally focusing greater interest on the Democratic candidates. All of these factors combined to produce unusual interest in the 2008 election, an unprecedented number of candidates, and an exceedingly long campaign.

Press coverage for each election cycle begins in the days and months immediately after the end of the previous one. News coverage during the first year of any election cycle focuses on "aspirants," individuals doing things that would clearly help them with a presidential bid. Aspirants might be traveling the country giving speeches, meeting with an unusual assortment of interest-group leaders, forming exploratory committees, visiting states important to early selection processes such as New Hampshire and Iowa, and otherwise getting more positive press coverage than usual. John Edwards and John McCain, among others, followed this pattern from 2004 to 2008. Louisiana Governor Bobby Jindal's trip to Iowa and his presentation of the Republican counter to President Obama's address to Congress during February 2009 are examples of such positioning for 2012.

A second set of individuals might better be thought of as potential aspirants; they do a few things that bring them press coverage but prove not to be serious candidates for that election cycle. However, such coverage in one cycle becomes a resource for future cycles. Speculation surrounding Hillary Clinton immediately after the 2000 election provided exactly this type of coverage. She often was mentioned as a potential candidate for 2004, and although she made no attempt to run in 2004, she stayed in the limelight. That speculation helped make her the heir apparent for 2008.

A third set of potential candidates is spotlighted because they have characteristics consistent with presidential candidates, although they may not have given serious consideration to a presidential bid. These individuals can be thought of as recruits; the mere fact that the press mentions them as potential candidates begins to build the perception of their viability. The press plays an influential role in this process. When the media mention an individual as a presidential candidate, they create the perception that she or he could be one, as was the case with Barack Obama after his well-received speech at the 2004 Democratic convention. With no mention in the press, regardless of his or her aspirations and credentials, an individual will not be a potential or actual candidate.

Consistent with the pattern, press coverage for the 2008 race began in November 2004. Table 1.1 shows the names of individuals mentioned by the *New York Times* or the *Washington Post* as possible candidates during the first three years of the cycle leading up to the 2008 election; the date each was first mentioned; and whether each proved to be an aspirant, a potential aspirant, or a recruit.

For the gendering of presidential elections a few matters are clear. Like the cycle leading up to the 2004 election, only three women made the list of those mentioned by the press as potential candidates for 2008: Democratic Senator Hillary Clinton of New York, Democratic Governor Janet Napolitano of Arizona, and Republican Secretary of State Condoleezza Rice. Hillary Rodham Clinton was again the first to be mentioned, and again she was mentioned the day after the election. Condoleezza Rice was mentioned the next day and Janet Napolitano a few days later in an article that listed seven potential candidates. Rice and Napolitano compare to New Hampshire's former governor Jeanne Shaheen during 2004, when she appeared only one time in a list of possible candidates, as did several other governors and senators. Like Shaheen, they made no gestures toward a candidacy, so this mention reflects a recruiting attempt. Rice, in particular, explicitly warded off several public attempts to recruit her as a candidate.

TABLE 1.1: Only three women were among the candidates mentioned early for the 2008 presidential election

Candidate	Party	Previous position	Date of first mention	Type of candidate
Hillary Rodham Clinton	D	First Lady, Senator (NY)	11/04/2004	Aspirant
John Edwards	D	Senator (NC)	11/04/2004	Aspirant
Barack Obama	D	Senator (IL)	11/04/2004	Aspirant
Condoleezza Rice	R	National Security Adviser, Secretary of State	11/05/2004	Recruit
Howard Dean	D	Governor (VT)	11/07/2004	Recruit
Mark Warner	D	Governor (VA)	11/07/2004	Potential
Bill Richardson	D	Congressman (NM), UN Ambassador, Governor (NM)	11/07/2004	Aspirant
Janet Napolitano	D	Governor (AZ)	11/07/2004	Recruit
Phil Bresden	D	Governor (TN)	11/07/2004	Recruit
Michael Easley	D	Governor (NC)	11/07/2004	Recruit
Rod Blagojevich	D	Governor (IL)	11/07/2004	Potential
John Kerry	D	Senator (MA)	11/09/2004	Potential
Mitt Romney	R	Governor (MA)	11/14/2004	Aspirant
Chuck Hagel	R	Senator (NE)	11/15/2004	Potential
Bill Frist	R	Senator (TN)	12/21/2004	Potential
Newt Gingrich	R	Congressman (GA)	1/19/2005	Potential
Rudolph Giuliani	R	Mayor (NYC)	1/20/2005	Aspirant
George Pataki	R	Governor (NY)	1/20/2005	Potential
Ken Brownback	R	Senator (KS)	4/21/2005	Aspirant
George Allen	R	Senator (VA)	4/29/2005	Aspirant
John McCain	R	Senator (AZ)	4/29/2005	Aspirant
Evan Bayh	D	Senator (IN)	4/29/2005	Potential
Joe Biden	D	Senator (DE)	6/22/2005	Aspirant
Haley Barbour	R	Governor (MS)	7/21/2005	Recruit
Tom Vilsack	D	Governor (IA)	7/21/2005	Potential
Mike Huckabee	R	Governor (AR)	7/21/2005	Aspirant
Tom Daschle	D	Senator (SD)	10/21/2005	Potential
Russ Feingold	D	Senator (WI)	10/24/2005	Potential
Tom Tancredo	R	Congressman (CO)	10/02/2005	Aspirant
Mike Gravel	D	Senator (AK)	4/17/2006	Aspirant
Chris Dodd	D	Senator (CT)	6/15/2006	Aspirant
Duncan Hunter	R	Congressman (CA)	10/31/2006	Potential
Tommy Thompson	R	Governor (WI)	1/17/2007	Potential
Ron Paul	R	Congressman (TX)	3/13/2007	Aspirant
Fred Thompson	R	Senator (TN)	3/13/2007	Aspirant
Dennis Kucinich	D	Congressman (OH)	4/18/2007	Aspirant

Note: Names mentioned in the *New York Times* and *Washington Post* in articles with search terms "presiden!" and "2008."

Importantly, these early mentions again indicate that the press has begun to take seriously women with presidential credentials (e.g., governors, senators, cabinet members) as possible candidates for both major political parties. This marks a distinct change from the past, as other chapters in this volume detail. As in 2004 when Carol Moseley Braun ran, however, only one female candidate ultimately emerged.

Noteworthy for this gender analysis of presidential election space is the fact that again only three women were mentioned, given the extraordinary opportunity for and interest in candidacies in the 2008 cycle. Whether this lack of attention to potential female candidates by the two leading political newspapers simply reflects or actually contributes to women's challenges in entering masculine presidential space is difficult to disentangle. Either way, it readily shows the glacial pace of progress in opening this space for women. Because the election was wide open, with no current or former presidents or vice presidents running, both parties had more opportunities. In 2008, thirty-seven names emerged in early mentions, compared with only twenty-three in 2004. Yet the two leading political newspapers mention only three women.

During the third year of a presidential election cycle, the pace quickens. Candidates become active in early states, strive for viability by raising considerable campaign funds, and use the opportunity of an official announcement of their candidacy to garner press coverage. The aspirants become separated from others during this time. During 2001 and 2002, Hillary Rodham Clinton was particularly subject to speculation, despite repeated claims that she would not run. These speculations subsided in 2003. By speculating often that a woman might become a candidate, the press helps to change the gendering of presidential election space, simply because the idea is in front of the attentive public. The 2008 election began to take shape during 2007 as the last of the candidate pool emerged; as recruits and potentials withdrew; and as aspirants tested the water, trying to tap top campaign talent, line up endorsements, and raise money. Unlike 2004, when President Bush received very little coverage explicitly related to his role as a candidate (although everything he did as president reflected on his candidacy), in 2008, there was no president in the race and thus no candidate had the advantage of presidential coverage. As in 2004, with a large cast of contenders and an impassioned desire to retake the White House, the Democrats opted again to hold a series of debates among their aspiring candidates. These began with a widely televised debate in South Carolina on April 27, 2007. Republicans began

May 3, 2007 at the Reagan Library in California. After Labor Day, the pace of polls conducted by news outlets, polling organizations, and campaigns quickened, and the polls themselves provided candidates frequent press coverage. However, such coverage tends to be limited and can become detrimental if a candidate is not polling well. In fact, a candidate's viability is heavily influenced by levels of both fund-raising and press coverage. Many candidates withdraw during year 3 as a result.

In election cycles prior to 2008, focus on the early states tended to escalate after Labor Day of year 3, when candidates undertook a whirlwind of visits to the early primary and caucus states of New Hampshire and Iowa and, to a lesser extent, South Carolina and Nevada. Polls and press coverage of these visits became critical. Do poorly in either and a candidate loses the "press election," in which the press vets candidates for their presidential viability and presidential timber. Activity has tended to kick into high gear during year 4 of an election cycle, during early November, with press coverage intensifying after January 1 as the campaign approaches the first contests in Iowa and New Hampshire.

In the 2008 cycle, this frenetic activity started during the summer of year 3 and escalated even more as year 4 approached. Because states wanted to have an impact on selecting candidates, many opted to move their primary or caucus dates earlier, causing a cascade of shifting dates because – with party approval – Iowa and New Hampshire insisted on remaining the first caucus and primary, respectively. The parties, especially the Democrats, sought more diversity and so had placed South Carolina and Nevada immediately afterward. South Carolina is also especially important to conservatives in the Republican Party. In fact, so many states wanted to move earlier that the Democrats sanctioned states that shifted their dates, and eventually said that they would not seat delegates from Michigan and Florida because they had moved their primaries into January. The consequence of the cascading dates was uncertainty about the start of contests, which eventually began in Iowa on January 2, 2008, earlier than they had in 2004 by seventeen days. New Hampshire followed with the first primary on January 5, three weeks earlier than in 2004.

During the last ten months of any campaign season, press coverage escalates greatly and presidential election space becomes highly visible and national, drawing interest from a much broader audience. Candidates generally withdraw from contention as their performance in polls, primaries, and caucuses falls short of expectations set by news coverage.

The Iowa caucuses and New Hampshire primary, which always come first, hold substantially more sway than any others. They are followed by a series of state primaries and caucuses whose rules are determined by states and political parties. For the past several presidential elections, Super Tuesday, a collection of many states' primaries, which takes place the first week of March, has determined the presumptive nominees, even though primaries continue until June. In 2008, Super Tuesday took place on February 5, a month earlier than it had in the previous two cycles, with twenty-four states holding primaries or caucuses, eight more than in 2004. John McCain emerged from the pack as the Republican nominee, but the Democratic contest continued. In practice, the general election season began after Super Tuesday, although the Democratic nominee was not confirmed until after the last primaries on June 3, when Hillary Clinton effectively stepped aside. As a result, unlike past years when campaign activities have subsided during late primaries and early summer, the late primaries in 2008 proved crucial for the Democrats. Throughout this time the Republican nominee, John McCain, struggled to capture any media attention. Not since 1968 had the late primaries played such an important role.

During the late summer of presidential election years, press coverage shifts to each party as it approaches its nominating convention. In 2008, the Democratic convention took place August 25–28, and the Republican convention ran September 1–4. Conventions officially nominate a party's candidate, but they also showcase the candidate and other party notables, including potential future nominees. In contrast to 2004, when the duration between conventions was unusually long, with a full month separating them, in 2008, they were close together, separated by less than a week. Importantly, John McCain selected Sarah Palin to be his vice presidential running mate on August 29, stealing the media limelight from the Democrats and generating enormous press coverage for the GOP. The choice captured media imagination so effectively that Palin garnered more coverage than the presidential nominees for a period. As Carroll and Dittmar detail in this volume, Palin faced stereotypical coverage that diminished public perception of her abilities and her capacity to serve as vice president.

The final throes of the general campaign begin in earnest after the conventions, becoming ever more frenzied as Election Day nears. For the 2008 election, presidential debates, which always attract considerable press coverage, were held on September 26, October 7, and October 15, and a vice presidential debate took place on October 2. With the emerging fiscal crisis, the polls showed the race gradually moving toward a comfortable Obama victory.

The campaigns came to a close on Election Day, November 4, 2008. Because television networks faced severe criticism for the way they "called" the election in 2000, they gave greater care in 2004 and continued the practice in 2008. Nonetheless, the moment the polls closed on the West Coast, Barack Obama was declared the winner by all the major outlets. Unlike 2000 and 2004, the electoral college victory was large enough so that charges of fraud did not mar the vote count, and the election ended in an ordinary fashion.

The next day, November 5, the newspapers mentioned five possible Republican candidates for 2012: Sarah Palin, Mitt Romney, Bobby Jindal, Tim Pawlenty, and Newt Gingrich. The 2012 presidential campaign space opened, once again with one woman mentioned.

THE GENDERED PRESIDENCY AND PRESIDENTIAL TIMBER

The term *presidential timber* implies the building products used to construct a president. So far, the human material that makes presidents has been male. Masculinity has been embedded through the traditions that dominate the presidency, but inside those traditions lie more implicit assumptions that make presidential elections masculine space: the test of executive toughness, a preference for military heroes, the sports and war metaphors of debates, and more. Implicit in the gendering of presidential election space is the common belief that the election picks a single leader and commander in chief of "the greatest nation on earth." This belief stands in a post–World War II context that includes the Cold War, the fall of communism, the emergence of the United States as the world's sole superpower, and the rise of terrorism.

In these conditions, Americans have carefully, albeit not necessarily systematically or rationally, sought the right man for the job. As judged from the number of candidates and the reaction to candidacies thus far, women had not been seriously considered as suitable to serve as president until Hillary Clinton's campaign of 2008, and then she did not win. Although many reasons can be proffered to explain this dearth of female attempts for the post, observations about the heavily masculinized character of the office, and hence masculinized selection process, remain among the strongest explanations, albeit the most difficult to establish. In essence, because the institution is itself perceived as masculine, contests for the presidency are, among other things, struggles over dominant or hegemonic masculinity. Presidential elections also present real challenges for women who must exhibit masculine characteristics (probably more so than males) while retaining their femininity if they want to succeed.

Evidence that institutions have been gendered toward masculinity became obvious when women entered them; their novel presence made visible the ways masculinity is "normal." Thinking of men as having gender instead of "naturally" coinciding with a universal standard has occurred only quite recently. An institution becomes gendered because it takes on characteristics or preferences of the founders, incumbents, and important external actors who influence it over time. In doing so, these founders and influential incumbents create the institution's formal and informal structures, rules, and practices, reflecting their preferred mode of organizing. If men have played an overwhelming role in an institution's creation and evolution, it is only "natural" that masculine preferences become embedded in its ideal nature. It takes on a masculine gender ethos. This is what has happened to the U.S. presidency.

But gender is not static, and neither is the gendering of an institution that operates inside a social context. One can expect continual gender transformations as a result of women's activism, equal employment opportunity policies in education and the workplace, generational change, and cultural experiences of Americans' daily lives. Similarly, campaigns and elections evolve from a particular history influenced by key people and processes that have gendered aspects. This evolution favors those whose preferences become reflected in presidential election processes, but those preferences can change over time. So, although men have clearly had the advantage in shaping the presidency and presidential elections over time, gender has been in considerable flux over the past forty years. Even if only men have been viewed as really possessing presidential timber thus far, these assumptions may change in the future. Recent polls, for example, show the many positive and nuanced changes in views toward women as political leaders, although 14 percent still think women are not tough enough and 16 percent think men are better leaders.[5]

So how might presidential timber be gendered? Informal use would suggest that it blends overlapping elements of charisma, stature, experience, and viability in a particular election. It has also included ideas of proper manliness. The presidential historian Forrest McDonald provides insights into presidential timber through his description of presidential image:

> [T]he presidential office...inherently had the ceremonial, ritualistic, and symbolic duties of a king-surrogate. Whether as warrior-leader, father of his people, or protector, the president is during his tenure the living embodiment of the nation. Hence, it is not enough to govern well; the president must also seem presidential. He must inspire confidence in his integrity, compassion, competence, and capacity to take charge in any conceivable situation.... The image thus determines the reality.[6]

The "king-surrogate,...warrior-leader, father..., protector" roles and images indisputably evoke men and masculinity.

Yet one could imagine a queen, mother, and protector with Joan of Arc warrior qualities. The former British prime minister Margaret Thatcher is often cited as having evoked these images, but British comedy often showed her baring a muscular, manly chest. Many argue that Britain's experience with highly successful queens opened the way for Thatcher.

In contrast, the United States has no such historical experience, so voters have a harder time considering women capable of fulfilling traditionally masculine leadership roles of the institution. This cultural incapacity to understand women as able public leaders likely is exaggerated because, according to Michael Kimmel, an expert on masculinity, the gendered public and private divide was much stronger in the United States than in Europe.[7]

Even more challenging, and perhaps most important for electing presidents, presidential timber derives from the perception of others. That is, others must see a potential candidate as possessing presidential timber. Forrest McDonald declares that a president must "seem presidential" and inspire confidence in his "capacity to take charge in *any* conceivable situation... with image determining reality" (emphasis added).[8]

If only men have been president, then having a presidential image presents a significant challenge for women who need political elites, party activists, and ultimately voters to perceive them as presidential. Further, men have more often been culturally imbued with a take-charge capacity, although women certainly do and can take charge, so this aspect of timber might be open for cross-gendering, for being understood as suitable for either women or men. However, because of stereotypes, the requirement that one be perceived as able to take charge in any conceivable situation undermines women, particularly during war or security threats such as 9/11. Jennifer Lawless found in post-9/11 America that considerable gender stereotyping reemerged, with a willingness to support a qualified female candidate falling to its lowest point in decades.[9] For these reasons, the ordinary usage of the term *presidential timber* and the potential gendering of it deserve scrutiny, because the term's use is both the center of analysis and invisible.

By examining how the term *presidential timber* is used in press accounts, we can better establish its meaning and its explicit and implicit gendering. To do so, I searched the North American Nexus database for all newspaper and news magazine articles including the term, for the years 2005 (N = 2), 2006 (N = 13), and 2007 (N = 10), for a total of twenty-five articles. Of these articles, fifteen highlighted the timber of only one candidate, a situation that cues that the candidate is worthy of particular scrutiny. Seven articles mentioned that an outside source considered a candidate to be presidential timber and five wrote of the candidate himself believing that he had presidential timber. A closer look suggests more about what presidential timber is constructed to be and its importance to gendered space.

In the 2004 election, George W. Bush's campaign repeatedly pointed to his post-9/11 performance and approval ratings whenever questions were raised about his credentials for the job. In essence, they positioned him as possessing timber by virtue of serving as president, although this has not always worked for other recent presidents. Jimmy Carter purportedly lost because he anguished too much in public, and many commentators – and arguably voters – perceived George H. W. Bush as lacking sufficient timber. Often, this perceived lack of timber has been linked to a "wimp factor" or another version of absence of the requisite image of presidential masculinity.[10] In an apparent response to this danger, George W. Bush has positioned himself as exceptionally masculine, a steadfast cowboy willing to stand firm as he takes on the world. Interesting for the 2008 cycle, John McCain was mentioned only once in terms of presidential timber, in association with many senator-candidate colleagues while working on a national security policy. This paucity may reflect the vicissitudes of his campaign as it waxed and waned, or it may reflect the extent to which he was already a known quantity. In terms of a gendered presidency, more likely it reflects the fact his biography and character unquestionably match the description proffered by Forrest McDonald of one who can take charge and inspire confidence as a warrior-leader, father, and protector. No one had reason to question his presidential timber because he was indisputably viewed as possessing it.

The importance of the idea of timber resides in impressions, which are still largely unformed. Media coverage early on "is considered an important chance to form opinions that could help shape later aspects of the campaign."[11] Key to the impressions and the opinions are "passion" and "appeal" that would help party activists "gauge which candidate could mount the strongest challenge." In other words, presidential timber involves a candidate's passion, appeal, and competitiveness as conveyed through early impressions reported by the press. None of these aspects appears to be particularly gendered, although a woman might be eliminated if she is not perceived – for reasons of sexism or feminine personal characteristics – as competitive with the other party's candidate. Appeal is a tricky thing, especially early on. The frequent references to Clinton as being too contentious to win suggest a reason to eliminate her, but the gender dimensions of her evocation of that response escape scrutiny.

The impressions involved in presidential timber are magnified in individual coverage of candidates, whether for better or for ill depending on the nature of that coverage. No place were the impressions of timber more favorable than for Fred Thompson, who definitely looked presidential but proved to be a weak candidate. For example, he was featured in a lengthy, well-timed December 2007 article in the *Washington Post* titled "Bigger Than Life," which painted a rags-to-riches story of a reluctant but able candidate. Little seems gendered here, unless one wonders why Thompson was so readily deemed to "look" presidential.

Of the fifteen articles focused on the presidential timber of only one candidate, three are devoted to Hillary Clinton and two to Barack Obama, while another two feature Obama and mention merely another candidate in passing. Considering that Hillary Clinton was the perceived Democratic front-runner until the Iowa caucus results, a focus on her presidential timber might be expected. In fact, she was the lone focus of one of two articles during 2005. Writing in the form of a memorandum to her, Frank Gaffney Jr. of the *Washington Times* proclaimed her front-runner and then laid out her problems:

> But to win the Oval Office, you will have to overcome a very different challenge – persuading enough independents and perhaps even Republicans you are the first Democrat in two generations who can

safely be entrusted with the presidency in time of active, global hostilities.[12]

At face value, this passage could as readily be written for any of the Democratic candidates and hence would not be particularly gendered. However, women have not been associated with proficiency in active, global
hostilities. Hence, even apparently neutral language can have gendered
ramifications. Gaffney goes on, however, to cast Hillary Clinton as inseparable from her husband: "Toward this end, you, your husband and other
political advisers are reportedly assiduously working." No other candidate
faced routine reference to his spouse.

Gendering need not be bad, but it should be recognized. For example,
Clinton was the subject of a glowing column about her presidential timber
in *Newsweek* that did just that:

> A presidential election will test how many voters can make the distinc-
> tion between feeling that Senator Clinton rubs them the wrong way
> and thinking that her considerable skills make her prime presidential
> timber. It's also expected to test whether Americans are ready for a
> female commander in chief. That may be less of an issue than conven-
> tional wisdom would suggest; the universe of those who would never
> elect a woman is a universe that significantly overlaps the hard-core
> Hillary haters. Thus her negatives may help neutralize her sex.[13]

Clinton's tendency to rub people the wrong way has seemed integrally
linked to her sex from the start. Among reasons often cited is the fact
she was a woman who did not shy away from her own power. The column offers encouragement for Clinton to run, going on to describe her as
"well informed, high profile, enormous war chest, works hard, speaks
eloquently, campaigns well," all traits that suggest the timber needed
to be president. But unlike most writings on presidential timber, here
the gendering is made explicit. Interestingly, despite its overtly positive
endorsement of Clinton, the column's title and references to "the Clinton question" imply that a question necessarily exists, even if unspoken.
This invidious questioning about a female president is itself a gendered
challenge to all women who would be president, standing in stark contrast to Fred Thompson, who looked presidential and so was cajoled into
running.

Gendering can occur in many subtle ways. For example, Clinton's
presidential timber was mentioned in a book review titled "Lionesses"
about one hundred years of "journalistas" and the best writing by female
journalists. Such placement suggests that Clinton, too, is a lioness, a

clearly gendered term, and that she is somehow insurgent as an "-ista." More important, though, the text itself sets up judging her presidential timber and touts an Erica Jong piece in the *Nation* to capture "her unquestionable smarts but also her penchant for striking bargains to acquire power. No one reading this piece could be surprised by Senator Clinton's multisided utterances on Iraq policy or the steely discipline that helped get her elected."[14] Her timber is negated because she strikes bargains to acquire power. One wonders which male presidential candidate has not done the same, but her conduct makes her suspect because of cultural norms for men, women, and political power.

Nowhere is the paradoxical presence and invisibility of gender more visible than with the term *commander in chief*. In another article that mentions several candidates, Clinton is said to need to "show her potential as commander-in-chief" and "regain her stature" as front-runner in an area considered to be her strength – national security – in the face of "Democratic darling-of-the-moment" Barack Obama.[15] Again, none of this may appear gendered if all candidates need to do these things to win. However, for a female to head the military breaks gender norms of one of the most masculine of all undertakings. Clinton had no choice but to demonstrate her prowess in national security.

Importantly, in a separate analysis of the term *commander in chief* in articles from eight major newspapers, this gendering becomes obvious. The analysis searched for McCain, Clinton, or Obama with the term in the same sentence and found a total of six, nineteen, and twenty mentions, respectively. McCain simply received less coverage, and again, no one doubted his capacity as commander in chief; all references were positive. The Clinton search produced a total of nineteen hits, seventeen of which were positive and two of which were negative about her capacity. This finding is remarkable in that, for the first time, a woman was treated by the press as fully capable of commanding the world's greatest military. Obama received a total of twenty hits. Even more remarkably considering that he won, all twenty spoke negatively about his qualifications and capacity to be commander in chief. Yet this did not disqualify him for the office. It is not possible to discern whether the economy so overshadowed everything else that his weakness as commander in chief did not matter or whether a black man was simply assumed to be able to function in the military realm.

Like most gendered aspects of the presidency, the nature of presidential timber coverage of Obama shows that it is simultaneously present and invisible. One straightforward article compares him directly to President Kennedy, ostensibly because everyone was doing so.

> It's been a virtual Obama-rama in recent days – Barack Obama on talk shows, news shows, magazine covers. Everywhere, all the time. The charismatic Obama on some level seems to be all things to all people. And he has a new book out. So he can write, but will he run? Should he, could he? He won't say yet, though Oprah says he ought. Every argument for has an argument against. He's too young, too inexperienced, he's barely been a U.S. senator, let alone shown presidential timber. Do we really want another president to learn on the job? Ah, comes the retort, you can't time timing. If not now – when, then? Still, no man – particularly one whose Senate seniority is next to dead last – has been elected to the presidency directly from that august body since, well, Jack Kennedy, which is the name invoked near the top of every Obama story. Fair enough. Just for fun, let's do it, too. Decide for yourself if comparing the two is sensible or simply silly.[16]

The article goes on to compare Obama to Kennedy on several counts, including military service, something that would have been unlikely for women even today. Further, a comparison to a former male president introduces masculinity without needing to do so explicitly. We naturally tend to compare a woman to other women and a man to other men. In doing so for the presidency, we inadvertently and invisibly introduce gender. Further, although seemingly balanced by recognizing arguments for and against, the article's structure sets up the validity of comparing him to Kennedy as well as cuing Obama's potential to win just like Jack Kennedy. So, while questions are asked about Obama's timber, they differ greatly in tone from those asked of Hillary Clinton.

The remaining four articles, focused on Obama and presidential timber, contain similar gender elements. One *USA Today* column also compares him to JFK, while a second references gushing journalists as well as his drug use during his youth that could have become "a fatal role for a would-be black man." It ends explicitly with a gender reference: "He deserves to be given a chance to show us the kind of man he has become – and the kind of president he could be."[17]

In a catch-22, women are less likely to be seen automatically as having adequate timber because we do not yet know how a woman president looks. Further, because masculinity is so normal, we do not readily recognize when masculinity is being cued and women stigmatized. Masculine presidents are ordinary, and hence masculinity is simply assumed.

CONTESTING MASCULINITY: EXPERIENCE AS EXPERTISE
AND CHANGE AS DOMINANCE?

Masculinity is neither fixed nor uniform. Just as there are several versions of a "proper" woman – often varying by class, cultural subgroup,
and gender ideology – men and masculinity are not singular. From the
perspectives of presidential candidates, political gatekeepers, and voters,
a president must meet certain expectations of masculinity. Nonetheless,
within broader ranges of gender expectations, analysis suggests that much
of the heat around gender performances, or the way individuals "do" gender, derives from contests to make one version of gender the hegemonic
form, the form that is recognized as right, just, proper, and good and the
form that is afforded the most value. It is the form most able to control all
other forms, and therefore it becomes the most "normal."

R. W. Connell has analyzed contemporary masculinity, finding ongoing contests between two major forms: dominance and technical expertise.[18] Dominance masculinity is preoccupied with dominating, controlling, commanding, and otherwise bending others to one's will. Often
rooted in physical prowess and athleticism, this competitive and hierar-
chical masculinity also can be rooted in financial prowess in the corporate
world or elsewhere. Michael Jordan and Arnold Schwarzenegger serve as
archetypal examples.

Expertise masculinity emerges from capacity with technology or other
intellectualized pursuits. Such masculinity also values wealth, a key
marker of masculine status, but the hegemony arises from mastery of
and capacity for dealing with complex technology or ideas. Bill Gates and
Carl Sagan serve as exemplars of technical expertise masculinity.

Connell says that these modes of masculinity "sometimes stand in
opposition and sometimes coexist," because neither has succeeded in dis-
placing the other.[19] Connell further argues that these modes of hegemonic masculinity always stand in relationship to other subordinated
masculinities and to femininity.

If this struggle for hegemonic masculinity plays out in presidential
elections, then it also has consequences for female candidates, because
expertise has been a prime base of power for women in leadership roles.
Whereas women gain credibility in leadership situations when they are
perceived as possessing expertise, they face a considerably greater challenge in being perceived as leaders when they try to dominate. In fact,
women often are punished for seeming too dominating. Therefore, the
nature of the contest for hegemonic masculinity has implications for

women, too. A strong showing of expertise masculinity would allow women easier access; a strong showing of dominance masculinity would cause women to face greater difficulty in the contest, or even in being seen as suited to participate in the contest.

The past gives clues to the present. In 1992, George H. W. Bush had won the Persian Gulf War but had also been labeled a "wimp" who could not project a vision for the nation. Bush had the possibility of employing dominance masculinity as commander in chief, but he failed. Bill Clinton portrayed himself as intelligent, a Rhodes Scholar, and a policy wonk. He projected expertise masculinity and won by being smart about the economy. Once in office, however, he backed down from a disagreement with the Joint Chiefs of Staff over gays in the military and let his wife lead his major health-care initiative. He was portrayed as weak until a showdown over the budget with House Speaker Newt Gingrich and the Republican majority in the 104th Congress, when he dominated and won. Strangely, when he was again attacked, this time over sexual misconduct, his popularity rose. While far too complicated to suggest a single cause, the manly vitality at stake – perhaps proof that he was not controlled by his strong wife, Hillary – figures as an aspect of dominance masculinity. Clinton did best as president when he projected dominance masculinity, not expertise masculinity.

The 2000 election might seem the perfect contest between expertise and dominance masculinity, with Al Gore, the smart and technically savvy vice president, against George W. Bush, a former professional baseball team owner whose intelligence was regularly questioned. In the 2004 election, Bush entered the contest from an explicit position of dominance masculinity. He could not, and likely would not choose to, project expertise masculinity. Although ironic, when Bush called on his expertise with the office of the presidency, he did so from a dominance masculinity stance, claiming that expertise mostly in terms of a war presidency. John Kerry tried to project both expertise and dominance masculinity; he was both smart and heroic. Kerry certainly had plenty of resources for expertise masculinity, from foreign policy to nineteenth-century British poetry. However, his primary election victories derived from his war-hero status, firmly rooted in dominance masculinity. He also projected his athleticism at every available opportunity. Apparently, his campaign recognized the potential liability of expertise masculinity, even though the liberal base values intelligence and expertise greatly, so Kerry tried to have both.

To test the prevalence of each broad category of masculinity, I identified words that could be associated with each. I searched short but critical

TABLE 1.2: Dominance words were more than four times more common than expertise words in articles about presidential candidates during 2008

Expertise masculinity		Dominance masculinity	
Words	No. of times used	Words	No. of times used
Technical	15	Dominate	26
Intelligent	24	Strong	309
Smart	49	Aggressive	86
Advocate	60	Attack	223
Wonk	3	Blast	14
Total	151	Total	658

Note: Articles analyzed from March and October 2008 in the *Washington Post, New York Times, Los Angeles Times, Atlanta Journal-Constitution, St. Louis Post-Dispatch, Houston Chronicle, Seattle Times,* and *Boston Globe.* Compiled by author.

election stages (April and October 2000, January 2004, and March and October 2008) and looked for words that suggested either dominance or expertise in candidates.[20] Quite simply, for all time periods, consistent with Table 1.2, words common to dominance masculinity outnumbered expertise masculinity words greatly: roughly two to one for 2000 and four to one for 2004 and 2008. This pattern strongly suggests that dominance, rather than expertise, drives the ethos of presidential campaigns. Women, therefore, face particular gendered challenges in their bid for the masculinized presidency.

The pattern suggests that expertise matters far less than dominance, posing particular challenges for women. A closer look at the 2000 Bush and Gore race shows that each candidate received about the same amount of dominance coverage. Nonetheless, Gore did not "do" dominance masculinity well, with many references to his aggressiveness and attacks being cast negatively: "a kind of sanctimonious aggressiveness [was] his principal weakness."[21]

For the gendered space of presidential elections, the facts that women and men do not "do" dominance the same way and that women are not culturally allowed to dominate in the public world like men matter greatly. Hence, a gender double bind. Any show of dominance by Hillary Clinton risked a similar claim of ill-performed aggressiveness, even though some aggressiveness is expected of a president. Clinton inspired now-legendary nutcrackers made in her likeness, cable news commentators likened her to the "first wife," and a nationally syndicated radio commentator called her a "testicle lockbox." No male candidate has faced such personal and sexualized derision. Female candidates must tread very lightly on dominance, and yet they must meet the demands of presidential timber.

Expertise has been central to women's advancement in the public realm. In fact, since the 1970s when women began to enter the public realm, they have relied on expertise, often presenting higher and better credentials than their male counterparts as a rational response to sexism. In 2008, Clinton staked out her credentials with expertise gained in her experience as first lady and in the Senate, a traditional route to the presidency. Because women tend to be punished for dominance displays, a strong showing of expertise becomes rational. In fact, both Clinton and McCain evoked expertise through experience, in large part because Obama lacked experience. McCain already had masculine dominance, though in comparison to Obama, age and vitality became the issue. Clinton faced a different challenge: she sought to transform expertise into dominance. Obama, in contrast, played on change and the dominance required to change the system. Indisputably, he dominated the big-campaign-rally format, and through his speeches, he demonstrated an ability to inspire committed followers.

Table 1.2 makes clear that dominance masculinity trumps expertise masculinity in presidential space. What remains unclear is whether the campaign themes of change (Obama) and experience (Clinton and McCain) somehow correlate with dominance and expertise masculinity. Because Obama won the election, one can hypothesize that change *somehow* cued dominance masculinity more than expertise. Similarly, because Clinton and McCain lost, one would expect that experience did not particularly cue dominance. To explore these hypotheses, I undertook a two-by-two search of all the newspaper mentions of the expertise and dominance words identified in Table 1.2, searching first by experience and then by change. I expected to find a stronger relationship between change and dominance than between any of the other conditions. My expectations were confirmed (see Table 1.3). I found change in the same paragraph as a dominance word in 40.1 percent of cases. The other three combinations each appeared in only about 30 percent of paragraphs. Thus, the theme of change was disproportionately associated with dominance masculinity.

TABLE 1.3: Change and dominance masculinity combined most often in articles about presidential candidates during 2008

	Expertise		Dominance	
	N	%	N	%
With Experience	49	32.4	195	29.6
With Change	48	31.7	**264**	**40.1**
Total Mentions	*151*		*658*	

Note: Articles analyzed from March and October 2008 in the *Washington Post, New York Times, Los Angeles Times, Atlanta Journal-Constitution, St. Louis Post-Dispatch, Houston Chronicle, Seattle Times,* and *Boston Globe.* Compiled by author.

CASTING THE GAZE AWAY: WHEN RACE AND GENDER MAKE MASCULINITY INVISIBLE

The use of particular words related to masculinity became the subject of explicit analysis and explicit campaign strategy during the 2004 and 2008 elections. Table 1.4 shows such words as they appeared in newspaper coverage of the election; the counts include all forms of the word, such as *manly* and *manliness,* or *masculine* and *masculinity.* The contrast is dramatic. The election of 2004 used *masculinity* as an overt tactic in ways 2008 seems not to have done. The words *manly* and *wimp* seem negligible in contrast.

For the 2004 cycle, campaigns overtly projected hegemonic masculinity. By 2003, conservatives were "draping George W. Bush in a masculine mystique.... [T]he president is hailed as a symbol of virility – a manly man in contrast to the allegedly effeminate Bill Clinton."[22] But not

TABLE 1.4: Masculinity was covered much more in 2004 than in 2008

	Manly	Masculine	Wimp	Testosterone
2004	101	26	69	22
2008	6	12	5	6

Notes: Numbers indicate the actual number of times the word appeared in article set on the presidential election. Articles analyzed from January 1, 2003, to November 16, 2004, in the *Washington Post, New York Times, Los Angeles Times, Atlanta Journal-Constitution, St. Louis Post-Dispatch, Houston Chronicle,* and *Boston Globe.* For 2008, words were gathered from January 1, 2007, to October 31, 2008, from the foregoing newspapers and from the *Seattle Times.* Compiled by author.

only Republicans were concerned. One extended headline read, "Who's the Man? They Are; George Bush and John Kerry stand shoulder to shoulder in one respect: Macho is good. Very good. It's been that way since Jefferson's day."[23] Many experts claimed, "A good portion of the presidential image-making in 2004 will center on masculinity. . . . Both candidates appear to come by their macho naturally." Both candidates also took every chance to overtly cultivate macho images, whether it was Bush powering his father's cigarette boat in Maine or Kerry taking shots and checks on the hockey rink. Despite use of explicit terms, most manly themes were "cast in more subtle and euphemistic terms, as pundits talk about the candidates' 'authenticity,' 'decisiveness,' and 'toughness.'"[24]

Toughness has had masculine associations, and discourse throughout the space of presidential elections drips with evocations of it. Despite women making tough decisions all the time, decisiveness has generally been associated with men. Therefore, Republican efforts to paint John Kerry as indecisive, a flip-flopper, and unable to make tough decisions extended into 2008. They cast him as a stereotypical woman who keeps changing her mind. This legacy of 2004 boxed Clinton in. To avoid association with the stereotypical indecisive woman, something that pulled Kerry down, she needed to make tough decisions and then stand by them. The feminized gendering of Kerry in 2004 left her no space to change her mind on issues, especially on Iraq. To do so would mark her as "not tough" and open her to one of the lingering doubts about a woman in the White House: could a woman make tough decisions, especially decisions in times of crisis?

Associating authenticity with masculinity presents a puzzle. The answer, however, emerged in perceptions of authentic masculinity itself. Authenticity was linked to masculinity because the Republicans particularly displayed a strategy of

> portraying opponents as less than fully masculine. Republicans retooled a Nixon plan from the 1972 campaign, and designed a plan to enable Bush to "capture the hearts and votes of the nation's white working men. . . . Nixon's plan was to build an image as 'a tough, courageous, masculine leader.'"[25]

Bush's advisers intended to do the same. A key component of such masculinity is dominance. To be the manly leader who can rally other men requires the enemy to "be feminized."[26] But this is not new. "American politicians have not been above feminizing their opponents dating back to the era of powdered wigs, playing on the stereotypical notion that only the 'manly' can lead." Bush supporters called John Edwards the "Breck girl" and mocked John Kerry.[27] They also succeeded in raising questions about Kerry's status as a hero. Such attacks pushed Kerry into ever more explicit displays of his own dominance masculinity. His advisers began to declare that masculinity. "Different voters... were really struck by John's presidentialness. He's big, he's masculine, he's a serious man for a serious time."[28] Kerry moved away from his expertise because it highlighted his "patrician airs" and did not play well with audiences, and the Bush camp systematically undermined Kerry's key weapon for the presidency, his heroic manliness.

Hillary Clinton's 2008 campaign emerged out of this hypermasculinity from 2004. How would she demonstrate sufficient masculinity to be seen as presidential? The failures of hypermasculinity may also have changed the terms of what would be valued in 2008. For example, *tough* has been an important word for presidential politics and has become integral to the discourse of elections. In fact, the most pronounced finding from word analysis is the extent to which presidential election space is infused with the concept of toughness; hence, one can predict that its regendering will hinge on the extent to which women can be seen as tough enough.

As a woman, Hillary Clinton faced a challenge of proving toughness to a standard beyond any of the men. Using the eight-newspaper data set, I searched for the term *tough* and a candidate's name in the same paragraph from January 2007 through May 2009. During that time, Clinton definitely became associated with toughness more than Obama did. Clinton received 542 mentions with *tough* compared to Obama's 498. McCain, who simply struggled for press coverage during the later primary season, was mentioned with *tough* 364 times. In other words, Hillary won the *tough* battle but may have lost the election in the process in part because, culturally, we do not necessarily want tough women, even though we want a tough president. If overt appeals to masculinity proved so common in 2004, where were they in 2008?

Rather than being framed as a contest of masculinity, the 2008 election was framed as a historic election. The question was whether a woman or a black man would receive the Democratic nomination. Of course, the woman, Clinton, faced the challenges of masculinity associated with the presidency. As a white woman, she did not face the racial barrier because all presidents heretofore have been white. The black man, Obama, faced challenges as a black *man*. He faced the usual questions about his masculinity discussed throughout this piece: Could he

Figure 1.1: Newspapers covered the "woman" candidate and the "black" candidate about the same until December, when race became the dominant story.

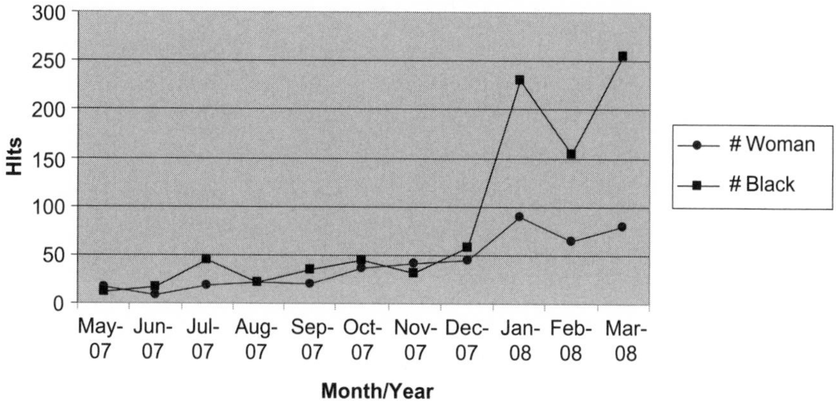

dominate? Would he inspire a large enough following to win? Would he be judged as possessing sufficient presidential timber? He, however, also needed to negotiate many obstacles of his blackness, such as whether white Americans would agree to a black man leading a national institution and how to not seem to fit the stereotype of an angry black man. His clear intellect and career as a law professor endowed him with sufficient expertise masculinity. In terms of dominance, white culture tends to assign hypermasculinity to black men. So, despite the uniformly negative coverage of his qualifications to be commander in chief discussed earlier, he faced a far different need to prove his warrior credentials than Clinton because whites tend to fear the martial capacities of black men and associate them with violence. Obama therefore began on a strong basis of masculinity, which he could foster through tales of his basketball prowess and other masculinity displays.

The overt discussions of masculinity so common in 2004 were diverted to the historic election frame. Gender was not about masculinity; gender was equated with the first woman candidate. Coverage of race was not about a black *man* but about the first black presidential candidate. This historic-first frame averted the gaze from masculinity almost entirely, as Figure 1.1 shows. In terms of gender, the woman frame and black candidate frame received about the same amount of coverage in the late months of the third year of the cycle, May through November 2007. However, by January 2008, with Obama's victory in Iowa, the frame turns to the first black president and race becomes the dominant story of the primary season.

By bringing implicit masculinity into awareness, the citizenry can think more clearly about masculinity as an assumed qualifier for office. Ideas of leadership, which have been adjusting to women leaders' successes in other realms, can inform judgments in presidential elections, too. To think explicitly about masculinity in presidential elections is to open the door wider for women. The 2008 election space offered the opportunity to think about both gender and sexism. Questions remain about whether and how masculinity and sexism will shape the 2012 presidential space.

NOTES

 1 Ron Fournier. November 6, 2004. "Exit Polls Can Lead the Way in Finding Mr. or Mrs. Right for a Run in 2008." *Wisconsin State Journal*.
 2 For information about the White House Project, see http://www.thewhite househouseproject.org/.
 3 R. W. Connell. 1995. *Masculinities*. Berkeley: University of California Press, and Whitehead and Barrett.
 4 David Collinson and Jeff Hearn. 2001. "Naming Men as Men: Implications for Work, Organization, and Management." In *The Masculinities Reader*, ed. Stephen M. Whitehead and Frank J. Barrett. Cambridge, MA: Polity Press, pp. 144–169.
 5 Celinda Lake. March 4, 2009. "Gender Gap in Politics Is Invitation for More Women to Run." *Women's eNews*. <http://www.womensenews.org/article. cfm/dyn/aid/3938/context/archive>, retrieved on March 5, 2009.
 6 Forrest McDonald. 1994. *The American Presidency: An Intellectual History*. Lawrence: University of Kansas Press.
 7 Michael Kimmel. 1996. *Manhood in America*. New York: Free Press.
 8 McDonald 1994.
 9 Jennifer L. Lawless. 2004. "Women, War, and Winning Elections: Gender Stereotyping in the Post–September 11th Era." *Political Research Quarterly* 57: 479–90.
10 Stephen J. Ducat. 2004. *The Wimp Factor*. Boston: Beacon Press.
11 James Gerstenzang and Mark Z. Barabak. May 3, 2003. "Democrats Gather for a Debate in Deep South; Nine Contenders for the Presidential Nomination Assemble Tonight in South Carolina in a Bid to Form Opinions and Capture Voter Interest." *Los Angeles Times*. All of the quotations in the remaining 2004 analysis of timber are from this article.
12 Frank Gaffney Jr. June 7, 2005. "Attention Senator Clinton." *Washington Times*.
13 Anna Quindlen. October 30, 2006. "The Hillary Questions." *Newsweek*.
14 Jill Abramson. January 8, 2006. "The Lionesses." *New York Times*.
15 Michael McAuliffe. December 5, 2006. "Iraq Hearing a Test for Three Prez Rivals." *New York Daily News*.

16 Jim Verhulst and Angie Drobnic Holan. October 29, 2006. "Obama? Just Like Jack?" *St. Petersburg Times*.

17 DuWayne Wickham. January 9, 2007. "Obama's Folly of Youth Shouldn't Hinder Rise." *USA Today*.

18 Connell 1995.

19 Connell 1995, 194.

20 For the 2000 election, I looked at news accounts in the *Washington Post* and the *St. Louis Post-Dispatch* for the months of April and October; Peter Bartanen assisted with the research. For 2004, I looked in all seven papers for the month of January, a key time for winnowing Democratic candidates; Sarah Bryner and Sara Hyler provided excellent research assistance. For 2008, I added the *Seattle Times*. Laura Sunstrom and Kevin Symanietz proved outstanding research assistants. I thank them all.

21 "In Gore-Bush Debates, Voters Will See Personal as Well as Political Differences, TV Setting May Magnify Strengths and Weaknesses." October 2, 2000. *St. Louis Post-Dispatch*.

22 Cathy Young. September 8, 2003. "We're Still Playing the Gender Card." *Boston Globe*.

23 James Rainey. March 18, 2004. "Who's the Man? They Are; George Bush and John Kerry Stand Shoulder to Shoulder in One Respect: Macho Is Good. Very Good. It's Been That Way since Jefferson's Day." *Los Angeles Times*.

24 Rainey 2004.

25 Arlie Hochschild. October 5, 2003. "NASCAR Dads Fuel Strategies for Bush in '04." *Los Angeles Times*.

26 Ducat 2004.

27 Maureen Dowd. March 11, 2004. "Whence the Wince?" *New York Times*.

28 Todd S. Purdum and David M. Halbfinger. February 1, 2004. "With Cry of 'Bring It On,' Kerry Shifted Tack to Regain Footing." *New York Times*.

2 The 2008 Candidacies of Hillary Clinton and Sarah Palin

Cracking the "Highest, Hardest Glass Ceiling"

On June 7, 2008, Hillary Clinton spoke for about thirty minutes to a large crowd of supporters at the National Building Museum in Washington, D.C., announcing the official suspension of her campaign and ending her bid to become president of the United States. This was hardly the speech she had envisioned giving when she posted the simple words "I'm in" on her Web site on January 20, 2007, declaring her candidacy for the Democratic Party's presidential nomination.

Clinton had won more votes and more delegates than any unsuccessful presidential primary candidate in history, and for several months, she had been viewed as the front-runner to win her party's nomination. As she bowed out of the race, Clinton, who had downplayed her gender throughout most of the campaign, explained, "When I was asked what it means to be a woman running for president, I always gave the same answer, that I was proud to be running as a woman, but I was running because I thought I'd be the best president." Acknowledging that gender "barriers and biases" remain, Clinton pointed to the fact that, as she spoke, the fiftieth woman astronaut was orbiting the earth. To a roar of approval from her supporters, she proclaimed:

> If we can blast 50 women into space, we will someday launch a woman into the White House. Although we weren't able to shatter that highest, hardest glass ceiling this time, thanks to you, it's got about 18 million cracks in it and the light is shining through like never before, filling us all with the hope and the sure knowledge that the path will be a little easier next time.[1]

What Clinton could not have known, and what few political observers anticipated, was that fewer than three months after she spoke those words, before a huge crowd in Dayton, Ohio, the Republican presidential nominee Senator John McCain would introduce his vice presidential choice, Alaska Governor Sarah Palin, to the millions of Americans for whom she was a political unknown. Palin spoke to the crowd of Republican supporters and curious reporters, echoing Clinton's comments about cracking the glass ceiling:

> I think, as well, today of two other women who came before me in national elections. I can't begin this great effort without honoring the achievement of Geraldine Ferraro in 1984 and, of course, Senator Hillary Clinton, who showed such determination and grace in her presidential campaign. It was rightly noted [at the Democratic Party convention] in Denver this week that Hillary left 18 million cracks in the highest, hardest glass ceiling in America. But it turns out the women of America aren't finished yet. And we can shatter that glass ceiling once and for all.[2]

Despite Palin's attempt to link her candidacy with Clinton's, the two women have little in common politically. Clinton, for example, is pro-choice on abortion, favors a more activist role for the federal government, supports some restrictions on the right to bear arms, and is a proponent of universal health care. Palin, in contrast, is opposed to abortion except when the life of the mother is threatened, wants to limit the role of government, opposes gun control as a lifelong member of the National Rifle Association, and believes that the market, rather than government, can best administer and provide affordable health care. As a U.S. senator, Clinton represented one of the most liberal states in the country, New York; had spent several years in Washington, D.C., as both senator and first lady; and had traveled widely in the United States and abroad. In contrast, Palin was governor of a conservative state; was living in a small town; and at the time of her candidacy, had traveled little outside of the borders of the United States.

Despite their many differences, Palin was able to draw parallels between her candidacy and Clinton's precisely because these two very different politicians did share one important commonality. In seeking the most powerful executive offices in the United States and perhaps the world, both women confronted strong and persistent gender stereotypes that their male opponents did not face.

Research by political scientists and pollsters has shown that voters have clear and specific stereotypes about women candidates and potential women political leaders.[3] Some of these stereotypes can work to the advantage of women seeking office, especially in elections where vot-ers want change and where domestic – as opposed to international – issues are at the forefront of voters' concerns. For example, when com-pared with male candidates, women candidates are commonly viewed as more honest, more caring, more inclusive and collaborative, more likely to bring about change, and more likely to have expertise on domestic issues such as education and health care.

However, just as there are positive stereotypes that can work to the advantage of women candidates, there are also strong negative stereo-types held by voters that can seriously disadvantage women, especially when they run for national and/or executive offices. Voters are less confi-dent that women can handle the emotional demands of high-level office, and they worry about whether women are tough enough and can act decisively. Voters are concerned about whether women are qualified to hold top executive positions while they readily assume that men have the necessary qualifications. Voters worry about whether women have the financial expertise to deal with big budgets, and they view women as less likely than men to be able to manage the military and to handle international crises. Finally, voters are more likely to scrutinize a woman candidate's family situation, expressing concern, for example, that the demands of running for office may lead her to neglect her family. When a man runs for office, his family is generally viewed as an important source of emotional and personal support. When a woman runs, her spouse and children are more often perceived as additional responsibilities that the candidate must shoulder.

Confronting these negative gender stereotypes, Hillary Clinton and Sarah Palin, as pioneers in seeking the country's top executive positions, faced challenges in their campaigns that male contenders for president and vice president did not. Because they are very different women with distinct life experiences and situations, the specific nature of the gender-related challenges Clinton and Palin faced varied, as did their responses. Nevertheless, in each case gender very much helped to shape the candi-date's campaign and the way the media and the public responded to her candidacy.

This chapter examines the ways that gender stereotypes influenced the strategies employed by the 2008 campaigns of Hillary Clinton and Sarah Palin, the media's coverage of their campaigns, and public reactions to the candidates. We begin with a brief historical review of women's efforts to run for president and vice president, focusing largely on major party candidates. We then provide short overviews of the backgrounds and accomplishments of both Clinton and Palin before turning our attention to several major gender stereotypes and the ways these stereotypes affected the campaigns.

HISTORY OF WOMEN CANDIDATES FOR PRESIDENT AND VICE PRESIDENT

While the nation's topmost executive posts – the presidency and the vice presidency – remain male preserves, a handful of women prior to Hillary Clinton and Sarah Palin have dared to put themselves forward as candidates for these offices. These women trailblazers slowly chipped away at the gender role expectations that have traditionally relegated women to the East Wing instead of the West Wing of the White House.

Two women became candidates for the presidency in the nineteenth century before they could even cast ballots themselves. Victoria Woodhull in 1872 and Belva Lockwood in 1884 were both nominated as presidential candidates by a group of reformers identifying themselves as the Equal Rights Party. Woodhull, a newspaper publisher and the first woman stockbroker, was only thirty-three years old when she was nominated, too young to meet the constitutionally mandated age requirement of thirty-five for the presidency, and as an advocate of free love, Woodhull spent Election Day in jail on charges that she had sent obscene materials through the mail.[4] Unlike Woodhull, who made no real effort to convince voters to support her, Lockwood actively campaigned for the presidency despite public mockery and even criticism from her fellow suffragists. As the first woman to practice law in front of the U.S. Supreme Court, Lockwood knew what it felt like to stand alone and did so again in her second presidential bid in 1888.

Before the next female candidate claimed a space on the presidential ballot, three women had been considered for vice presidential slots. Nellie Tayloe Ross of Wyoming, a true pioneer as the nation's first female governor, won thirty-one votes for the vice presidency on the first ballot at the Democratic convention in 1928. Twenty-four years later, in 1952, two Democratic women – India Edwards and Sarah B. Hughes – were considered for the vice presidency, but both withdrew their names before convention balloting began.

In 1964, Republican Senator Margaret Chase Smith from Maine became the first female candidate to have her name placed in nomination for president at a major party convention, winning twenty-seven delegate votes from three states. Eight years later, in 1972, Congresswoman Shirley Chisholm of New York, the first African American woman elected to Congress, became the first woman and the first African American to have her name placed in nomination for the presidency at a Democratic National Convention, winning 151.95 delegate votes.[5] At the same convention, Frances (Sissy) Farenthold won more than four hundred votes, finishing second, for the vice presidential slot.[6]

Smith and Chisholm, like their predecessors Woodhull and Lockwood a century earlier, recognized the improbability of their nomination, measuring success in other terms. Smith prioritized normalizing the image of a woman running for executive office, and Chisholm sought to pave the way for women after her, proving that "it can be done."[7]

Despite the presence of women on some minor party ballots, no woman was nominated to a major party's presidential ticket until 1984, when New York Congresswoman Geraldine Ferraro was chosen as former vice president Walter Mondale's Democratic running mate. Her candidacy was shaded with questions surrounding her gender, from whether she was schooled enough in military and foreign policy to how she should dress and interact with presidential nominee Mondale. Much attention, too, was paid to her husband, a trend that continued with female candidates who came after her, from Elizabeth Dole to Hillary Clinton.

While the defeat of the Mondale-Ferraro ticket in 1984 disappointed voters looking to make history, many supporters of women in politics had their hopes renewed in 1987 as they watched Congresswoman Patricia Schroeder of Colorado prepare to make a presidential bid. Despite the fact that Schroeder raised more money than any woman candidate in U.S. history, she was not able to raise enough. Her decision, long before the first primary, not to officially become a candidate resulted in the tears of her supporters and of Schroeder herself. Those tears, unacceptable for a woman candidate, made national news and provoked public debate about gender traits and presidential politics.

In 1999, two-time presidential cabinet member Elizabeth Dole established an exploratory committee and mounted a six-month campaign for the Republican nomination for president, taking the next step toward putting a woman in the White House. Although Dole consistently came in second in public opinion polls behind George W. Bush and benefited from name recognition, popularity, and political connections, many people doubted that she could win. Even her husband, Senator Bob Dole, who had been the Republican nominee for president in the previous election, expressed reservations about her campaign, telling a *New York Times* reporter:

> [that] he wanted to give money to a rival candidate [McCain] who was fighting for much of her support. He conceded that Mrs. Dole's operation had had growing pains, was slow to raise money early and was only beginning to hit its stride. And while Mr. Dole was hopeful, he allowed that he was by no means certain she would even stay in the race.[8]

In mid-October, five months after Bob Dole's comments and a few months before the first primary, Elizabeth Dole withdrew from the race for the Republican nomination.

In 2003, Carol Moseley Braun, the first African American woman to serve in the U.S. Senate and a former ambassador to New Zealand, was the only woman among ten candidates who contended for the presidential nomination of the Democratic Party. Her appearance in six televised debates among the Democratic hopefuls helped to disrupt the white, masculine image of presidential contenders so strongly embedded in the American psyche. Although major women's groups endorsed her, Moseley Braun dropped out of the race in January 2004, shortly before the first primaries and caucuses took place.

Ruth B. Mandel has described the legacy of the women who ran for the office of president before Hillary Clinton: "They made a claim on public awareness by attaching voices and living images of accomplished woman leaders to the idea that one day a woman could conceivably be president. Their actions made the idea less outrageous to conceive."[9] These women blazed paths, opened doors, and challenged established gender stereotypes and gender role expectations.

HILLARY CLINTON

Hillary Clinton's claim that she was "in to win" the 2008 presidential election moved women candidates from novelty to viability. Standing on the shoulders of the pioneering women who came before her, Clinton took a major step forward in normalizing the idea of a female American president. Her candidacy, popularity, and challenge to gender norms had a near-immediate impact on American politics, as Republican John McCain noted the excitement over a woman candidate and chose Alaska Governor Sarah Palin as his running mate, only the second woman – and the first Republican woman – to win a spot on a major party's presidential ticket.

Accustomed to making news and, more important, to making history, Hillary Clinton built on a lifetime of leadership and trailblazing in her bid as the first serious female contender for the U.S. presidency. Clinton's political activism began early on, as a "Goldwater girl" in the early 1960s and later as a college student supporting the Democratic, antiwar candidate, Senator Eugene McCarthy, in 1968. As president of her college government association, she became the first student to speak at a Wellesley College commencement. After graduation, Clinton earned a law degree from Yale University, married Bill Clinton, and as a practicing attorney was twice named to the list of the one hundred most influential lawyers in America.

Hillary Clinton's political and professional credentials became the subject of debate and discussion as she moved into the role of a political wife – albeit one who was far from traditional and at many times controversial. Even before her move to the White House, Clinton was making news for challenging traditional roles and for balancing work and family as the first lady of Arkansas. Once she was in Washington, D.C., she continued to defy established expectations for a first lady, made most evident in her move of the first lady's office from the East Wing to the West Wing of the White House. Within five days of becoming first lady, Clinton was named by her husband to head the President's Task Force on Health Care Reform, living up to his earlier promise that voters supporting his candidacy would be getting "two for one." Many criticized Hillary Clinton's policy role as evidence of her unrestrained ambition, and the failure of the Clinton health-care plan only fueled greater vilification of her by many political foes.

Dealt both a personal and a professional blow with the defeat of health-care reform, Hillary Clinton restored her political capital internationally with her famous 1995 address to the United Nations in Beijing. Reminding the Chinese government, and the world, that "women's rights are human rights," Clinton cemented a role as an advocate and a role model for women.[10] In 1997, she continued her long-standing advocacy for children and families by initiating federal efforts for the Children's Health Insurance Program. Despite these successes, Clinton's reputation was tarred by her rejection of a traditional role as first lady, her deep involvement in White House policy, repeated allegations about her possible involvement in political scandals, and her decision to stay with a cheating husband. Clinton left the White House as a controversial and polarizing figure, deeply admired by some and intensely disliked by others.

Unsurprisingly to most of her closest friends and political peers, Hillary Clinton began her own political campaign for the U.S. Senate from New York even before exiting the White House. After a tough campaign in which her motives and loyalty to the Empire State were questioned, Hillary Clinton became the first former first lady ever elected to public office. Clinton won over New Yorkers through a county-by-county listening tour, a strategy that she would later use to launch her presidential bid, and she defeated her Republican opponent, Congressman Rick Lazio, by a comfortable margin. Continuing a path that has proved anything but typical, Clinton joined the U.S. Senate in 2001, prepared to leave a lasting imprint there while casting an ambitious eye to her political future.

Clinton built her political credentials through service on the Senate Armed Services Committee and trips to Afghanistan and Iraq. Her work for the people of New York combated the carpetbagger claims that had plagued her first Senate campaign, resulting in a landslide victory in her 2006 reelection race. She proved to be a popular and effective senator.

However, speculation that she would seek the presidency began even before she was elected to the Senate. Just days after President George W. Bush was reelected in 2004, Clinton emerged as the top contender in the Gallup Poll's trial heats of Democratic candidates for 2008, and she maintained the front-runner position in subsequent polls over the following three years.[11] After years of denying her ambition to run, Hillary Clinton announced that she would form an exploratory committee for her presidential bid on January 20, 2007, exactly two years before a new president would be sworn into the White House.

Holding the front-runner position throughout her first year of campaigning for the Democratic nomination, Hillary Clinton blazed a new trail, crossing the country with a motto of "making history" and exciting voters – especially women of all ages, for whom the prospect of a female president became real. Many observers thought her background, political clout, and wide coalition of supporters made her nomination inevitable. Historians and analysts will, for decades, look back to her campaign to see what shifted the narrative from almost-certain winner to underdog. Poor campaign management and strategy, perceptions of her status as a Washington insider, her vote on the Iraq War, the role of her husband Bill Clinton, the altered primary season calendar, and the phenomenon of her major opponent, Senator Barack Obama, are some of the many possible reasons for Clinton's downslide in polls and, later, in the Democratic primaries. After Clinton's initial defeat in the nation's first contest, the Iowa caucuses, the real battles stretched from the snowy terrain of New Hampshire – where Clinton, like her husband before her, became the state's "comeback kid" – to the deserts of Nevada. The historic primary season of 2008 was unprecedented not only in length but also in the frequency with which front-runner status changed. Over the course of six months, Hillary Clinton and Barack Obama competed in state primaries and caucuses from coast to coast and faced each other in seventeen debates.

After winning nine of the last sixteen primaries and caucuses and nearly 18 million votes nationwide, Hillary Clinton conceded the Democratic nomination on June 7, 2008. Despite calls for her to contest the nomination at her party's convention in Denver, Clinton's preference for unity and loyalty to her party prevailed when she took to the convention floor to stop the roll-call vote and move that her primary rival, Barack Obama, be nominated by acclamation. Although she made history as only the second woman to have her name formally placed into nomination for president at the Democratic National Convention, Clinton took the opportunity to heal primary wounds, telling the crowd, "Whether you voted for me, or voted for Barack, the time is now to unite as a single party with a single purpose. We are on the same team, and none of us can sit on the sidelines."[12] With those words, the general election campaign season began, and Hillary Clinton shifted her role from history-making candidate to strong supporter and campaign surrogate for Obama.

SARAH PALIN

While the Democratic convention in Denver marked the end of Clinton's history-making campaign, it signaled the start of the 2008 campaign for another prominent woman. John McCain announced his choice of Alaska Governor Sarah Palin as the Republican candidate for vice president on the morning after Barack Obama's media-spectacle acceptance speech at Invesco Field. Motivated by hopes of curbing Obama's momentum, McCain's strategy proved successful, as Palin quickly became the focus of news media and water-cooler conversation. Palin was an unexpected candidate, novel for her outsider identity, her colloquial candor, and – for many – her gender. According to a Gallup Poll taken on the day following her first address to the nation, 71 percent of Americans reported that they either had no opinion of her or had never heard of her.[13] While nearly everyone in the country had an (often strong) opinion of Hillary Clinton after her nearly two decades in the national spotlight, Sarah Palin's route to celebrity was condensed into a two-and-a-half-month period between McCain's announcement of his choice of running mate and Election Day of 2008. By mid-September, almost 81 percent of Americans held an opinion of Palin, and by Election Day, Palin and Clinton were almost equally well known, according to public opinion polls.[14]

Palin was not politically active as an adolescent or young adult, but she did crosscut gender role boundaries as an avid hunter and outdoors-woman, a star point guard on her high school basketball team, and a contestant in beauty pageants. She attended five colleges in six years, ultimately graduating from the University of Idaho. After working as a sports journalist and commercial fisher, Palin began her political career in 1992 when, at the age of twenty-eight, she was elected to the city coun-cil of the small Alaskan town of Wasilla. Palin became mayor of Wasilla in 1996, unseating a three-term incumbent, and she later served as pres-ident of the Alaska Conference of Mayors. It was not long before her political ambitions grew. In 2002, she sought the Republican nomination for lieutenant governor but was defeated for the first time in her polit-ical career. She was soon appointed to the Alaska Oil and Conservation Commission – gaining knowledge and experience that she used in later races – but resigned from the board in 2004 citing ethics violations by its members, thereby helping to shape her image as a pro-reform candidate for governor in 2006.

After defeating the incumbent governor to win the Republican nom-ination, Palin entered the 2006 general election race for governor as the clear front-runner. She campaigned as an outsider on an ethics reform platform, turning criticisms of her inexperience into evidence that she was not tied to established interests and would be a fresh face for Alaskan government. Her political skills were evident. Profiling herself as an antiestablishment underdog and agent of change, she became the first woman, and the youngest person, ever to serve as governor of Alaska.

Faced with an energized Democratic electorate and the wide appeal of Barack Obama's historic nomination, the 2008 McCain campaign needed a vice presidential candidate who could bring attention and excitement to the Republican ticket. Palin not only was a popular governor, a rousing speaker, and a crowd pleaser but also had a reputation as a reformer and a maverick with strong ties to the social conservative base of the party. Moreover, her gender was viewed as a potential lure for any Clinton sup-porters harboring resentment over Clinton's loss.

As Palin took to the campaign trail, she did bring considerable energy and attention to the Republican ticket, attracting strong reactions, both positive and negative, from voters – particularly women, social conservatives, and working-class Republicans. She took the Republican National Convention by storm, demonstrating that she would gladly be John McCain's loyal surrogate and an attack dog when necessary. In the week following the convention, Palin received more media attention than either John McCain or Barack Obama, with more than half of the campaign news stories focused on her.[15] Throughout the remaining weeks of the campaign, Palin remained the subject of much media analysis and commentary, although the economic crisis chipped away at the Republican ticket's hope for a general election victory.

Over the two months she spent on the campaign trail, Sarah Palin's persona became fodder for public debate and speculation. While she was unknown early on, Americans soon had strong opinions of Palin. The McCain campaign, realizing that she had little knowledge of international politics and little experience with national political issues, initially tried to keep her away from the press while they schooled her on policy. This made the press all the more eager for interviews with her, and when Palin stumbled in her first major interviews with news anchors Charlie Gibson of ABC and Katie Couric of CBS, the public impression grew that she was unprepared to be one heartbeat away from the presidency. Nevertheless, Palin continued to draw large and enthusiastic crowds at her campaign events. By the end of the 2008 presidential campaign, few voters seemed indifferent toward Palin; her supporters were as passionate in their enthusiasm for her as her detractors were in their criticism. Sarah Palin emerged from the 2008 election as one of the most fascinating women on the political scene and a likely contender for the Republican presidential nomination in 2012.

GENDER STEREOTYPES AND THE CANDIDACIES
OF CLINTON AND PALIN

While Palin was unable to break the glass ceiling cracked by Hillary Clinton's candidacy, both women's candidacies demonstrate the gender-related struggles of women in American politics, particularly at the national executive level. As noted by the Women's Media Center, the 2008 election may have been "sexism's coming out party."[16] The 2008 election experiences of Hillary Clinton and Sarah Palin cannot be understood and appreciated without serious consideration of the gender stereotypes that influenced their campaign strategies and perceptions of their campaigns.

EXPERIENCE AND QUALIFICATIONS

Women are assumed to be less qualified than men to hold public office, even when they have more experience and stronger credentials. This stereotype is evident not only in research on voters but also in studies of women officeholders. For example, research on women state legislators conducted by the Center for American Women and Politics has found that women legislators tend to be more qualified than their male counterparts on every single measure of political experience except for holding previous elective office – an indication that women who run for office know that they need to accumulate more experience to be perceived as equally qualified as male candidates.[17]

To counter this stereotype, Hillary Clinton made experience the centerpiece of her campaign for the Democratic nomination. Her campaign advisors knew they still needed to convince voters that Clinton was qualified to be president, even though her credentials included seven years in the U.S. Senate, eight years as first lady, and many years of advocacy work on public policy. On the campaign trail, Clinton proclaimed that she would be "ready to lead on day 1," and she made frequent references to her more than thirty-five years of experience. While Barack Obama talked in broad strokes with appealing rhetoric, Hillary Clinton emphasized her mastery of the details of public policy, demonstrating the knowledge she had gained through her years of experience in public life.

Of course, by emphasizing experience as the major theme of her campaign, Clinton ceded the issue of change to Obama, who made it the centerpiece of his campaign. Ironically, the Clinton campaign may have believed that it did not need to explicitly emphasize change. The campaign may well have assumed that, as a woman, Clinton would, by default, be seen as an agent of change. After all, a well-documented finding in the literature on women candidates is that women, as traditional outsiders in politics, are viewed by voters as the embodiment of change. Thus, women candidates tend to do well in elections where voters are dissatisfied and are looking to throw the rascals out, as they did in congressional races in 1992, for example.

The gender-based benefit expected by the Clinton campaign was unexpectedly lost as she faced an opponent, Barack Obama, who also embodied change through his physical appearance and adopted "Change We Can Believe In" as his campaign theme. Although Obama did not have a lengthy record of political experience at the beginning of his campaign, having served for only two years in the U.S. Senate and for seven years as a state senator in Illinois, his campaign did not have to worry, as Clinton's did, that its candidate's gender would make him appear less qualified. Consequently, Obama chose to emphasize, as well as to embody, change. Thus, in one of the great ironies of the 2008 campaign, the first woman to make a serious run for the White House came to be seen as the representative of the status quo.

Because of the stereotype that women are less qualified than men to hold public office, and because Clinton was seeking a highly masculinized position (see Chapter 1, in this volume) whose previous occupants had all been men, Hillary Clinton and her campaign had no choice but to emphasize experience. However, her campaign may have made a strategic error in failing to transition successfully at some point from an emphasis on experience to an emphasis on change or, even better, in finding a workable and catchy campaign theme that would have encompassed both experience and change. Clinton and her campaign did, at times, talk about change as well as experience. For example, in ads airing in Iowa and New Hampshire, the campaign added *change* to Clinton's list of credentials: "If we have the will, she has the strength. If we have the conviction, she has the experience. If we're ready for change, she's ready to lead."[18] However, the Clinton campaign's occasional references to change failed to build on positive ideals of women as change agents by alluding to gender-related differences in background and life experiences, and instead were always overshadowed by references to masculine traits of leadership and experience.

Hillary Clinton's campaign was very successful in countering the stereotype of women as unqualified for office. A *USA Today*/Gallup Poll taken February 21–24, 2008, found that 65 percent of Americans agreed that Hillary Clinton had the necessary experience to be a good president.[19] In contrast, Sarah Palin was never able to overcome perceptions of inexperience. According to the national exit poll conducted on Election Day, only 38 percent of voters thought Palin was qualified to be president if necessary.[20]

The McCain-Palin campaign did make some attempts to address the issue of Palin's experience. For example, the campaign ran a thirty-second ad arguing that Palin's record as a reformer was stronger than Obama's. The McCain-Palin campaign also argued both in an ad and through campaign spokespeople that Palin's experience as a governor "who oversees 24,000 state employees, 14 statewide cabinet agencies and a $10 billion budget" exceeded that of "Barack Obama's experience as a one-term junior senator from Illinois."[21] But none of this seemed to work. Perhaps the campaign's attempts to compare Palin with Obama to counter the perception of Palin as inexperienced were not very compelling. Perhaps the short amount of time Palin was a candidate – only two months as opposed to two years for Hillary Clinton – was simply insufficient to combat such a strong gender stereotype. Or perhaps the fact that Palin was propelled onto the national stage before accumulating more experience made the problem insurmountable.

Regardless, one factor that clearly contributed to Palin's problem with the experience issue was her treatment by the press. She was repeatedly characterized by the media as lacking the experience necessary to be vice president or, if need be, president. Her first major interview after being selected as a vice presidential nominee was with Charlie Gibson, the anchor of the evening news on ABC. Gibson's very first question was, "Governor, let me start by asking you a question that I asked John McCain about you, and it is really the central question. Can you look the country in the eye and say 'I have the experience and I have the ability to be not just vice president, but perhaps president of the United States of America?'" Gibson continued to pursue the experience issue in his next question, "And you didn't say to yourself, 'Am I experienced enough? Am I ready? Do I know enough about international affairs? Do I – will I feel comfortable enough on the national stage to do this?'" When Palin answered that she "didn't hesitate, no," Gibson responded, "Didn't that take some hubris?"[22]

One wonders whether Gibson would have asked an equally inexperienced man, "Didn't that take some hubris?" Interestingly, Gibson never asked this question of Barack Obama or George W. Bush, although neither had impressive political or international experience before becoming a presidential candidate and president.

In another early interview with Palin, Katie Couric, anchor of the CBS evening news, asked a similarly unusual question about what newspapers and magazines Palin read "to stay informed and to understand the world."[23] Although Palin's answer was less than satisfying, this question has never before been asked of candidates for president and vice president, even those who were relatively inexperienced before running.

Given the media's treatment of Palin, it is not surprising that she was unable to counter the impression of her as inexperienced and unqualified.

The media continually reinforced this impression of Palin in the minds of their audiences.

Unfortunately for Palin, so did the McCain campaign itself. The campaign tried to keep Palin away from reporters for several weeks after she was nominated, which created the impression that they thought she was not experienced and informed enough to handle herself with the press. This treatment prompted Campbell Brown, anchor of an evening show on CNN, to call on the campaign to "Free Sarah Palin" and to "stop treating Sarah Palin like she is a delicate flower who will wilt at any moment."[24] After the campaign and the election were over, Palin herself expressed some discontent over her treatment by her handlers in the campaign, suggesting, "If I would have been in charge, I would have wanted to speak to more reporters because that's how you get your message out to the electorate."[25] In keeping Palin from the press, those who were "in charge" in the McCain campaign played into and reinforced the stereotype of the inexperienced, unqualified woman instead of giving Palin an opportunity to try in some way to overcome this stereotype.

TOUGHNESS

Just as voters are concerned about whether women candidates are qualified and have sufficient experience to serve in high-level political office, they also worry that women may not be tough enough to take command and handle the emotional demands of the job. This stereotype is especially problematic for women running for executive positions such as governor or president, held by only one person at a time. Fortunately, we have progressed since 1972, when Dr. Edgar F. Berman, a member of the Democratic Party's Committee on National Priorities, argued that women's "raging hormonal imbalance" made them unfit to hold top executive positions.[26] Nevertheless, some voters still believe that men are better suited for the demands of the office. As a recent Barbara Lee Foundation study of voters' attitudes toward women governors reported, "Even when voters assume a woman is qualified for the job in terms of prior experience, they question whether she would be tough enough to be a good executive."[27]

What makes this toughness stereotype particularly difficult and tricky for women candidates is that those who behave in assertive and dominant ways are often labeled as "aggressive" or "bitchy." Acceptable behavior for men is not necessarily acceptable for women. Voters also expect women candidates to be feminine – compassionate, nurturing, nice, womanly. As the Barbara Lee Foundation study explained, "Voters want women who are as tough and decisive as men, but voters do not want to elect 'manly' women.... Female candidates walk a tightrope in attempting to present a persona that's neither too strong and aggressive – too 'male' – nor too soft."[28] Women who aspire to the highest levels of political leadership must somehow find a way to strike a balance between masculine and feminine behavior, between toughness and niceness.

As the first woman to make a serious run for the presidency, Hillary Clinton faced great challenges, both in establishing her toughness and in walking the line between masculinity and femininity, between toughness and niceness. Her campaign clearly recognized the need to portray her as strong and decisive, and they succeeded in doing so. She was rarely, if ever, described as weak. From the very beginning of her campaign, Clinton presented herself as tough as nails, as a fighter who would never give up. Campaigning in Ohio, she told a crowd of supporters, "I'm here today because I want to let you know, I'm a fighter, a doer and a champion, and I will fight for you."[29] Governor Mike Easley of North Carolina described Clinton as someone "who makes Rocky Balboa look like a pansy."[30] A union leader in Indiana even introduced her at a campaign event by describing her as a person who has "testicular fortitude!"[31]

Depictions of Clinton's strength were not always positive or benefi-cial, however, as criticisms of her toughness fused with sexist attacks. In an egregious example of misogyny, Tucker Carlson, MSNBC's senior campaign correspondent, exhibited mock castration fears, proclaiming on more than one occasion, "When she [Hillary Clinton] comes on televi-sion, I involuntarily cross my legs."[32] Accompanying such commentary were visual portrayals of Hillary Clinton as an emasculator, such as edi-torial cartoons of Clinton with a whip and Hillary nutcrackers (where the nut was cracked between her thighs) for sale on the Internet and in shops across the country. Images and descriptions of Clinton as Satan also appeared on the Internet and in political cartoons. She was repeatedly characterized as a bitch. Anti-Hillary bumper stickers proclaimed "Stop the bitch" and "Life's a bitch so don't vote for one." In a well-publicized incident, John McCain was asked at a campaign event, "How do we beat the bitch?" His response, "That's an excellent question," received far less publicity.[33] Glenn Beck of CNN and ABC observed of Clinton, "There's something about her vocal range.... She is like the stereotypical...bitch, you know what I mean?"[34] The pundit Alex Castellanos on CNN said of Clinton being called a bitch, "Some women are named that and it is accu-rate.... She can be a very abrasive, aggressive, irritating person."[35] The characterization of Clinton as a bitch occurred so often that it prompted a comedic counterattack in the form of a *Saturday Night Live* skit in which Tina Fey famously proclaimed that "bitches get stuff done" and "bitch is the new black."[36]

While the public clearly came to perceive Clinton as strong, many voters did not see her as particularly likable. Clinton's campaign, caught in a common trap for women trying to balance toughness and niceness, may ultimately have placed too much emphasis on toughness without showing enough of her humanity and humor. Clinton appears to have won over some New Hampshire voters when she teared up on the eve of that state's primary. Behind in the polls, she went on to win the primary the next day, perhaps an indication that people longed to see more of her human side. However, Clinton's boost did not last long, as some political pundits and reporters suggested that her tears were not authentic but rather a political ploy, as though Clinton were a veteran stage actress who could turn tears off and on at will. The media's frequent interpretation of many of Clinton's moves as "calculated," exemplified in stories about her forced laugh, or "cackle," reinforced perceptions that Hillary Clinton was neither genuine nor likable.

While Hillary Clinton had great difficulty walking the difficult line between toughness and niceness, Sarah Palin, in her brief two months in the public eye, seemed to fare better. In her speech before the Republican National Convention on the evening before she was formally nominated for the vice presidency, Palin referred to herself as "just your average hockey mom" and then went on to ask, "You know, they say the difference between a hockey mom and a pit bull? Lipstick."[37] With this one metaphor Palin was able to define herself, with humor, in a way that perfectly balanced masculine and feminine; she was tough as a pit bull, but she tempered her toughness with lipstick.

Palin's convention speech helped to convey her toughness in other ways. Palin presented herself as a reformer who, as governor, had "stood up to the special interests, and the lobbyists, and the Big Oil companies, and the good-old boys." She also claimed that she had taken a tough posture on a federal government earmark viewed by most as an unnecessary expenditure; as she explained, "I told the Congress, 'Thanks, but no thanks,' on that Bridge to Nowhere."[38]

Moreover, as her supporters and detractors alike frequently noted, Palin not only was a hunter but also was the only candidate in the 2008 race who could field dress a moose. Even the mockery of Palin portrayed a tough, but feminine, woman. A widely circulated, Photoshopped picture on the Internet showed Palin's head on the shapely body of a woman, clad in a bikini with a U.S. flag motif and holding a rifle with her finger on the trigger. In summary, although Clinton and Palin were both successful in conveying toughness, Palin may have been more successful in combining niceness with toughness.

COMMANDER IN CHIEF

Related to concerns that women may be inexperienced and weak, a third stereotype plaguing women candidates is that women are less prepared than men for the role of commander in chief and less able than men to handle the military, national security, and foreign affairs. Voters worry that women lack experience and expertise in these areas and that they will be too "soft" in dealing with U.S. enemies. As an example of how this stereotype comes into play when a woman runs for high-level office, Geraldine Ferraro, when she was the Democratic nominee for vice president in 1984, was asked on *Meet the Press* if she would be able, if necessary, to push the button to launch nuclear weapons. No man seeking the presidency or vice presidency had ever been asked a similar question on national television.

Clinton took strong steps to counter this stereotype even before announcing her candidacy for president. As first lady, Hillary Clinton had traveled extensively outside the borders of the United States, and while some questioned how much she had actually engaged in diplomacy, few doubted that she had a strong knowledge of international affairs. Perhaps in anticipation of a presidential bid, Clinton tried to gain the knowledge and experience she would need to be commander in chief from the moment she was elected to the U.S. Senate by obtaining an appointment to the Armed Services Committee. When she decided to run for president, she lined up a long list of military brass who supported her; more than thirty former admirals and generals endorsed her candidacy.[39] Clinton was very careful as a candidate never to show any sign of weakness on military and foreign policy issues, going so far as to say, in a very controversial statement, that if Iran attacked Israel, "we would be able to totally obliterate them."[40]

As a U.S. senator, Hillary Clinton voted to authorize the war in Iraq, and as a candidate, she repeatedly refused to renounce this vote, even though she was heavily criticized by activists on the Left and by her primary opponents, especially Barack Obama and John Edwards, for taking these positions. The media tended to interpret her refusal to call her war vote a mistake as either a character flaw or a strategic mistake. But this refusal is perhaps more accurately interpreted as a response to a strong and persistent gender stereotype. Clinton and her campaign knew that, as a woman, she needed to counter the stereotype that women are soft on defense and military issues. Clinton undoubtedly would have been accused of flip-flopping and portrayed as weak and indecisive on defense if she had renounced her vote on the war. She chose instead to project strength and consistency on issues of military involvement and foreign affairs, even at the cost of some votes among Democrats.

While Hillary Clinton worked hard and took serious steps to overcome the stereotype that women are weak on defense and foreign affairs, Sarah Palin was thrust onto the national stage with little knowledge or preparation in these areas. Foreign policy and military expertise do not always matter greatly for a vice presidential candidate, but the precarious state of the world in 2008, as well as John McCain's advanced age and history of melanoma, ensured that the Republican vice presidential candidate's credentials in these areas would be more closely scrutinized. Governors seldom deal with international issues, and Palin's experience with the military was limited to overseeing the Alaskan National Guard and being a "military mom" whose son was sent to Iraq shortly after her nomination. Unlike Hillary Clinton, who had traveled extensively outside the United States, Palin had not obtained a passport until 2006, and other than visiting Canada, she traveled outside the United States only once, visiting National Guard troops from her state who were serving in Iraq, Kuwait, and Germany. Moreover, in her very first major media interview as a vice presidential candidate, with Charlie Gibson of ABC News, she said of Russia, "They're our next door neighbors and you can actually see Russia from land here in Alaska, from an island in Alaska."[41] Palin's critics and detractors construed and ridiculed this as a statement of her foreign policy experience, and in her *Saturday Night Live* comedic portrayal of Palin, Tina Fey proclaimed, "And I can see Russia from my house."[42] In an astounding example of art imitating life, made more credible by the stereotype that women are not prepared to deal with defense and foreign policy, many Americans came to believe that it was actually Palin, not Fey, who had uttered those words about seeing Alaska from her house. Because Palin had little experience to counter the stereotype that women are not prepared to be commander in chief and deal with international relations, she was particularly vulnerable to the negative gender stereotype and came to be seen as much less prepared than the numerous men, including George W. Bush and Bill Clinton, who had assumed national executive offices with very little military or foreign policy experience.

CHILDREN AND SPOUSES

Private lives pose particular challenges for women candidates. Every woman who runs for office must decide how she will present her children and spouse – or the fact that she has none – to the public. Maternal roles are especially tricky for female candidates. Although voters value the communalism and compassion that they consider attached to women's familial roles, they often worry that women may neglect their maternal responsibilities in seeking office, especially if they have young children. Male candidates are rarely asked the kinds of questions that female candidates face about their parental roles. Instead, the public and the media assume the candidates' wives are taking care of day-to-day family responsibilities. In addition, because voters still see men as playing the dominant role in family decision making, with women being more dependent, a spouse's finances and other affairs are subject to greater scrutiny when a woman runs. The public and the media also are often concerned about how a husband will respond to having his wife in the political limelight. Hillary Clinton and Sarah Palin took decidedly different approaches in confronting these voter concerns and balancing their roles as mothers, wives, and candidates in their campaigns.

Because Hillary Clinton's only daughter, Chelsea, was an adult by the time Clinton decided to seek the presidency, Clinton did not have to deal with voter concerns that she might somehow be neglecting her family responsibilities in running. Nevertheless, she still had to figure out whether to highlight or downplay her maternalism. In a December 2006 memo, Mark Penn, Clinton's chief campaign strategist, wrote that voters "do not want someone who would be the first mama" because such a person would be viewed as too "soft." He added, however, that voters are "open to the first father being a woman," suggesting that Clinton should embrace this paternalistic role by displaying toughness and experience.[43] Perhaps as a result of this advice, Clinton rarely mentioned her maternal role in discussing her policy goals and qualifications for office. For example, when she appeared on ABC's *The View* before formally announcing her candidacy and was asked whether being a mother would give a would-be president an advantage over a male rival, Clinton dodged the question.[44] It was not until her concession speech, after Penn's "first father" strategy failed to secure Clinton the nomination, that she talked about the implications of motherhood for her candidacy:

> I ran as a mother who worries about my daughter's future and a mother who wants to lead all children to brighter tomorrows. To build a future I see, we must make sure that women and men alike understand the struggles of their grandmothers and mothers, and that women enjoy equal opportunities, equal pay, and equal respect.[45]

While Clinton rarely presented herself as a mother in campaigning for office, her campaign did not completely neglect the potential benefits of touting her maternal and familial roles. Seeking to reconcile the image of a tough, experienced candidate with more traditional gender stereotypes, the campaign deployed Dorothy Rodham, Clinton's mother, and Chelsea Clinton, her daughter, to campaign across the country, introducing voters to Clinton's "softer" side. Neither woman focused primarily on Clinton's maternalism, but Chelsea Clinton reminded voters that Clinton was both an extraordinary candidate and a dedicated mother. For example, in a fund-raising appeal for Mother's Day 2008, Chelsea Clinton narrated a video in which she described Hillary Clinton as a loving and devoted mother who had successfully balanced child rearing with professional goals.

While Hillary Clinton seldom emphasized her identity as a mother in campaign images or media coverage, Sarah Palin took to the national scene with her motherhood in tow. She confronted voters' concerns over whether a woman candidate could simultaneously be an adequate mother head-on by presenting herself as a mother-candidate. Introducing her five children to America on the day she was announced as the vice presidential candidate and labeling herself a "hockey mom" in her first national speech at the Republican National Convention, Palin attempted to turn what could have been a liability into an asset by using her maternal identity to forge a connection with voters – particularly women. She was surrounded by her husband and children at the convention, and she was regularly seen with at least one of her children – from baby Trig to seven-year-old Piper to teenager Willow. Even when her children were not with her, Palin made mention of her maternal inclinations in mentioning the faith that she had in John McCain to command her son Track, a young soldier, in war. She also spoke frequently about her concern for families with special-needs children, discussing her decision to carry Trig to term despite his Down syndrome diagnosis and emphasizing how her personal experience would influence the McCain-Palin policy agenda.

Sarah Palin emerged, then, as a candidate who tried to connect to average Americans, not only as a person with small-town, working-class roots but also as a mother of five who was both blessed with and challenged by a special-needs child. Palin used her motherhood to create a sense of camaraderie with working mothers struggling to balance work and family as well as to reassure supporters on the Right who might otherwise have been put off by an ambitious woman pursuing a high-powered career.

Nevertheless, Palin was not completely successful in turning her motherhood into an asset. Many women feared that Palin's "super-woman" or "supermom" image would create unrealistic expectations for women candidates (and women) who came after her. And the question of whether she could be a good mother while seeking high-level political office never really disappeared.

Usually, the strongest criticism of women who try to "do it all" by combining career and family comes from social conservatives on the political Right. However, social conservatives were largely silent in the case of Palin, who shared their political platform and concern for traditional values, while more liberal media questioned her ability to be governor, vice presidential candidate, and mother simultaneously. For example, on NBC's *The Today Show*, coanchor Meredith Vieira observed, "It seems like the conservatives, who would probably advocate that moms stay home, are backing Governor Palin and a lot of the other working moms are questioning her decision."[46] Jodi Kantor and Rachel Swarns of the *New York Times* noted working women's skepticism of Palin's ability to "have it all" and, more specifically, to have it all at once. They described women's commentary on the appropriateness, ability, and influence of Palin's decision to accept the nomination as "Mommy Wars: Special Campaign Edition."[47] For a campaign looking to balance stereotypical expectations and limitations on its female candidate, arguing that Palin represented the juggling everywoman made strategic sense. However, its success was limited.

As was the case for the women who preceded her in American politics, Palin's parental role was evaluated much more thoroughly than that of her male counterparts. Although John Edwards's young children were on the campaign trail for months during the primaries without much public concern or scrutiny, commentators and citizens alike began asking how Palin's children were being schooled and whether Trig should be in front of stage lights or even out in public past a certain time of night. The concern over whether Palin was somehow a bad mother who was putting her personal ambition ahead of her children's welfare was amplified when the public learned that Palin's teen daughter, Bristol, was pregnant. Female commentators were particularly critical. For example, Campbell Brown of CNN questioned a McCain-Palin campaign adviser about Palin's maternal responsibility:

> This [is] obviously putting this young woman, Bristol Palin, smack in the media spotlight at what's already got to be a very challenging time in her life, I mean, how do you respond to people who wonder why her mother would have subjected her to this kind of scrutiny by accepting this high-profile position? ... And so do you risk putting her through an incredibly difficult process by accepting this job if you're her mother?[48]

The *Washington Post*'s Sally Quinn made similar claims about Palin's flawed priorities and returned to the larger question of whether Palin could or should attempt to be both candidate and mother simultaneously. In a piece that demonstrates vividly the fears over whether women can fulfill both private and public responsibilities and that assumes women's primordial role as caregiver, Quinn proclaimed, "Her first priority has to be her children. When the phone rings at three in the morning and one of her children is really sick, what choice will she make?"[49]

Children are not the only private-life issue with which candidates must deal; spouses pose a challenge as well. In 2008, both Hillary Clinton and Sarah Palin sought to portray their independence, challenging stereotypical expectations that female spouses cannot or should not act alone.

Hillary Clinton's primary campaign was particularly challenged to combat the stereotype of spousal dependence because her spouse is former president Bill Clinton. For much of the primary season, debates over his role and influence raged, and his words and actions were closely analyzed. While Clinton's chief strategist hoped to present Hillary as the "new Clinton," many in the media and the public continued to frame her as the former first lady. The campaign struggled to balance Clinton's emphasis on her past experiences in the White House with her forward-looking plans as presidential candidate. Moreover, when she did add first lady to her credentials for the Oval Office, skeptics and competitors alike accused her of exaggeration. Even Barack Obama challenged the claim that a president's wife can act both independently and substantively. Just before the primary season began, he compared Hillary Clinton to his wife, Michelle, arguing that neither woman could claim experience on the basis of their spousal ties:

> There is no doubt that Bill Clinton had faith in her and consulted with her on issues, in the same way that I would consult with Michelle if there were issues. On the other hand, I don't think Michelle would claim she is the best qualified person to be a U.S. Senator by virtue of me talking to her on occasion about the work I've done.[50]

The criticism of Clinton's credentials as first lady blended into more direct claims that she would not have advanced in U.S. politics without the assistance of her husband, thus deriding her Senate victories as not won through her own merit. Chris Matthews of MSNBC commented after Hillary Clinton's comeback in the New Hampshire primary:

> Let's not forget – and I'll be brutal – the reason she's a U.S. Senator, the reason she's a candidate for president, the reason she may be a front-runner is her husband messed around. That's how she got to be senator from New York. We keep forgetting it. She didn't win there on her own merit. She won because everybody felt, "My God, this woman stood up under humiliation," right? That's what happened.[51]

Matthews's analysis, crude in its expression, illustrates the struggle that Clinton faced to be viewed as a worthy, credentialed, and independent candidate for president.

Hillary Clinton also confronted suggestions that she would not act alone should she assume the nation's highest office. Again, the Clinton campaign sought to minimize these fears by avoiding "two for the price of one" reminders and challenging claims that Bill Clinton was a cocandidate seeking a third term in the Oval Office. Unlike the other candidates' spouses, Bill Clinton did not attend public forums and debates and was rarely at Hillary Clinton's side at campaign appearances. Despite these efforts, Bill Clinton continued to influence Hillary Clinton's campaign – at times for better and at other times for worse.

Sarah Palin's spousal relationship was less scrutinized by the public and the media than was Hillary Clinton's. However, similar patterns were evident. In numerous profiles of Palin, Todd Palin was described as a persistent influence not only on her life but also on her governing. Michelle Cottle, of the *National Review*, wrote that "Todd Palin is Hillary Clinton circa 1992," commenting on a *Washington Post* profile of the couple that cited them as commonly referred to in tandem – "Sarah and Todd." She added that Todd Palin was privy to high-level meetings and official e-mail, in addition to informally lobbying lawmakers, traveling on state business, and counseling the governor on major policy decisions.[52] Cottle's commentary and similar profiles were not without some factual basis. In an ethics report filed by the Alaska Legislature in October 2008, Todd Palin was charged with having "unusual access" to the governor and "significant influence" on her decision making. In reacting to the report, the McCain campaign compared him to Hillary Clinton and Eleanor Roosevelt, calling his influence typical of first spouses who had come before him. Although the historical comparisons might be valid, the genders of the candidate and spouse were reversed in the case of the Palins, so the idea of a spousal invisible hand influencing Sarah Palin's priorities served to reinforce the traditional stereotype of women's dependence on men in decision making.

Despite media commentary about his possible influence on her as governor of Alaska, Todd Palin did not play an overshadowing role on the campaign trail. Palin traveled with his candidate-wife at times, being introduced as the "first dude" and often shown holding his youngest child, Trig. However, he rarely spoke at campaign events, and his media exposure was slim and often unnoticed. His backseat role in the campaign was an apparent strategic choice, quieting most fears that he might have a strong influence on his wife's actions as vice president.

SEXUALITY

Beyond familial roles, female candidates are subjected to more blatant evaluations of femininity and sexuality based largely on their appearances. Voters want women candidates who are tough but feminine – and attractive but not too attractive. Women who are too unattractive or too unfeminine are often branded disparagingly as lesbians. Women who are too attractive can be perceived as bimbos and sex objects and find that they have a hard time being taken seriously. For years, scholars and media critics have noted the greater attention paid to female candidates' clothing, hair, age, and looks, arguing that such attention detracts from women's personas as substantive candidates for office. The same questions and criticisms emerged in the 2008 election, as comments on Hillary Clinton's pantsuits and Sarah Palin's beauty were all too common. While the attire and attractiveness of both women received far more attention than did the physical presentation of most of their male competitors, these women represent quite different examples of sexual imagery, commentary, and reaction.

Hillary Clinton has never been associated with traditional norms of femininity. As first lady, her appearance was criticized; her sexuality questioned; and her character profiled as masculine, tough, and bitchy. Clinton has largely been viewed as almost asexual. Her pantsuits, the fodder for many jokes, are more symbolic of a woman who has worked to blend the masculine and feminine, to emphasize her competence over her appearance.

The androgyny of Clinton's self-presentation and reactions to it have led to great discomfort among many commentators who have questioned whether Clinton really is a woman. Conservative shock jock Rush Limbaugh has called her the only man he knows in the Democratic Party and, with others, has perpetuated speculation that she might be a lesbian. The claim that Clinton lacked feminine sexuality was even used in the late 1990s to explain (and sometimes justify) her husband's infidelity. While references to Hillary Clinton's masculine or androgynous self-presentation may have made her seem less likable or sympathetic, her disassociation from the traditional feminine image has afforded her a greater claim to toughness and competence, traits vital to a campaign for commander in chief.

While Clinton is often perceived as asexual, she did not completely avoid evaluations based on stereotypical notions of femininity throughout her presidential campaign, nor did commentators, supporters, or the campaign stay silent in response. Robin Givhan of the *Washington Post* sparked a public debate about candidate gender and coverage of appearance in July 2007 when she wrote about Clinton's unprecedented show of cleavage on the Senate floor. Her commentary went beyond a basic critique of Clinton's outfit to imply more about the candidate's sexuality and gender-based strategy. Givhan wrote:

> Showing cleavage is a request to be engaged in a particular way. It doesn't necessarily mean that a woman is asking to be objectified, but it does suggest a certain confidence and physical ease. It means that a woman is content being perceived as a sexual person in addition to being seen as someone who is intelligent, authoritative, witty and whatever else might define her personality. It also means that she feels that all those other characteristics are so apparent and undeniable, that they will not be overshadowed.[53]

While Givhan may have been attempting to commend Clinton on her newfound sense of sexual confidence, female critics, Clinton supporters, and even the Clinton campaign reacted with both rage and disappointment that such attention was being paid to a presidential candidate's appearance.

Givhan's surprised reaction to Clinton's dipping neckline makes clear the more persistent image of Clinton as unfeminine, especially in appearance. This lack of femininity was somewhat related to Hillary Clinton's age. Women are typically subjected to age-based criticism much earlier and more frequently than their male counterparts, and women in the public eye are at risk of losing ties to sexuality as they age. Rush Limbaugh incited debate over Hillary Clinton's age and image. In a lengthy rant in December 2007, Limbaugh posed a question to his listeners about the prospect of Hillary Clinton as president: "Will the country want to actually watch a woman get older before their eyes on a daily basis?"[54] While the idea of watching John McCain – the oldest of the potential candidates for president in 2008 – age in the White House was never discussed on the airwaves, this bias against older women was also apparent in other comments by reporters and pundits that described Clinton's appearance as "tired," "wrinkled," or "aged." Whether because of age or wardrobe, Hillary Clinton faced broad-based characterizations as a woman lacking sexuality and the expressions of femininity so expected from women.

Whereas Hillary Clinton's public image has been one devoid of much feminine sexuality, vice presidential candidate Sarah Palin's public image was hypersexualized from the moment she took to the national scene in August 2008. From her nickname "Caribou Barbie" to media emphasis on her days as a beauty pageant contestant, Sarah Palin's image as candidate was uncomfortably paired with her sex appeal. Much of the commentary surrounding Palin's appearance can be described within the frame of a Madonna-whore dichotomy. While she was often portrayed as the beautiful, pure, and down-to-earth mother-politician, Palin was also viewed as less innocent at times, strategically employing her sex appeal for political benefit. In a *Salon* article, Tom Perrotta explored these two sides of Palin, describing her as the "sexy puritan" who symbolizes a new Christian Right archetype of the political woman:

> Sexy Puritans engage in the culture war on two levels – not simply by advocating conservative positions on hot-button social issues but by embodying nonthreatening mainstream standards of female beauty and behavior at the same time. The net result is a paradox, a bit of cognitive dissonance very useful to the cultural right: You get a little thrill along with your traditional values, a wink along with the wagging finger. Somehow, you don't feel quite as much like a prig as you expected to.[55]

The GOP itself emphasized Palin's attractiveness at the Republican National Convention. Selling buttons with Palin's image and the words "Hottest Governor from the Coldest State," the Republican Party linked Palin's political appeal to her physical appearance. The Republican National Committee immediately assigned a stylist to Palin and purchased thousands of dollars worth of wardrobe, hair, and makeup assistance to propagate the image that Palin had garnered in Alaska as one of America's "hottest governors." As she did with Hillary Clinton, Robin Givhan of the *Washington Post* commented on what Palin's image said about her sexuality:

> Palin's power isn't in her physical looks as much as in the packaging. Palin seems to dress for pretty rather than powerful. She is willing to be sexual, with the occasional fitted jacket and high heels. She wears dangly earrings. Campaign photographers can't seem to resist shooting her legs, as if they've never seen an American female politician with bare gams wearing three-inch heels. (Then again, they probably haven't.)[56]

Katha Pollitt, one of many feminists critical of Palin, preferred the whorelike characterization of a woman substituting sexuality for substance, conceding to a stereotype that bars women from pairing brains and beauty together. After Palin's nomination, she wrote, "As has been known to happen in less exalted workplaces, Palin got the promotion because the boss just liked her."[57] Kathleen Parker, conservative columnist and Palin critic, described a deeper psychological root to Palin's selection, commenting that McCain was swayed by Palin's attractiveness as Antony succumbed to Cleopatra.[58] Amanda Fortini of *New York Magazine* portrayed Palin as campaigning on a "platform of charm rather than substance." She cited Michelle Goldberg, who criticized Palin's style as "a brazen attempt to flirt [her] way into the good graces of the voting public."[59]

The attention paid to Palin's image – from her hairdo to her rimless glasses – often masked both Palin's political achievements and questions about her competence for national executive office, at least early on. Media pundits, particularly men, were taken by Palin's attractiveness. Rush Limbaugh labeled Palin a "babe," Fred Barnes of the *Weekly Standard* noted she was "exceptionally pretty," Jay Nordlinger of the *National Review* described Palin as "a former beauty-pageant contestant, and a real honey, too," and Bill Kristol called her "my heartthrob."[60] The most blatant sexualization came when Donny Deutsch admitted, "I want her to lay in bed next to me," during a CNBC segment on the candidate.[61] Even Palin's political counterparts commented on her appearance, with Joe Biden calling her "good-looking" and Pakistani president Asif Ali Zardari describing Palin as "gorgeous" in a political meet and greet. Thus, even in formal political settings, Palin's attractiveness seemed to overshadow her image as politician. In her case, sexuality proved to be a blessing in garnering candidate attention and even favorability but a curse in that such attention and favorability were rooted in image over substance and sexuality over politics.

CONCLUSION

Gender stereotypes present female candidates for the top executive offices in the United States with several obstacles and challenges that their male counterparts do not confront. Men who seek the presidency or vice presidency do not have to continually prove themselves qualified for office, capable of making difficult decisions, and tough enough to handle the world's crises. Unlike female candidates, men rarely face questions about their parental responsibilities interfering with their professional lives. Men are rarely burdened by questions of spousal influence and are not usually characterized by journalists or pundits on the basis of appearances or perceptions of sexuality.

While fundamentally different in ideology and persona, Hillary Clinton and Sarah Palin faced similar gender-based challenges, although popular criticisms and their campaigns' reactions differed. Hillary Clinton, a political celebrity and knowingly ambitious legislator, focused her campaign on strength and experience, avoiding the stereotypic hurdles faced by women who came before her. While successful in demonstrating the qualifications and toughness necessary for executive office, Clinton's masculine emphasis failed to take advantage of the positive traits of change, warmth, compassion, and communalism often attributed to female candidates. Sarah Palin, in contrast, took full advantage of her feminine identity, becoming the mother-candidate who could appeal to new swaths of conservative voters. Although the McCain-Palin campaign attempted to balance Palin's "soft" image with a no-nonsense frontierswoman persona, it was Palin's lack of national political exposure and international experience that proved to be her Achilles' heel. Finally, the popular obsession with both women's sexuality provided unwanted attention for women asking to be taken seriously as presidential or vice presidential contenders.

Clinton's and Palin's struggles are not new to female candidates, nor will they disappear for women running in the near future. However, these challenges are uniquely amplified in candidacies for the nation's highest executive offices – the presidency and the vice presidency. As both women move on in their political careers – Hillary Clinton as secretary of state and Sarah Palin as a potential 2012 Republican presidential candidate – political observers and scholars alike are left asking what might be different the next time a woman runs for president of the United States. Has the 2008 campaign altered perceptions of gender and the presidency? Have Clinton and Palin changed expectations of presidential candidates' images, traits, and experiences? And, finally, how much longer will it take to finally crack that highest, hardest glass ceiling in American politics? While Hillary Clinton's and Sarah Palin's history-making candidacies may have made the presence of women's names on future presidential ballots less remarkable, and perhaps even expected, the 2008 race demonstrated all too well the power of the sexism and gender stereotypes that will likely continue to influence the candidacies of the women who seek the presidency in upcoming elections.

NOTES

1 Washingtonpost.com. Transcript: Hillary Rodham Clinton Suspends Her Presidential Campaign. <http://www.washingtonpost.com/wp-dyn/content/article/2008/06/07/AR2008060701029.html> February 12, 2009.

2 Clips and Comment: News, Politics, and Society: Ohio and the World. <http://www.clipsandcomment.com/2008/08/29/transcript-sarah-palin-speech-in-dayton-ohio/> February 12, 2009.

3 For example, see Leonie Huddy and Nayda Terkildsen. 1993. Gender Stereotypes and the Perception of Male and Female Candidates. *American Journal of Political Science* 37(1): 119–47; Leonie Huddy and Nayda Terkildsen. 1993. The Consequences of Gender Stereotypes for Women Candidates at Different Levels and Types of Office. *Political Research Quarterly* 46(3): 503–25; Kim Fridkin Kahn. 1996. *The Political Consequences of Being a Woman: How Stereotypes Influence the Conduct and Consequences of Campaigns*. New York: Columbia University Press; and Barbara Lee Family Foundation. 2001. *Keys to the Governor's Office*. Brookline, MA: Barbara Lee Family Foundation.

4 Jo Freeman. 2008. *We Will Be Heard: Women's Struggles for Political Power in the United States*. Lanham, MD: Rowman and Littlefield.

5 Ibid.

6 Center for American Women and Politics. August 2008. Women Presidential and Vice Presidential Candidates. This fact sheet is available in pdf form at www.cawp.rutgers.edu/fast_facts/elections/historical_trends.php.

7 Shirley Chisholm. 1973. *The Good Fight.* New York: Harper Collins.

8 Richard L. Berke. May 17, 1999. As Political Spouse, Bob Dole Strays from Campaign Script. *New York Times.* <http://query.nytimes.com/gst/fullpage .html?res=9B06E1DF153EF934A25756C0A96F958260> February 12, 2009.

9 Ruth Mandel. 2007. She's the Candidate! A Woman for President. In *Women and Leadership: The State of Play and Strategies for Change,* ed. Barbara Kellerman and Deborah L. Rhode. San Francisco: Jossey-Bass, 283–311.

10 Patrick E. Tyler. September 6, 1995. Hillary Clinton, in China, Details Abuse of Women. *New York Times.* <http://query.nytimes.com/gst/fullpage.html? res=990CEFDF133DF935A3575AC0A963958260> February 17, 2009.

11 Gallup. November 16, 2004. Hillary Clinton, Giuliani Early Favorites for 2008. <http://www.gallup.com/poll/14053/Hillary-Clinton-Giuliani-Early-Favorites-2008.aspx> February 17, 2009.

12 National Public Radio. August 26, 2008. Transcript: Hillary Clinton's Prime-Time Speech. <http://www.npr.org/templates/story/story.php?storyId= 94003143> February 17, 2009.

13 Gallup. August 30, 2008. Palin Unknown to Most Americans. <http://www .gallup.com/poll/109951/Palin-Unknown-Most-Americans.aspx> February 17, 2009.

14 Gallup. Favorability: People in the News. <http://www.gallup.com/poll/ 1618/Favorability-People-News.aspx> February 17, 2009.

15 Pew Project for Excellence in Journalism. October 22, 2009. Winning the Media Campaign: Sarah Palin. <http://www.journalism.org/node/13310> February 17, 2009.

16 Hannah Seligson. November 21, 2008. Sexism's Coming Out Party. *Wall Street Journal.* <http://online.wsj.com/article/SB122727851066847919.html> February 17, 2009.

17 Susan J. Carroll and Wendy S. Strimling. 1983. *Women's Routes to Elective Office: A Comparison with Men's.* New Brunswick, NJ: Center for the American Woman and Politics.

18 Marc Ambinder. September 5, 2007. Obama, Clinton Air "Change" Ads. *The Atlantic.* <http://marcambinder.theatlantic.com/archives/2007/09/ obama_clinton_air_change_ads.php> February 17, 2009.

19 Gallup. March 4, 2008. The Experience Paradox. <http://www.gallup.com/ video/104737/Experience-Necessary.aspx> February 12, 2009.

20 CNN. Election Center 2008. President: National Exit Poll. <http://www .cnn.com/ELECTION/2008/results/polls/#val=USP00p4> February 12, 2009.

21 Politico. Mike Allen. Ad: Palin More Qualified Than Obama. <http://www .politico.com/news/stories/0908/13111.html> February 12, 2009.

22 ABC News. September 11, 2008. EXCERPTS: Charlie Gibson Interviews Sarah Palin. <http://abcnews.go.com/Politics/Vote2008/story?id=5782924&page= 1> February 12, 2009.

23 CBS News. CBS Evening News with Katie Couric. Palin Opens Up on Controversial Issues. <http://www.cbsnews.com/stories/2008/09/30/eveningnews/ main4490618.shtml> February 12, 2009.

24 CNN. Campbell Brown. Commentary: Sexist Treatment of Palin Must End. <http://www.cnn.com/2008/POLITICS/09/24/campbell.brown.palin/> February 12, 2009.

25 Huffington Post. Rachel Weiner. Palin: McCain's Biggest Mistake Was Sheltering Me from the Press. <http://www.huffingtonpost.com/2008/12/22/palin-mccains-biggest-mis_n_152857.html> February 12, 2009.

26 Patsy Mink, Veteran Hawaii Congresswoman, Dies at 74. September 30, 2002. *New York Times*. <http://query.nytimes.com/gst/fullpage.html?res=9A06E0DC1538F933A0575AC0A9649C8B63> February 12, 2009.

27 Barbara Lee Family Foundation. 2001. *Keys to the Governor's Office*. Brookline, MA: Barbara Lee Family Foundation, 28.

28 Ibid., 29.

29 Rick Pearson. March 2, 2008. Hillary Clinton: "A Fighter, a Doer and a Champion." *Chicago Tribune*. <http://www.swamppolitics.com/news/politics/blog/2008/03/hillary_clinton_a_fighter_a_do.html> February 17, 2009.

30 Governor Mike Easley of North Carolina Endorses Hillary. <http://www.youtube.com/watch?v=zbqFEaP4Vow> November 1, 2008.

31 Fernando Suarez. April 30, 2008. From the Road: Union Boss Says Clinton Has "Testicular Fortitude." CBS News. <http://www.cbsnews.com/blogs/2008/04/30/politics/fromtheroad/entry4059528.shtml> November 1, 2008.

32 Media Matters for America. July 18, 2007. Tucker Carlson on Clinton: "[W]hen She Comes on Television, I Involuntarily Cross My Legs." <http://mediamatters.org/items/200707180009> November 1, 2008.

33 Media Matters for America. November 18, 2007. AP Reported McCain "Didn't Embrace the [Bitch] Epithet" Not That He Called the Question "Excellent." <http://mediamatters.org/items/200711180001?f=h_latest> November 1, 2008.

34 Media Matters for America. March 15, 2007. CNN's, ABC's Beck on Clinton: "[S]he's the Stereotypical Bitch." <http://mediamatters.org/items/200703150011> November 1, 2008.

35 Women's Media Center. May 23, 2008. CNN's Alex Castellanos – "Bitch" Is OK If It's Accurate? <http://mediamatters.org/items/200711180001?f=h_latest> November 1, 2008.

36 Salon.com. February 25, 2008. Tina Fey: Bitch Is the New Black. <http://www.salon.com/mwt/broadsheet/2008/02/25/fey/> February 12, 2008.

37 Palin's Speech at the Republican National Convention. September 3, 2008. Election 2008. *New York Times*. <http://elections.nytimes.com/2008/president/conventions/videos/transcripts/20080903_PALIN_SPEECH.html> February 12, 2009.

38 Ibid.

39 The Page by Mark Halperin. Clinton Campaign Memo Touting Military Supporters. *Time*. <http://thepage.time.com/clinton-campaign-statement-touting-military-supporters/> February 12, 2009.

40 David Morgan. April 22, 2008. Clinton Says U.S. Could "Totally Obliterate" Iran. <http://www.reuters.com/article/topNews/idUSN2224332720080422> November 1, 2008.

41 Rachel Sklar. September 29, 2008. Huffington Post. The *New Yorker* Can See Russia from Sarah Palin's House. <http://www.huffingtonpost.com/2008/09/29/the-emnew-yorkerem-can-se_n_130354.html> February 12, 2009.

42 Ibid.

43 Penn's "Launch Strategy" Ideas. December 21, 2006. *The Atlantic.* <http://www.theatlantic.com/a/green-penn-12–21–06.mhtml> February 17, 2009.

44 Fox News. December 20, 2006. Behar Goes Easy on Hillary Clinton Following Rumsfeld-Like-Hitler "Faux Pas." <http://www.foxnews.com/story/0,2933,237607,00.html> February 17, 2009.

45 Washingtonpost.com. Transcript: Hillary Rodham Clinton Suspends Her Presidential Campaign. <http://www.washingtonpost.com/wp-dyn/content/article/2008/06/07/AR2008060701029.html> February 12, 2009.

46 Howard Kurtz. September 8, 2008. Palin & Press: A Testy Start. *Washington Post.* <http://www.washingtonpost.com/wp-dyn/content/article/2008/09/07/AR2008090702646_pf.html> February 12, 2009.

47 Jodi Kantor and Rachel L. Swarns. September 2, 2008. In Palin, a New Twist in the Debate on Mothers. *New York Times.* <http://www.nytimes.com/2008/09/02/us/politics/02mother.html?partner=rssnyt> February 17, 2009.

48 CNN. September 5, 2008. Brown: Tucker Bounds Interview Becomes Lightning Rod. <http://www.cnn.com/2008/POLITICS/09/05/brown.bounds/> February 17, 2009.

49 Sally Quinn. August 29, 2008. Palin's Pregnancy Problem. *Washington Post.* <http://newsweek.washingtonpost.com/onfaith/panelists/sally_quinn/2008/08/sarah_polin.html> September 25, 2009.

50 ABC News. November 26, 2007. Nightline. Transcript: On the Trail with Barack Obama. <http://www.abcnews.go.com/Nightline/story?id=3916663&page=1> February 17, 2009.

51 Media Matters for America. January 9, 2008. After vowing not to underestimate Clinton, Matthews asserted, "[T]he reason she may be a front-runner is her husband messed around." <http://mediamatters.org/items/200801090008> February 17, 2009.

52 Michelle Cottle. September 22, 2008. Todd Palin is Hillary Clinton. *National Review.* <http://blogs.tnr.com/tnr/blogs/the_plank/archive/2008/09/22/todd-palin-is-hillary-clinton.aspx> February 17, 2009.

53 Robin Givhan. July 19, 2007. Hillary Clinton's Tentative Dip into New Neckline Territory. *Washington Post.* <http://www.washingtonpost.com/wp-dyn/content/article/2007/07/19/AR2007071902668.html> February 17, 2009.

54 The Rush Limbaugh Show. Hillary Monologue Fallout Ripples Across the Drive-By Media. December 19, 2007. <www.rushlimbaugh.com/home/daily/site_121907/content/01125108.html.guest.html> February 17, 2009.

55 Tom Perrotta. September 26, 2008. How Sarah Palin Embodies the Christian Right Archetype of the Sexy Puritan. Slate. <http://www.slate.com/id/2200814/> February 17, 2009.

56 Robin Givhan. September 28, 2008. Sarah Palin's Unassertive Fashion State-
    ment. *Washington Post.* <http://www.washingtonpost.com/wp-dyn/content/
    article/2008/09/26/AR2008092600859_pf.html> February 17, 2009.

57 Katha Pollit. September 24, 2008. Sarah Palin, Affirmative Action Babe.
    The Nation. <http://www.thenation.com/doc/20081013/pollitt> February 17,
    2009.

58 Kathleen Parker. October 24, 2008. Tragic Flaw. National Review Online.
    <http://article.nationalreview.com/?q=
    Njc2YzU3MjE4Nzk0YmVlM2ZlMjZkODRiNDA4YmQyODE=> February 17,
    2009.

59 Amanda Fortini. November 24, 2008. The "Bitch" and the "Ditz." *New York
    Magazine.* <http://nymag.com/news/politics/nationalinterest/52184> Febru-
    ary 17, 2009.

60 Ibid.

61 Rebecca Traister. September 11, 2008. Zombie Feminists of the RNC.
    Salon.com. <http://www.salon.com/mwt/feature/2008/09/11/zombie_
    feminism/> February 17, 2009.

3 Voter Participation and Turnout

Female Star Power Attracts Women Voters

Women make up a majority of the U.S. voting-age population, registered voters, and actual voters. These facts explain why both major political parties – Democrat and Republican – and women's advocacy groups from across the ideological spectrum worked hard to mobilize women voters in 2008. Democrats did a slightly better job than Republicans of getting out the vote – the reverse of 2004.

Democrats, particularly the Obama campaign, were more successful at tapping into the powerful new media of the day – social networking sites and online video. YouTube, Twitter, Facebook, MySpace, and Flickr each played a vital role in keeping voters, particularly younger ones, interested in the presidential election from start to finish by revolutionizing modes of communication between the candidates and the electorate. In addition, the extraordinary involvement of "celebrity" women (candidates, spouses, entertainers, and news media stars) made the campaign even more intriguing for women of all ages.

At the same time, the highly competitive, protracted fight between Hillary Clinton and Barack Obama for the Democratic Party's presidential nomination, followed by Sarah Palin's nomination as Republican John McCain's vice presidential running mate, made it crystal clear that even women within the same political party are not always a politically cohesive group. In the early stages of the campaign (primaries and caucuses), many Democratic women's votes were split between Obama and Clinton. And Palin's nomination as McCain's vice presidential running mate alienated some moderate GOP women, prompting them to vote for Obama. Democratic women's votes often split along generational lines, while Republican women's votes more often differed along ideological lines.

* This work could not have been completed without the invaluable assistance of Corttney Penberthy.

In this chapter, I begin by reflecting on the historical aspects of the 2008 presidential election, with a focus on the gender-versus-race dilemma facing women voters, particularly in the Democratic presidential nomination process, and on perceptions of sexism in media coverage. A short history of how women won the right to vote and an in-depth look at changes in registration and turnout rates over the years and through the election of 2008 follows. The remainder of the chapter focuses on strategies, candidate appearances, the role of influential female celebrity surrogates, and high-tech ways of targeting and mobilizing women voters in 2008. As the chapter shows, the get-out-the-vote game has become more important over the years, and women are now highly-sought-after players. This is nothing short of amazing, considering that women were denied the right to vote under the original U.S. Constitution.

HISTORICAL ASPECTS OF 2008 – AND DILEMMAS FACING WOMEN VOTERS

There was plenty of female star power in the 2008 election. Hillary Clinton, Sarah Palin, Michelle Obama, Cindy McCain, Oprah Winfrey, Tina Fey, Amy Poehler, Caroline Kennedy Schlossberg, the women of *The View*, Katie Couric, and Greta Van Susteren, even Britney Spears and Paris Hilton, were some of the more prominent women who played major roles in reaching out to and influencing women voters. Also, along with many female elected officials at the national, state, and local levels were numerous women's groups, whether liberal, conservative, or nonpartisan. Technological advances, especially those related to the Internet, made it easier to microtarget specific slices of the women's vote.

Throughout the process, both the Obama and the McCain campaigns saw women voters as crucial to their victory. Some were easier to mobilize than others. The most difficult to engage were those who felt estranged from the candidates as a consequence of perceived sexism or racism.

Progress or Retrogression in 2008?

Women's dominance at the ballot box is a relatively recent phenomenon. Women did not possess the right to vote in all the states until 1920, with the ratification of the Nineteenth Amendment to the U.S. Constitution. Since then, in the words of an old advertisement, "We've come a long way, baby" (or "sister," "mama," "grandma"), but not far enough in the eyes of some female voters, particularly older women.

The 2008 campaign left many Clinton and Palin supporters feeling disappointed with the outcome, but even angrier with the media coverage of female candidates, which they perceived as biased and sexist – retrogressive, not progressive. These women were incensed by the disproportionately negative, often crude treatment of Clinton and Palin in the mainstream media. They found the references to Clinton's and Palin's looks, clothing, and life choices particularly upsetting. The tabloid-like treatment of these accomplished candidates infuriated women. In many instances, it made women more determined to vote; for others, it prompted them to stay home. Across the board, women saw a double standard being applied by the press to Clinton and Palin as compared with their male colleagues. In a postelection poll of women (voters and nonvoters), 65 percent of the women surveyed – majorities in every demographic and political group – said that women candidates are held to different standards on the campaign trail.[1]

Cross-Pressure between Gender and Race

Women voters from both parties, and independents as well, faced a tough choice in the 2008 election. For many Democratic women, the most difficult decision occurred at the nomination stage – whether to support the woman, Hillary Clinton, or the African American man, Barack Obama. Both candidacies were pathbreaking. One would break the race barrier; the other would crack the gender glass ceiling. Women, especially those who were activists during the women's movement of the 1970s, faced a dilemma. They well understood and appreciated the significance of electing an African American president, yet felt that a man, regardless of his race, was still more advantaged than a woman when seeking the nation's top office. Many would concur with the words of feminist icon Gloria Steinem: "Gender is probably the most restricting force in American life."[2] Older women voters were more likely than their younger counterparts to feel cross-pressured between gender and race.

Clinton's Primary and Caucus Supporters: Analyses of Democratic exit polls conducted in numerous states showed that Hillary Clinton's supporters were more likely to be women who were working class, ardent feminists, older, married or widowed, and Hispanic or white. Her support from the working class came from those who longed for the good economy during the Bill Clinton presidency and from union members. As Christine Marie Sierra explains in Chapter 5 of this volume, much Hispanic support for Hillary Clinton stemmed from the Clinton campaign's outreach to Hispanic elected officials and voters. Bill Clinton also reached out to the Hispanic community during his presidency; several of his cabinet members were Hispanics. But observers also speculated that some

Hispanics might have supported Hillary Clinton because she is not black. (Social scientists have long documented tensions between blacks and Hispanics in large metropolitan areas, where they compete for jobs and political positions).

Among women, Clinton was the choice of the baby boomers who fought women's movement wars and the older women (married and widowed) who wanted to see a woman president in their lifetime. As for the black women who voted for Clinton in the primary, many were older and had experienced more sex discrimination than their male counterparts, whether in the workplace or in the world of politics.[3]

Obama's Primary and Caucus Supporters: Obama's strength was greatest among younger voters, blacks, men, highly educated and affluent whites (including professional women), singles and divorcees, and those who describe themselves as very liberal. There was a great deal of early speculation as to why some women voted, or would vote, for Obama:

> Many will wonder in the years to come why so many professional women and female students so readily deserted her [Clinton]. Was it because they chose to rise above identity politics and judge the candidates on what they took to be individual merit (even while African-Americans remained staunchly attached to one of their own?) Or was it because, in the deepest recess of most liberals' souls, race trumps sex? Or was it because these women found the younger, kinetic Mr. Obama a more attractive figure, able to command them with more audacity?[4]

Another theory was that gender would have very little impact on the vote choice of younger women: "They absolutely believe a woman will be president during their lifetime. They don't feel that it [gender] is their battle at all. And these women believe that they as women will benefit just as much from an African-American man who is going to work to impact racial disadvantages. Women know that, historically, when minorities are positively influenced, so are women."[5] At a minimum, the splintering of the women's vote during the Democratic primaries and caucuses highlighted the need for the candidates to target specific slices of the women's vote using different media and messages.

Microtargeting on the Upswing

Getting women to register and then to vote were key goals of each party from the primaries and caucuses all the way to the general election. The presidential campaigns varied their outreach to women, microtargeting them differently according to age, race and ethnicity, education, and – to a lesser degree – by income and employment, marital, parental, and/or sexual orientation. Microtargeting as a mobilization strategy began in the 2004 campaign and escalated in 2008. It recognizes that using one-size-fits-all tactics to energize women voters can result in a candidate's defeat. As Donna Brazile, a Democratic strategist and manager of Al Gore's 2004 presidential campaign, has advised:

> To pull more women into the voting process – and to win votes – the two major parties should drop any idea of a "one size fits all" approach to women. Instead, they should target their messages to diverse groups of women. . . . Political campaigns will have to address single women, married women, suburban soccer moms, security moms, on-the-go female professionals, urban-base[d] voting women, Jewish women, Latinas, senior moms, want-to-be-moms and soon-to-be moms.[6]

Throughout the 2008 campaign, political parties and advocacy groups alike used a variety of voter mobilization tools. These included everything from text messages to online social networks, recorded ("robo") phone calls from candidates and celebrities, and appearances by the candidates and high-profile surrogates to precisely targeted mail, radio spots, and broadcast and cable television ads. Online ads and links to YouTube ads were new forms of voter outreach in 2008, generally aimed at energizing younger voters. Feedback and insights from focus groups and public opinion surveys were used to craft the content, format, and placement of political ads to narrowly defined groups of potential female voters. The importance of the women's vote was evident every step of the way – a world apart from the days when American women were left out of the process altogether.

A BRIEF HISTORY OF WOMEN'S SUFFRAGE

The struggle for women's voting rights began at the nation's birth (see Text Box 3.1). In 1776, women like Abigail Adams urged the men writing the Declaration of Independence to include women. "Remember the Ladies," wrote Adams to her husband, John, a delegate to the Continental Congress. "If particular care and attention is not paid to the ladies, we are determined to foment a rebellion, and will not hold ourselves bound by any laws in which we have no voice or representation." Was she ever right!

TEXT BOX 3.1: The history of the women's vote

Today, every U.S. citizen who is eighteen years of age by Election Day and a resident of the local precinct for at least thirty days is eligible to cast a ballot. However, women, African Americans, Native Americans, and members of certain religious groups were not allowed to vote during the colonial period and the early years of the country's history. In 1787, the U.S. Constitution granted each state government the power to determine who could vote. Individual states wrote their own suffrage laws. Early voting qualifications required that an eligible voter be a white man, twenty-one years of age, Protestant, and a landowner. Many citizens who recognized the importance of the right to vote led the suffrage movement.

One Hundred Years Toward the Women's Vote

Compiled by E. Susan Barber

1776

Abigail Adams writes to her husband, John, at the Continental Congress in Philadelphia, asking that he and the other men – who are at work on the Declaration of Independence – "Remember the Ladies." The Declaration's wording specifies that "all men are created equal."

1848

The first women's rights convention in the United States is held in Seneca Falls, New York. Many participants sign the "Declaration of Sentiments and Resolutions," which outlines the main issues and goals for the emerging women's movement. Thereafter, women's rights meetings are held on a regular basis.

1861–1865

The American Civil War disrupts suffrage activity as women, North and South, divert their energies to "war work." The war, however, serves as a training ground, as women gain important organizational and occupational skills they will later use in postwar organizational activity.

1866

Elizabeth Cady Stanton and Susan B. Anthony form the American Equal Rights Association, an organization for white and black women and men dedicated to the goal of universal suffrage.

(continued)

TEXT BOX 3.1 (continued)

1868

The Fourteenth Amendment is ratified. It extends to all citizens the protections of the Constitution against unjust state laws. This Amendment is the first to define citizens and voters as "male."

1870

The Fifteenth Amendment enfranchises black men.

1870–1875

Several women – including Virginia Louisa Minor, Victoria Woodhull, and Myra Bradwell – attempt to use the Fourteenth Amendment in the courts to secure the vote (Minor and Woodhull) and right to practice law (Bradwell). They all are unsuccessful.

1872

Susan B. Anthony is arrested and brought to trial in Rochester, New York, for attempting to vote for Ulysses S. Grant in the presidential election. At the same time, Sojourner Truth appears at a polling booth in Grand Rapids, Michigan, demanding a ballot; she is turned away.

1874

The Woman's Christian Temperance Union (WCTU) is founded by Annie Wittenmyer. With Frances Willard at its head (1876), the WCTU becomes an important force in the struggle for women's suffrage. Not surprisingly, one of the most vehement opponents of women's enfranchisement was the liquor lobby, which feared women might use the franchise to prohibit the sale of liquor.

1878

The Woman Suffrage Amendment is introduced in the U.S. Congress. (The wording is unchanged in 1919, when the amendment finally passes both houses.)

1890

Wyoming becomes the first women's suffrage state on its admission to the Union.

1893

Colorado becomes the first state to adopt a state amendment enfranchising women.

1896

Mary Church Terrell, Ida B. Wells-Barnett, Margaret Murray Washington, Fanny Jackson Coppin, Frances Ellen Watkins Harper, Charlotte Forten Grimké, and the former slave Harriet Tubman meet in Washington, D.C., to form the National Association of Colored Women (NACW).

1903

Mary Dreier, Rheta Childe Dorr, Leonora O'Reilly, and others form the Women's Trade Union League of New York, an organization of middle- and working-class women dedicated to unionization for working women and to women's suffrage. This group later becomes a nucleus of the International Ladies' Garment Workers' Union (ILGWU).

1911

The National Association Opposed to Woman Suffrage (NAOWS) is organized. Led by Mrs. Arthur Dodge, its members include wealthy, influential women and some Catholic clergymen – including Cardinal Gibbons, who, in 1916, sent an address to NAOWS's convention in Washington, D.C. In addition to the distillers and brewers, who work largely behind the scenes, the "antis" also draw support from urban political machines, southern congressmen, and corporate capitalists – like railroad magnates and meatpackers – who support the "antis" by contributing to their war chests.

1912

Theodore Roosevelt's Progressive (Bull Moose/Republican) Party becomes the first national political party to adopt a women's suffrage plank.

1913

Alice Paul and Lucy Burns organize the Congressional Union, later known as the National Women's Party (1916). Borrowing the tactics of the radical, militant Women's Social and Political Union (WSPU) in England, members of the Woman's Party participate in hunger strikes, picket the White House, and engage in other forms of civil disobedience to publicize the suffrage cause.

1914

The National Federation of Women's Clubs – which by this time includes more than 2 million white women and women of color throughout the United States – formally endorses the suffrage campaign.

(continued)

TEXT BOX 3.1 *(continued)*

1916

Jeannette Rankin of Montana becomes the first American woman elected to represent her state in the U.S. House of Representatives.

AUGUST 26, 1920

The Nineteenth Amendment is ratified. Its victory accomplished, NAWSA ceases to exist, but its organization becomes the nucleus of the League of Women Voters.

Source: Adapted from *Election Focus 2004* 1, no. 8, April 14, 2004. Available at http://usinfo.state.gov/dhr/img/assets/5796/elections04_14_043.pdf.

In the 1800s, white women began working outside the home, mostly at mills, as America changed from an agrarian to a more industrialized society. The long working hours and dangerous conditions led many women to organize. Meanwhile, stay-at-home, middle-class women began banding together for charity work, temperance, and the abolition of slavery. Black women like Sojourner Truth and Harriet Jacobs rose to oppose sexism, slavery, and the white activists who "saw themselves as the sole liberators of passive, childlike slaves."[7]

The birth of the women's suffrage movement in the United States is usually dated to July 20, 1848, at the country's first women's rights convention in Seneca Falls, New York. The three hundred attendees issued a document proclaiming that men and women were created equal and, therefore, that women should be allowed to vote.

After the Civil War, groups led by Susan B. Anthony and others organized to push for universal suffrage. They made substantial progress in 1870, when the Fifteenth Amendment extended the franchise to African American men.

In 1890, rival suffrage groups merged to form the National American Woman Suffrage Association (NAWSA). Conservative and liberal women's groups alike, including the Woman's Christian Temperance Union, the Young Women's Christian Association, and the National Association of Colored Women, began to see that voting was the only way for women to affect public policy.

Western States ahead of the Nation

Ultimately, it was in the Wild West where women first tasted success. Historically, most public policy innovations in America occur not at the national level but in the states. So it was with women's suffrage. In 1890, Wyoming became the first women's suffrage state on its admission to the Union. In 1893, Colorado extended the right to vote to women through an amendment to its state constitution. Neighboring western states soon jumped on the bandwagon. By 1900, women could vote in thirteen western and midwestern states as well as in Michigan and New York.

The Ladies Get Testy

The successes of the women's suffrage movement spurred strong opposition from antisuffragists, many of whom were also women. Then, as now, different views on women's societal and political roles resulted in a traditionalist/antisuffragist versus revisionist/suffragist schism.

Even within their own ranks, suffragists disagreed about the pace of the movement. One faction of NAWSA broke off to form another group that became the National Woman's Party in 1916. They used protests and hunger strikes to rally support for an amendment to the U.S. Constitution. (It was known as "the Anthony Amendment" in honor of Susan B. Anthony and ultimately became the Nineteenth Amendment to the U.S. Constitution in 1920.)

During World War I, women suffragists split into prowar and antiwar blocs. (The same schism characterized women voters in 2004 over the war in Iraq.) But the leaders of suffragist groups, like Alice Paul of the National Woman's Party and Carrie Chapman Catt of the Woman's Peace Party, put aside their personal feelings about the war, fearing a backlash against women's suffrage. The tactic paid off. Their refusal to campaign against the war made it more politically palatable for President Wilson and other politicians to support the Nineteenth Amendment.

At Last, Ratification!

It was not until June 4, 1919, that the U.S. Congress formally presented the Nineteenth Amendment to the states for ratification.[8] More than a year later, on August 18, 1920, by a single vote in its legislature, Tennessee became the thirty-sixth state to approve of the amendment. The young legislator who cast the deciding vote confessed that he had been led to do so by a telegram he had received from his mother urging him to vote in favor of the amendment. On August 26, 1920, the U.S. secretary of state officially proclaimed that the required thirty-six states had ratified the Nineteenth Amendment, thus giving women the right to vote. However, it would be years before African American women had full voting rights. Discriminatory practices such as literacy tests and poll taxes, along with threats and violence, kept many from voting until these barriers were outlawed by court rulings, voting rights acts passed by Congress, and a constitutional amendment eliminating poll taxes.

The Nineteenth Amendment as proposed and ratified read:

> The right of citizens of the United States to vote shall not be denied or abridged by the United States or by any State on account of sex.
>
> Congress shall have power, by appropriate legislation, to enforce the provisions of this article.

The suffragists finally prevailed. It had been a long haul – 140 years after the Declaration of Independence was signed in 1776 and 72 years after women had issued their first formal demand for the right to vote at Seneca Falls. In its editorial on Sunday, August 29, 1920, the *New York Times* applauded those who had worked so long and hard for this right: "Women in fighting for the vote have shown a passion of earnestness, a persistence, and above all a command of both tactics and strategy, which have amazed our master politicians." But the editorial went on to warn against presuming that women would all vote alike: "It is doubtless true that women will divide much as men have done among several parties. There will be no solid 'woman vote.'"

There certainly was no solid "woman vote" in the election of 2004: Democrat John Kerry won 51 percent of the women's vote and Republican George W. Bush, 48 percent – a difference of only three percentage points. In the election of 2008, the women's vote was somewhat more cohesive but still by no means monolithic. Democrat Barack Obama won 56 percent of the female vote; Republican John McCain, 43 percent; and other minor party candidates, 1 percent.

REGISTRATION RATES

Convincing people to register is often more difficult than getting them to vote once they have registered. Some states, like Maine, Minnesota, Wisconsin, Wyoming, New Hampshire, and Idaho, allow citizens to register on Election Day. But most states require them to register in advance, usually fifteen to thirty days before the election.[9]

Figures from the U.S. Census show that in every election cycle since 1980, a greater percentage of women than men has registered to vote (see Figure 3.1). Younger women (under age forty-five) have outregistered younger men since the 1970s. It is only among the oldest cohort,

Figure 3.1: **Women have registered to vote at higher rates than men in recent elections.**

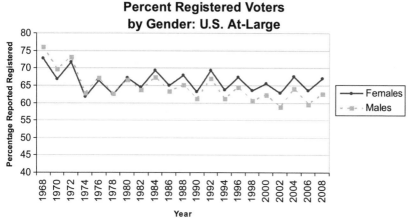

Source: U.S. Census, Current Population Survey, November 2008 and earlier reports.

sixty-five and older, that women's registration rates consistently lag behind men's.

After close presidential elections in 2000 and 2004, both the Democratic and the Republican parties realized they had to spend considerably more time and money registering voters for 2008. The parties knew they would have to identify nonregistrants more precisely and begin registration drives earlier to win. Naturally, women were a prime target, especially those who had never registered to vote (first-time voters).

The long Democratic nomination process, which continued into the month of June (when the last states held their primaries or caucuses), allowed Democrats to easily beat Republicans at the registration game. The Obama campaign was particularly adept at registering young, female, and minority voters who attended large-scale rallies, concerts, and debates. The campaign gathered e-mail addresses from event attendees via cell phones and text messages, then provided online links to registration information, making it easy for those who had not registered on the spot to do so.

Once he secured the nomination, Obama's tremendous money advantage allowed him to open campaign offices in key battleground states and hire young staffers to aggressively continue to conduct registration drives on college campuses, at concerts and movies, outside churches and bookstores, at political rallies and civic group meetings – anywhere eligible but unregistered persons were likely to be. (Voter eligibility requirements

include age – eighteen years of age or older – U.S. citizenship, and resi-
dence at the location where one is registering. In most states, one is not
eligible to register if convicted of a felony and not yet finished with the
sentence. The same is true of persons declared mentally incapacitated by
the state.)

The Republicans had a more difficult time registering new voters in
2008. The money simply was not there in 2008 for the McCain campaign
or the GOP as it had been in 2004 for George W. Bush. By 2008, the
country at large (especially its younger, female, and Hispanic voters) was
trending Democratic. This made it even harder for the Republicans to
stay even with Democrats in the registration game. Republicans ended up
having to rely more on state party organizations and unpaid volunteers
to register voters. And there simply were not as many of them to do so,
given the tepid enthusiasm of some conservatives for the more moderate
McCain.

Registration efforts were not limited to events. Citizens' mailboxes
(postal and Internet) were flooded with voter registration forms, along
with the telephone numbers and mail and Internet addresses of election
officials. Parties and advocacy group representatives went door-to-door
offering to help people register or leaving forms for them to complete.
Naturally, the registration outreach efforts were targeted at high-growth
areas and places with heavier concentrations of unregistered people. Public service announcements reminding voters of how and when to register
ran on just about every cable and broadcast television and radio station.
These PSAs were tailored to fit the demographics of each station's viewers
or listeners.

By 2008, Democrats and Republicans alike heavily targeted Spanish-
language television and radio stations, reflecting Latinos' status as the
fastest-growing minority group in the United States. In a number of key
battleground states, such as Florida, Nevada, and New Mexico, Hispanics already outnumbered African Americans and were perceived as vital
swing voters. Democrats were more successful at registering Hispanic
females. It paid off, as Latinas ended up supporting Obama more heavily
than their male counterparts (68 percent versus 64 percent, respectively,
according to the national exit poll).

Women's Groups Are Active in Registration Efforts

Clinton's early lead in presidential horse-race polls, along with the entry
of many formidable women candidates into gubernatorial, U.S. Senate,
and U.S. House races, led many in the press and in women's political
circles to predict that 2008 would be a particularly good year for women.

Photo Section 3.1:   The Feminist Majority Leadership Alliance was quite active in the 2008 election. Its Facebook page announced the group was also "Twittering," "YouTubing," and "Flickring."
Source: http://www.facebook.com/pages/Feminist-Majority-Leadership-Alliance/ 23452514809.

Consequently, a number of women's groups placed an even higher priority on registering women voters in 2008 than they had in 2004. Specifically, Democratic-leaning groups including the National Organization for Women (NOW), EMILY's List, Women's Voices. Women Vote, and the Feminist Majority Foundation, among others, played a bigger role than in 2004, when non–gender-specific groups like America Coming Together, MoveOn.org, and various labor union political action committees took the lead in registration efforts targeting potential Democratic voters. Many of these groups, particularly those addressing young women, relied heavily on the use of social networking and online video Web sites (see Photo Section 3.1). In 2008, Democratic-leaning women's groups' registration efforts were targeted at young, unmarried, minority, and blue-collar working women. Perhaps the most aggressive efforts were by Women's Voices. Women Vote, which conducted a nationwide voter registration drive "You Count. Be Counted!" targeting some 1 million unmarried (single, separated, divorced, or widowed) women. According to the group, unmarried women were nine percentage points less likely to be registered than married women and thirteen percentage points less likely to actually vote.[10]

Local Republican Party women's clubs (part of the umbrella National Federation of Republican Women) at the state and local levels played the major role in registering new GOP-leaning women voters. Less well funded than the major Democratic-leaning women's groups, Republican women's clubs reached out to friends and neighbors with whom they regularly came in contact outside the world of politics. Specifically, they focused their registration efforts on married women with young children, fellow female churchgoers and social conservatives in suburban and rural areas, working women, and female small-business owners concerned about growing tax burdens.

The nonpartisan League of Women Voters was very active in distributing information about voter registration laws and processes in the various states to its chapters and to the media. And the White House Project, a nonpartisan, nonprofit organization, whose goal is to advance women's leadership in all communities and sectors, was also quite active in encouraging women to register, as well as in getting mothers to take their daughters to the polls with them.

There is evidence that these registration efforts made a difference. In six states that collected registration data by gender in 2004 and 2008, the new-registration rate among women was up 89 percent, compared with 74 percent for men.[11]

TURNOUT RATES

Intense Get-Out-The-Vote (GOTV) efforts, ranging from calls, text messages, e-mails, and transportation assistance to heavily targeted television, radio, Internet, and direct mail ads prompted 131.1 million people to vote in 2008 – 5 million more than in 2004. However, the turnout *rate* relative to the voting age population fell slightly from 63.8 percent in 2004 to 63.6 percent in 2008 because the voting age population grew as well. (The turnout rate is the proportion of the voting age population that voted.)

Turnout rate is measured in two ways – (1) the percent of the vot-ing age population (18 and over) that voted, or (2) the percent of reg-istered voters that voted. The U.S. Census conducts a post-election tele-phone survey to determine what percent of the 18 and older population voted (self-reported). While official, the Census Bureau's survey inflates turnout rates, primarily because more people say they voted than actually did. State election officials generally measure turnout rates using actual voters as a percent of registered voters. Unfortunately, not all states report turnout rates among registered voters by gender.

According to the U.S. Census Bureau's 2008 post-election survey, women had a higher turnout rate (60.4 percent) than men (55.7 per-cent).[12] Compared to 2004, women's turnout rate increased slightly (+0.3 percent) while men's declined (−0.6 percent). Some analysts attribute the increased female turnout rate in 2008 to higher participation levels among new voters – younger women, especially African Americans and Latinas. In fact, for the first time in history, black women turned out at a higher rate than any other racial, ethnic, or gender group.[13]

Women Catch Up with – and Pass – Men

For years after the passage of the Nineteenth Amendment, the partici-pation rates of men were greater than those of women in presidential elections, even though there were more women than men of voting age. This was true whether male-female comparisons were made using the sheer number of men and women voting or the relative percentage of each gender who voted (the turnout rate). It was not until 1964 that the number of women voters surpassed the number of men voting in presi-dential elections. But women continued to vote at a lower rate until 1980, when the percentage of women voting slightly exceeded that of men (see Figure 3.2). Since 1980, the turnout rate of women has exceeded that of men, and with each successive election, women have outvoted men at increasingly higher rates. Early on, the civil and women's rights move-ments of the 1960s and 1970s played a large role in improving the turnout rate among women. More recently, GOTV efforts by women's groups and political parties have targeted females who make up a majority of the vot-ing age population.

Female and male turnout rates are lowest among the young, the poor, the unemployed, and the least educated. Studies have found that turnout rates are also lower than average among renters, new-comers to a community, infrequent churchgoers and non-churchgoers, Asians, Latinos, single parents living in poor neighborhoods, persons with

Figure 3.2. **Women have voted at higher rates than men in recent elections.**

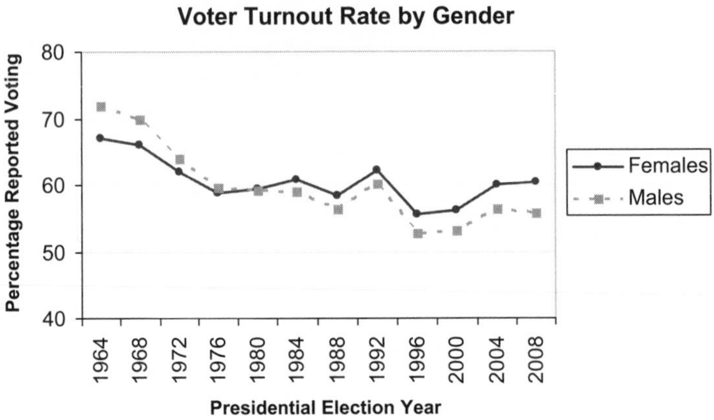

Voter Turnout Rate by Gender

Note: The turnout rate for each gender is the percentage of the eligible population that voted (the number voting as a percentage of the total number of voting-age persons of that gender).

Source: U.S. Census, Current Population Survey, November 2008 and earlier reports.

physical disabilities, blue-collar and service-sector workers, and independents.

The relative turnout rates of men and women differ across age groups. For decades, older men (sixty-five and older) have turned out to vote at higher rates than older women. The same pattern held true among the age group of forty-five to sixty-four until 1992, when female turnout rates surpassed male voting rates. In contrast, since the early 1970s, women age eighteen to forty-four have voted at higher rates than have males their age. The lone exception was in 1996, when the turnout rate of the youngest group of voters – women age eighteen to twenty-four – dipped below that of their male counterparts. Higher turnout rates among younger women are attributed in part to a rise in the educational level of women; today, more women than men attend college.

Women Benefit from Election Reforms Like Early Voting

Recent improvements in the electoral process, especially those allowing more flexibility in the way one votes, have been particularly beneficial to women voters. Since 2000, a number of states have adopted or expanded laws making it easier to vote by mail (absentee voting) or in person at designated voting sites. Both forms of pre–Election Day balloting are jointly referred to as early voting. It is a growing trend throughout the United States. By one estimate, nearly 32 million Americans voted early in 2008, up from 2004. Not all states break down early voters by gender, but in three that do, a much greater percentage of the early voters were women (Georgia and North Carolina, 56 percent; Louisiana, 57 percent).[14] Unmarried women were more likely to vote by mail than married women (46 percent versus 36 percent).[15] In 2008, more Democrats than Republicans voted early, while more Republicans than Democrats voted at a precinct on Election Day itself (November 4).

Targeted Ads Promote Early and Absentee Voting

Educating women about early and absentee voting was a major component of GOTV efforts in many states. The direct-mail pieces in Photo Section 3.3 (which appears later in the chapter) are visual proof of how precisely the pieces were targeted by both parties to women of different ages, races or ethnicities, and family situations in the key battleground state of Florida.

WOMAN-TO-WOMAN MOBILIZATION EFFORTS RULE THE DAY

High-profile women played key roles in the election of 2008, drawing big crowds or large viewing audiences. Some were candidates (Clinton, Palin) or the presidential nominees' spouses (Michelle Obama, Cindy McCain). Others were television celebrities – anchors (Katie Couric), interviewers (Oprah Winfrey, women of *The View*, Campbell Brown, Rachel Maddow, Greta Van Susteren), or comedy show personalities (Tina Fey, Amy Poehler). Still others starred as debate moderators (Gwen Ifill), political ad personalities (Paris Hilton, Britney Spears), or significant endorsers (Caroline Kennedy, the daughter of former President John Kennedy, and Carly Fiorina, the former chief executive officer of Hewlett-Packard).

Each woman sparked strong, and often opposite, reactions among women voters depending on the voters' age, race or ethnicity, education and income level, marital status, and/or political ideology. For example, conservative women saw Palin as a feminist; liberal women strongly disagreed. Media coverage highlighted just how much American women differed in their assessments of these well-known women. Blogs exploded with point-counterpoint exchanges about just how well these individuals really represented the women of America. But there was little debate over the fact that the woman-to-woman aspect of election coverage in 2008 affected turnout and vote choices. The following subsections present a few examples.

Senator Hillary Clinton

Heading into 2008, it was presumed by just about everyone that Hillary Clinton would be the Democratic presidential nominee. It was also assumed that the nomination fight would be over by Super Tuesday (February 5). Instead, the fight did not end until the Democratic National Convention in August. Clinton did not do well in caucuses. While some blamed her campaign for having miscalculated the importance of caucuses in amassing large blocs of delegates, others acknowledged that caucuses attract a disproportionate number of younger voters – always one of Obama's strongest groups of supporters.

Clinton did best in primaries in which women made up a greater-than-average portion of the electorate. Female turnout went up when women perceived that press coverage was extraordinarily sexist – maligning her for shedding a tear, which they saw as exemplary of her compassion rather than as a weakness or a staged event, or calling for her to bow out of the race before every state had voted. Unfair press treatment of Clinton even angered some Republican women who changed their party registration specifically to vote for her in the primary.

The treatment Clinton received from the media and, to a lesser degree, from the Obama campaign left many of her supporters angry and disgruntled. A sizable portion vowed not to vote for Democratic nominee Obama in the general election. Just how large a group this was is debatable – but it was big enough to worry the Obama campaign and to prompt Republican John McCain to name a woman as his vice presidential running mate. McCain spent a sizable amount of money to mail a large, four-page, full-color ad to older female Democrats, the staunchest Clinton supporters, in an effort to convince them to vote for the McCain-Palin ticket (see the ad in Photo Section 3.2). The ad had some effect but not enough; exit polls showed that 15 percent of those who voted for McCain-Palin would have voted for the Democratic ticket had Clinton been the nominee.[16]

Governor Sarah Palin

The surprise pick of a female running mate stunned even the savviest of pundits. Without question, Palin energized conservative Republicans, who had been rather lukewarm toward the moderate McCain, even after he had secured his party's nomination relatively early. Palin consistently drew larger crowds – sixty thousand at one Florida appearance – than McCain when he appeared solo. Republican women gleefully attended her rallies in droves as Democratic women had Clinton's. They were ecstatic at having gender diversity on a GOP ticket for the first time in history.

As with Clinton, it was not long before Palin's supporters became incensed at what they perceived as vicious treatment by the media. For some women, it was déjà vu – Clinton's treatment all over again. But for others, the press critiques were justified. To many liberal women, Palin was both unqualified and unacceptable. They labeled McCain's selection of her as pure tokenism and insulting to women. A senior female Obama adviser dismissed her as "just like any other politician, male or female."[17]

Nothing in the campaign of 2008 more clearly revealed the differences among female voters in 2008 than feelings toward Palin. She reignited a long-simmering debate between conservative and liberal women over just who is a feminist. Conservative women interviewed at Palin rallies stated emphatically that traditional feminist groups, like NOW, did not represent them. They took great umbrage at what they perceived as a definition of feminism that excludes women with pro-life beliefs:

> It is . . . foolish to expect that feminism must for all time be inextricably wed to the pro-choice agenda. There is plenty of room in modern thought for a pro-life feminism – one in fact that would have far more appeal to third-world cultures where motherhood is still honored and where the Western model of the hard-driving, self-absorbed career woman is less admired.[18]

In the eyes of more liberal women, Palin's brand of feminism is not feminism at all. In the words of a female blogger who warned Clinton supporters not to vote for Palin:

> Not only is Sarah Palin not a feminist, she is as anti-woman as Bush and McCain combined. . . . Feminism means to stand up for human rights; it means to stand up for equality and the freedoms and liberties of people and Sarah Palin is disgustingly right wing, anti-choice and has no record of representing women's interests; though her record in general is quite miniscule . . . Sarah Palin stands for everything Hillary Clinton is against so please, Hillary supporters, do not be fooled.[19]

While Palin was a very polarizing candidate who never was able to win over large numbers of Democratic or independent women voters, she definitely mobilized Republican women voters. Without her on the ticket, Republican McCain would not have even come close to beating Obama. In the words of the *Washington Post*'s Chris Cillizza, "It's hard to imagine conservatives rallying to McCain – even to the relatively limited extent that they did – without Palin on the ticket. And without the base, McCain's loss could have been far worse."[20] Even with Palin, turnout among conservative white Republican women most likely was lower than in 2004. This is a reminder that, for many voters, the candidate at the top of the ticket draws them to the polls more than the running mate. Some conservative women simply weren't drawn to McCain.

The Presidential Candidates' Wives: Michelle Obama and Cindy McCain

Debates over the "proper" role of women extended into press coverage of the presidential nominees' spouses. While neither spouse attracted huge crowds, they did attract considerable press coverage – Obama more than McCain. Both were subjected to sexist stereotyping – not just from the press but also from women with opposing ideological dispositions. Michelle Obama was described by some conservative women as "pushy" and "brash"; Cindy McCain by liberal women as a "rich, plastic-looking Barbie Doll." Both are mothers, and both have worked tirelessly to help poor women. Obama was outspoken, and McCain quite reserved. Both played important roles in reaching specific subsets of women voters.

When President Bush could not attend the first evening of the Republican National Convention because a major hurricane was threatening a number of southern states, Cindy McCain stepped onto the stage with First Lady Laura Bush and helped make the nationally televised event a success. Her work with Mother Teresa's orphanage in Bangladesh and her family's adoption of a child from the orphanage resonated well among conservative women strongly favoring adoption over abortion.

Michelle Obama played a large role in mobilizing women voters, especially African Americans. The thought of having a highly successful, well-educated black woman as the nation's first lady was inspiring. She was seen as someone who could "put a refreshing face on America's image of African-American women" and knock down "old stereotypes of black women: Sapphires, the angry black woman; Mammy, the caretaker and nurturer of her own children and everybody else's; and Jezebel, the loose woman."[21] Michelle Obama's efforts on the campaign trail appear to have been effective. According to the national presidential exit poll, black women made up 7 percent of the electorate; black men, 5 percent. Black women cast 96 percent of their ballots for Barack Obama; black men, 95 percent.

Caroline Kennedy: A Giant Step onto the National Stage to Endorse Obama

For most of her life, Caroline Kennedy has stayed out of the political limelight, choosing to focus on writing and numerous philanthropic activities. That changed in 2008, when she published a high-profile endorsement of Barack Obama in the *New York Times*, breaking with her previous policy of not endorsing candidates. That endorsement, deemed "huge" by the Obama campaign, led the news cycle that January day. The press's gushing over the endorsement did little to reverse the belief among many Clinton supporters and Republican women that, early on, the national media was favoring Obama.

Later, Kennedy agreed to serve on Obama's vice presidential selection committee, which selected Senator Joseph Biden as his running mate, much to the chagrin of many Clinton supporters who thought she should have been tapped. Then Kennedy appeared on stage at the nationally televised Democratic Party Convention to introduce her uncle, Senator Edward Kennedy, in a rousing tribute to him. By the campaign's end, Kennedy's highly publicized efforts on behalf of Obama helped win over some older Democratic women, who had contemplated voting for McCain because of Obama's lack of experience. These women loved Kennedy's father, President John F. Kennedy, and were moved by the fact that Caroline Kennedy felt so strongly about Obama that she would sacrifice her privacy to campaign for him.

Carly Fiorina: A High-Tech CEO Endorses John McCain

Like Caroline Kennedy, Carleton S. "Carly" Fiorina, had avoided making political endorsements until she announced her support for Republican John McCain. Well-known in the world of business, Fiorina had served as the chief executive officer of Hewlett-Packard, one of the country's largest corporations. The recipient of many awards, Fiorina was once named the most powerful woman in American business by *Fortune* magazine. McCain chose her to serve on his economic advisory team to improve his image as a candidate who understood the high-tech industry. She was also charged with reaching women voters, many of whom control the purse strings in their households. She became one of McCain's most visible surrogates on national television shows and was at one time even mentioned as a possible vice presidential running mate.

Female Television Celebrities: Oprah Winfrey, Amy Poehler, Tina Fey, Women of *The View*

Women celebrities reach large television audiences and are quite influential with them. A prime example is Oprah Winfrey. By one account, "No matter what you're selling, there's no greater single guarantee of success than getting yourself booked on the *Oprah Winfrey Show*."[22] In the election of 2008, Winfrey was herself "selling" Obama. Her endorsement of him,

Photo Section 3.2: *Saturday Night Live*'s stars Tina Fey and Amy Poehler, portraying Sarah Palin and Hillary Clinton, were hilarious, but in the eyes of some quite sexist and damaging to the candidates.
Source: Photographer Dana Edelson for NBCU Photo Bank.

made on the *Larry King Live* show, was also a first. Up to that point, she, like Caroline Kennedy, had refused to endorse candidates. Both Obamas appeared on her show several times.

For those who want to reach baby boomers and younger voters, an appearance on *Saturday Night Live* during an election year is manda-tory. Sarah Palin accepted the challenge because comedian Tina Fey had been so wildly successful at impersonating her that Palin felt compelled to appear alongside her. The result was the largest audience to watch *Saturday Night Live* in years.

The *Saturday Night Live* stars Amy Poehler and Tina Fey played major roles in affecting viewers' images of Hillary Clinton and Sarah Palin (see Photo Section 3.2). Their impersonations were superbly executed and quite hilarious. To many, they were simply great entertainment. To some, the impersonations were even seen as helpful, softening their images. But to others, they were seen as quite sexist, even cruel, especially the carica-ture of Palin.

Many believe that Tina Fey greatly harmed Palin, particularly among women voters who initially leaned her way, by defining her in a highly unflattering way:

> Tina Fey never "did" Sarah Palin. She took certain traits of Palin's, even traits Palin was simply assumed to have, then exaggerated them. Because Palin wasn't that well known, Fey had close to a blank slate, a rare advantage in the world of impressionists. And because her

impression was entertaining and funny, it drew us in. But the impression ridiculed Palin, and went far to define her in the public mind as someone not quite up to the job, a political airhead. It wasn't the only factor, of course, but it played an important role in sending Palin from her starring role at the Republican convention, crashing down to her later image as someone grasping for respect.[23]

Record audiences also tuned into ABC's popular daytime television program, *The View*, featuring five female cohosts – four liberals (Barbara Walters, Whoopi Goldberg, Sherri Shepherd, Joy Behar) and one lonely conservative (Elisabeth Hasselbeck). Designed to be argumentative, provocative, and controversial, the program led all networks in reaching women between eighteen and forty-nine years of age in the coveted daytime slot during the fall 2008 sweeps. In fact, during the two weeks leading up to the election, the program drew two of its largest weekly audiences in the program's history (more than 4 million). Cindy McCain appeared as a cohost on one telecast; Michelle Obama, on another. So, too, did John McCain and Barack Obama, but the latter fared much better than the former. Hasselbeck took a lot of heat for trying to defend McCain throughout the fall; the younger demographic was more in step with Obama than with McCain. The day after the election was *The View*'s most-watched telecast ever (6.17 million viewers).

Each of these celebrities had an impact on women's participation in the election of 2008. Without question, Winfrey had a major impact on Obama's ascension to the top:

> The most decisive moment in Hollywood's attempt to influence the election was Oprah Winfrey's introduction of Barack Obama on her daytime television show. This simply had never happened before.... But Oprah not only introduced Obama, she vouched for him, she gave him what Joan Crawford once called "the big okay," her seal of approval. Almost instantly, Winfrey transformed Obama from an ambitious young politician into a cultural star. He suddenly rocketed beyond politics. He became larger than all that. And there he remained, all through the campaign and up to Election Day, a man who was as much culture as candidate.[24]

Winfrey's strong endorsement was not without controversy. As her show's ratings fell, some analysts attributed the fall-off to a drop in white female viewers who were offended that she had endorsed Obama over Clinton. Overall, however, Winfrey's passion for Obama's candidacy likely prompted many of her viewers to vote – and to vote for Obama.

The dearth of celebrity conservative females on highly rated television discussion shows no doubt frustrated some young conservative women in the eighteen- to forty-nine-year-old demographic. Some gave up and either tuned in to the Fox News Channel or watched local television news magazine shows. Others just lost interest in television as a source of political information and discussion.

Television's Women News Stars

The vast majority of Americans get most of their political news from television during the evening hours. In 2008, the number of females anchoring or hosting evening political news shows increased slightly but was still rather low, including Katie Couric on CBS, Gwen Ifill on PBS, Campbell Brown on CNN, Greta Van Susteren on Fox, and Rachel Maddow on MSNBC. Nonetheless, these women gave much-needed female voices to political news shows. In addition, "The presence of women candidates...pushed media executives to showcase more women experts on the cable shows as guests."[25] Each of these women attracted and influenced different types of female – and male – voters in 2008, because networks have become more ideologically segmented. Fox attracts more conservatives; MSNBC, more liberals; and CNN, those who fall more in the middle of the ideological continuum.

As anchor of *CBS Evening News*, Katie Couric ultimately had the greatest influence on women's opinions and voting behavior. Her interview of Sarah Palin was in many minds a key factor in shifting some women voters away from the McCain-Palin ticket. It was Palin's first high-profile interview with the sole female evening news anchor. Some had presumed Couric would be more sympathetic to a woman candidate than Charles Gibson, anchor of *ABC Evening News*, had been. But Couric was a tough interviewer, and Palin did not do especially well in responding to her questions. What happened after the interview is exemplary of how regular news coverage is greatly enhanced by other media. The interview, spread out over two evenings on CBS, was subsequently played (or spoofed) on CNN, YouTube, *Saturday Night Live*, and thousands of blogs. Cumulatively across these venues, millions who had not watched the *CBS Evening News* nonetheless got a glimpse of Palin's performance.

In the end, some analysts concluded that Couric's interviews "might have shaped the view of Palin as not ready for primetime more than anything in the campaign."[26] But to many citizens, they merely exemplified media bias. At one point, 69 percent agreed that the national media was trying to support one candidate over the other.[27] At the very least, women's differential reactions to Couric were proof yet again that women are not a highly cohesive bloc of voters.

Hollywood "Accidentals": Paris Hilton and Britney Spears

Who would have thought that Paris Hilton and Britney Spears would play an important role in the 2008 presidential election? At a time when McCain was struggling to get much-needed media attention, the McCain campaign ran a television ad with clips of "divas" Hilton and Spears. The ad flashed shots of the two megacelebrities and likened Senator Barack Obama to them, short on leadership skills: "He's the biggest celebrity in the world. But is he ready to lead? With gas prices soaring, Barack Obama says no to offshore drilling and says he'll raise taxes on electricity. Higher taxes, more foreign oil – that's the real Obama" the ad's narrator says, while crowds screaming "Obama!" are shown.[28]

Hilton initially shied away from the debate over the ad and its effectiveness. But then she responded with a spoof aired on the comedy Web site Funny or Die:

> "Hey America, I'm Paris Hilton and I'm a celebrity, too. Only I'm not from the olden days and I'm not promising change like that other guy. I'm just hot," Hilton said, speaking as she reclined in a pool chair in a revealing bathing suit and a pair of pumps. "But then that wrinkly, white-haired guy used me in his campaign ad, which I guess means I'm running for president. So thanks for the endorsement white-haired dude. I want America to know that I'm, like, totally ready to lead."[29]

Hilton went on to discuss energy policy and recommended a combination of McCain's offshore oil-drilling plan and Obama's incentives for new energy technology. "Energy crisis solved! I'll see you at the debates," she said.

Both ads were widely distributed in all forms of media, as was the Couric interview. The McCain ad resonated more with older women, the Hilton spoof with younger women. They were aired in August, prior to the national party conventions. At the time, polls were showing Obama leading among women but by considerably less among some groups than others. The significance of this ad exchange reflected the reality-show nature of the 2008 campaign that kept female voters engaged from start to finish by showcasing women stars.

PRECISION AD TARGETING OF WOMEN VOTERS ON THE ISSUES

"In the political sphere, television is viewed as the ultimate persuasion medium and the Web more akin to direct mail."[30] In 2008, the candidates and their campaign strategists worked hard to create effective television, radio, online (including YouTube), and direct mail ads. (Very little advertising was done in the print media – newspapers or magazines.)

Television and radio ads are especially powerful in reaching young and new voters, the majority of whom are female. The campaigns selected the stations whose viewers or listeners the candidates most wanted to reach and the times those viewers would most likely be tuned in. In each ad, the words and images were finely focused on a desired group of viewers.

Although radio and television ads can beam specific campaign messages to specific audiences, direct mail is considered the most precise. It can reach far narrower audiences (by ZIP code, for example) and also reaches only registered voters who are eligible to vote in a particular electoral contest. Campaign managers can subdivide or cross-reference registered voter lists according to a personal characteristic such as race or gender or an issue such as membership in religious or environmental group, and mail pieces to only those names.

While one might argue that direct mail is junk mail and that recipients are likely to toss it in the trash, this is only partially borne out. Surveys conducted in the heat of the 2008 election campaign found that 40 percent of unmarried women voters found political mail from campaigns or candidates valuable.[31] And according to Women's Voices. Women Vote, unmarried women made up 26 percent of the voting age population in 2008. Ultimately, these women swung heavily for Obama (70 percent to 29 percent). Some attribute at least part of his success with these women to having had more effective direct mail than McCain. In fairness, the Obama campaign had three times as much money to spend on polls, focus groups, and marketing experts to help design these ads because of his superior fund-raising.

Overall, analysts agree that the 2008 election was characterized by the most precise demographic targeting in American campaign history. As shown in the direct-mail pieces found in this chapter (see Photo Section 3.3), the ads were specially crafted to appeal to different groups of women on the basis of their age, race or ethnicity, marital and parental status, employment and income, ideology, and religion, among

Direct Mail Ad 1

Front

Inside Left

Inside Right

Back

Ad Sponsor: Republican Party of Florida
Target: Older Democratic women who may have supported Clinton

Photo Section 3.3: Microtargeted direct-mail ads.

Direct Mail Ad 2

Front

Inside Left

Inside Right

Back

Ad Sponsor: Florida Democratic Party
Target: Working Women

Photo Section 3.3 *(continued)*

others. Reflective of the dominant issue of the campaign, the economy, both campaigns used ads featuring worrying women – worried about a job, equal pay for equal work, rising gas prices, the prospects for Social Security and Medicare, college education and health care for their children, and abortion rights.

The trick is to capture the recipient's attention. The time to do that is short, according to direct-mail specialists; it has to happen between the time a person picks up a mailer and the time she reaches the first trash can. It is more likely to happen if the recipient can immediately see something of herself and her sentiments in the piece. That means compelling pictures and a simple, straightforward message. The outside panels are

Direct Mail Ad 3

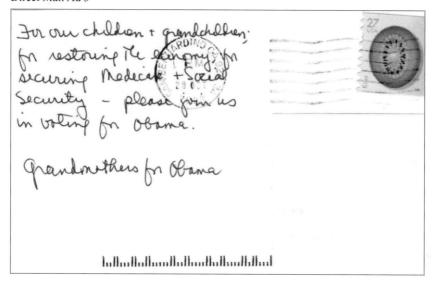

For our children + grandchildren; for restoring the economy; for securing Medicare + Social Security – please join us in voting for Obama.

Grandmothers for Obama

Ad Sponsor: Obama Campaign
Target: Grandmothers

Direct Mail Ad 3

Think you're paying too much at the pump?
Barack Obama doesn't

Ad Sponsor: Republican National Committee
Target: Young women

Photo Section 3.3 (*continued*)

Direct Mail Ad 4

Ad Sponsor: Florida Democratic Party
Target: Moms

Direct Mail Ad 5

Front   Back

Ad Sponsor: Republican Party of Florida
Target: Retirees

Photo Section 3.3 (*continued*)

Direct Mail Ad 6

Front   Back

Ad Sponsor: Florida Democratic Party
Target: Retirees

Photo Section 3.3 (*continued*)

often designed to look less like a political ad and more like a human-interest informational piece because, as direct-mail specialists know, politics is a lower priority with many voters than are children, work, health, and other aspects of their lives. Mailers in 2008 were considerably more visual and creative than those sent in 2004.

Timing of direct-mail ads is getting trickier, especially in the growing number of states that have early voting. If an advertisement is mailed too early, nobody remembers it. If it is mailed too late, it gets lost in the shuffle and has no impact on a voter's decision. In addition, the more mail pieces a candidate sends, the more likely a voter is to remember the candidate's name. All direct-mail consultants preach that repetition is critical, whether for mail, ads aired on television and radio, or those appearing online.

Mobilizing Voters: The Electronic Media and the Internet
The 2008 presidential contest has been dubbed by many media analysts and campaign consultants as the "YouTube Election." The founder of the

Direct Mail Ad 7

Front

Back

Ad Sponsor: Florida Democratic Party
Target: Parents

Photo Section 3.3 (*continued*)

Web site TechPresident aptly described Google's YouTube as America's
new "town square."[32] It enabled the introduction of videos as a new
form of campaign ad that quickly became an engaging and entertaining way to reach voters. The video-sharing site generated an estimated
81 million viewers a month. Some thirteen hours worth of videos were
uploaded each minute. It is hardly surprising, then, that nearly 40 percent

Direct Mail Ad 8

Front

Inside

Back

<u>Ad Sponsor</u>: Republican Party of Florida
<u>Target</u>: Pro-Life Women

Photo Section 3.3 (*continued*)

of all voters reported that they had watched a campaign-related video online – greater than the proportion who said that they had visited a candidate's Web site or accessed political blogs or social networking sites, such as Facebook, MySpace, Twitter, or Flickr.[33]

Seven out of 16 presidential candidates, including Hillary Clinton, announced their candidacies on YouTube through videos. Virtually every

John McCain says that Roe v. Wade "must be overturned."

(www.johnmccain.com)

"Most Americans believe these decisions should be between a woman and her doctor. John McCain's support for a total ban on abortion will take us back to those dark times." *- Valerie Baron, Nurse Practitioner*

Florida Democratic Party
214 S. Bronough St.
Tallahassee, FL 32301

Paid for by Campaign for Change, a project of the Florida Democratic Party.

Non. Profit Org.
U.S. Postage
PAID
Florida Democratic
Party
33010

ECRLOT**R030

Check for yourself at
www.johnmccainrecord.com/choice

Valerie Baron, FNP

Ad Sponsor: Florida Democratic Party
Target: Pro-Choice Women

Photo Section 3.3 (*continued*)

major aspect of the campaign ended up there – from candidates' speeches, interviews, debates, ads, and news clips to supporters' catchy homemade videos and personal stories.[34] Video postings came from both directions – top down from the political parties and candidates; bottom up from videos posted by individual voters. YouTube postings frequently were covered in regular television newscasts (e.g., Obama Girl's "I Got a Crush . . . on Obama"). Clever YouTube videos even ended up in candidate ads or being linked in mass e-mails or text messages sent to those who had signed up to receive campaign news from the candidate.

Online ads were utilized by both presidential campaigns, but more by Obama. From January to August of 2008, he spent around $5.5 million on online ads, $4.4 million of which went to Google. He bought both AdWords ads on Google and display ads seen through the AdSense network. However, online advertising did not come close to what was spent on television advertising. It was less than 1 percent of what was spent on television and not as effective.[35] Nor were online ads as effective as the free advertising the candidates did on YouTube.

The candidates used the Internet to send out mass e-mails to inform voters of special announcements to be made via the Web, to solicit contributions, and to recruit volunteers.

Photo Section 3.4: Candidate use of e-mailed messages and pleas for help.

The number of online ads run by both candidates increased in the final weeks of the campaign. Each went after specific audiences in key battleground states, usually women and younger voters, who are harder to actually get to the polls. Obama's online ads aimed to get voters in states with early voting to the polls, while McCain's were primarily persuasion ads featuring either Sarah Palin or Joe the Plumber[36] (see Photo Section 3.4).

THE FINAL WORD

In this chapter, I began with a brief discussion of the historical dimensions of the 2008 election from a gender and race perspective, followed by a short history of how women won the right to vote in 1920. I then tracked changes in female registration and turnout rates over the years through the election of 2008. By 1964, more women than men were voting, and by 1980, the percentage of women voting was greater than the percentage of men voting. The growing clout of female voters is attributable to the simple facts that women outnumber men among the population at large and have higher voter-turnout rates.

The election of 2008 resulted in record registration and high turnout levels among female voters. Candidates, political parties, and women's advocacy groups all worked hard to get more women registered and to the polls. They used virtually every advertising and mobilization tool available in this high-tech era: interactive Web sites; YouTube; online ads; and precisely targeted mail, radio spots, and television ads, both broadcast and cable. But it was the plethora of high-profile women – female star power – that worked best to mobilize women in a once-in-a-lifetime election.

The bottom line? A huge factor in energizing women voters, albeit different women voters at different times, was the very real possibility that a woman would break the glass ceiling and become either the nation's first female president or the nation's first female vice president. The issues were important, too, but hearing them articulated by strong women candidates and powerful female surrogates resonated with a lot of female voters. Perhaps the most lasting impact of the 2008 election was the realization that fielding an all-white-male ticket is no longer pragmatic and that choosing a woman who has broad appeal to all women voters is probably not possible. It is also highly likely that the technologies used to reach women voters of all stripes in 2008 will be replaced by newer mechanisms in time for the 2012 election. Far less likely is any abandonment of the woman-to-woman outreach strategies that have been used so effectively in recent presidential campaigns.

NOTES

1 Telephone poll of six hundred women conducted November 21–24 for Lifetime Network by Republican pollster Kellyanne Conway and Democratic pollster Celinda Lake, margin of error is plus or minus 4.4 percent.
2 Gloria Steinem. January 8, 2008. Women Are Never Front-Runners. *New York Times*.
3 DeNee L. Brown. March 24, 2008. A Vote of Allegiance? In the Obama-Clinton Battle, Race & Gender Pose Two Great Divides for Black Women. *Washington Post*.
4 James W. Caesar. April 2, 2008. What a Long, Strange Race It's Been. *Wall Street Journal*.
5 Lynn Sanders, quoted in Kirsten Scharnberg. April 7, 2008. Clinton Focusing on Females. *Chicago Tribune*.
6 Donna Brazile. July 3, 2004. Energize the Women's Vote in 2004. *Women's eNews*. <http://www.womensenews.org/article.cfm/dyn/aid/1856/context/archive.>
7 Carol Andreas and Katherine Culkin. 2003. Women's Rights Movement: The Nineteenth Century. In *Dictionary of American History*, 3rd ed., Stanley I. Kutler. New York: Charles Scribner's Sons, volume 8, 512.
8 On June 4, 1919, the U.S. Senate voted to add the Nineteenth Amendment to the U.S. Constitution by a vote of fifty-six to twenty-five. The House had passed it two weeks earlier by a vote of 304 to 89.
9 North Dakota has no registration requirement.

10 Women's Voices. Women Vote. July 30, 2008. "News Articles – Voter Registration Drive Begins in Arkansas, 23 Other States." <http://www.wvwv.org> December 18, 2008.

11 Associated Press. May 6, 2008. Historic Election Inspiring Millions of New Voters. <http://www.cnn.com/2008/POLITICS/05/06/new.voters.ap/index.html> December 18, 2008.

12 U.S. Census Bureau. July 20, 2009. Voter Turnout Increases by 5 Million in 2008 Presidential Election, U.S. Census Bureau Reports, Press release. <http://www.census.gov/Press-Release/www/releases/archives/voting/013995.html> Table 2, Reported Voting and Registration, by Race, Hispanic Origin, Sex, and Age, for the United States: November 2008. Current Population Survey, Internet release date, July 2009.

13 Sam Roberts. July 21, 2009. 2008 Surge in Black Voters Nearly Erased Racial Gap. *The New York Times*.

14 U.S. Elections Project. November 4, 2008. 2008 Early Voting Statistics. Compiled by Michael McDonald, George Mason University. <http://elections.gmu/early_vote_2008.html> December 18, 2008.

15 Women's Voices. Women Vote. Women's Tracking Survey: Unmarried Women Driving a New American Electorate, survey of 1,030 female likely voters, conducted October 26–28, 2008, in fifteen battleground states by Greenberg Quinlan Rosner Research, margin of error plus or minus 3.10 percent.

16 The published poll does not report what proportion of the 15 percent were women.

17 Anne E. Kornblut. September 10, 2008. Palin Energizing Women from All Walks of Life. *Washington Post*.

18 Camille Paglia. September 10, 2008. Fresh Blood for the Vampires. Salon.com. <http://www.salon.com/opinion/paglia/2008/09/10/print.html> December 21, 2008.

19 Sarah Palin Is Not a Feminist. August 30, 2008. Menstrual Poetry. <http://menstrualpoetry.com/sarah-palin-feminist> December 21, 2008.

20 Chris Cillizza. November 16, 2008. 5 Myths about an Election of Mythic Proportions. *Washington Post*.

21 Cassandra Spratling. July 10, 2008. Michelle Obama Credited with Helping Recast Image of U.S. Black Women. *Detroit Free Press*; also see Dahleen Glanton. December 21, 2008. In Multifaceted Michelle Obama, Black Women See a Mirror. *Chicago Tribune*.

22 Bill Tancer. May 9, 2007. Under the Influence of Oprah. Time.com. <http://www.time.com/time/printout/0,8816,1618910,00.html> December 18, 2008.

23 William Katz. Tina Fey, Kingmaker. Power Line Blog. <http://www.powerlineblog.com> December 1, 2008.

24 Ibid.

25 "Carol Jenkins & Glennda Testone: The Women's Media Center." December 5, 2008. feministing.com. <http://www.feministing.com/archives/012541.html> December 22, 2008.

26 Carla Marinucci. November 1, 2008. Campaign '08 Nears Its Cliffhanger Conclusion. *San Francisco Chronicle*.

27 Rasmussen. September 10, 2008. 69% Say Reporters Try to Help The Candidate They Want to Win. <http://www.rasmussenreports.com/public_content/politics/election_20082/2008_presidential_election/69_say_reporters_try_to_help_the_candidate_they_want_to_win> December 22, 2008.

28 Alexander Mooney. McCain Ad Compares Obama to Britney Spears, Paris Hilton. CNN.com. <http://cnn.com> December 22, 2008.

29 CBS. Paris Hilton Responds to McCain in New Video. <http://wbztv.com/national/paris.hilton.commercial.2.788651.html> December 22, 2008.

30 Kate Kaye. Web Ads Mattered More Than Ever in '08 Election. <http://www.clickz.com> November 4, 2008.

31 Greenberg Quinlan Rosner Research. October 2008. Women's Tracking Survey: Unmarried Women Driving a New American Electorate. <http://www.wvwv.org/research-items/women-s-tracking-survey> December 20, 2008.

32 Nikki Schwab. November 7, 2008. In Obama-McCain Race, YouTube Became a Serious Battleground for Presidential Politics. *U.S. News & World Report*.

33 Jessica Ramirez. November 10, 2008. The Big Picture. Newsweek Web Exclusive. <http://www.newsweek.com/id/168269> December 20, 2008.

34 Nikki Schwab. November 7, 2008. In Obama-McCain Race, YouTube Became a Serious Battleground for Presidential Politics. *U.S. News & World Report*.

35 Kaye (see *supra* note 30).

36 "Joe The Plumber" was an Ohio plumber named Joe Wurzelbacher. During an Obama campaign appearance, Wurzelbacher complained that Obama's proposal to raise taxes on people making more than $250,000 a year, while cutting taxes on everyone else, would prevent him from purchasing the plumbing company that employed him. McCain then held up Joe as a real life example of what was wrong with the Obama tax plan. "He [Obama] wants the government to take Joe's money and give it to someone else. His hard-earned tax dollars. We're not going to stand for that," said McCain. Joe then became the centerpiece of numerous McCain campaign ads attacking Obama's tax plan and accusing him of planning to redistribute wealth in America. CBS/Associated Press. October 16, 2008. Campaigns Battle Over 'Joe The Plumber', <www.cbsnews.com/stories/2008/10/16/politics/2008debates/main4526503.shtml> July 28, 2009.

4 Voting Choices

The Politics of the Gender Gap

Women voters have received special attention from the presidential candidates in recent elections primarily because of differences between women and men in their political preferences, a phenomenon commonly referred to as the gender gap. Statistically, a gender gap can be defined as the difference in the proportion of women and the proportion of men who support a particular politician, party, or policy position. In the 2008 election, Senator Barack Obama received 56 percent of women's votes compared with 49 percent of men's, resulting in a gender gap of seven percentage points.

A gender gap in voting has been evident in every general election for president since 1980. In each of the previous eight presidential elections, a greater proportion of women than men have voted for the Democratic candidate. In 2004, when Republican President George W. Bush was reelected, 51 percent of women compared with only 44 percent of men cast their votes for his Democratic opponent, Senator John Kerry. Bush received just 48 percent of women's votes but 55 percent of men's, resulting in a gender gap of seven percentage points – the same size as in 2008.[1]

Prior to the 1980 election, it was widely believed that women and men took similar positions on most issues, had similar political preferences, and voted in much the same ways. In other words, the assumption before 1980 was that gender did not matter much in voting. Today the assumption is exactly the opposite – gender does matter for politics, and women and men, in the aggregate, have different positions on many issues and tend to vary in their party identification and support for political candidates. The gender gap is now viewed as an enduring part of the political landscape, and candidates, parties, and politicians must pay specific attention to women voters if they want to win elections.

This chapter begins with an overview of the role that women voters and the gender gap played in the 2008 presidential elections. It then traces the origins of and explores possible explanations for the gender gap. It also examines the strategies candidates have employed in attempting to appeal to women voters. The gender gap has led to increased political influence for women, although that influence has been somewhat tempered by the fact that candidates have often used symbolic appeals, rather than strictly issue-based appeals, to respond to the growing influence of women voters.

WOMEN VOTERS AND THE 2008 PRESIDENTIAL ELECTION

Women voters received more attention in 2008 than in any previous election, and the candidacy of Senator Hillary Clinton was perhaps the major reason. Clinton did not win her party's nomination for president and was not a candidate in the general election, but throughout her many months of campaigning for the Democratic nomination, Clinton attracted strong support from women voters.

While the gender gap has become a recurring feature of the electoral landscape in general elections for president, gender gaps are seldom seen in primary elections where candidates of the same party face off against each other and policy differences are generally small. In such elections, women and men tend to divide their support and votes among the candidates in similar proportions. For example, several candidates vied for the Republican presidential nomination in 2008, including Senator John McCain, Governor Mitt Romney, Governor Mike Huckabee, Mayor Rudy Giuliani, Senator Fred Thompson, and Representative Ron Paul. Polls showed that women and men supported each of these candidates in roughly equal proportions.

The fact that Hillary Clinton attracted stronger support from women than from men in a primary election was thus an exception to the rule. Throughout the 2007 preprimary period and throughout the Democratic primaries in 2008, a gender gap was evident in support for her candidacy. For example, a national poll conducted by the Pew Research Center for the People and the Press in late November 2007, just a few weeks before the primaries began, found that, among likely Democratic voters, 52 percent of women, compared with 42 percent of men, supported Hillary Clinton over the other candidates. Similarly, Pew polls conducted at about the same time with likely Democratic voters in Iowa, New Hampshire, and South Carolina – the first three states to hold caucuses and primaries in early 2008 – found gender gaps in Clinton's support in each of these three states, with women more likely than men to support Clinton.[2]

As 2008 proceeded and various state primaries were held, gender gaps in support for Hillary Clinton were evident in voting in state after state. Clinton won some state primaries and caucuses while she lost others, but regardless of whether she won or lost, in most states, Clinton drew stronger support from women than from men. Two of the earliest primaries were New Hampshire, on January 8, 2008, which Clinton won, and South Carolina, on January 29, which she lost to Obama by a sizeable margin. Yet gender gaps were evident in support for Clinton in both primaries. In New Hampshire, the exit poll showed that Clinton won 46 percent of women's votes but only 29 percent of men's, for a seventeen-point gender gap. In South Carolina, only 30 percent of women voted for Clinton, but even fewer men – 23 percent – did, for a seven-point gender gap. Contests that were held later in the year showed a similar pattern of greater support for Clinton among women than men, regardless of the outcome of the election. For example, Clinton lost the Wisconsin primary on February 19 with a nineteen-point gender gap and won the Pennsylvania primary on April 22 with a ten-point gender gap.[3]

The gender gap evident in support for Clinton was not primarily due to issue differences between Clinton and Obama or the other Democratic contenders. For the most part, Clinton and Obama took very similar positions on issues. Their main differences were on health care, where Obama's plan was not quite as comprehensive as Clinton's, and the war in Iraq, where Clinton, as a U.S. senator, had voted to authorize the war while Obama, who was not in the U.S. Senate at the time, had opposed it. Nevertheless, both candidates pledged to end the war in Iraq and shared a common goal of providing health-care coverage to the vast majority of Americans. Polls showed that most Democratic voters liked the issue stances of both Clinton and Obama and would have been satisfied to have either candidate as their party's nominee. Because there were not major differences between Clinton and Obama on the issues, it seems likely that Clinton's greater support among women was related to her gender. Many Democratic women supported Clinton because they liked her issue positions (just as they liked Obama's) and because they wanted to see a woman in the White House.

When John Edwards dropped out at the end of January 2008, the race for the Democratic presidential nomination became a two-person contest. Because Hillary Clinton attracted stronger support from women than from men, this meant that the opposite was true for her opponent, Barack Obama, who was supported by greater proportions of men than of women. Thus, when it became clear that Clinton was going to lose her bid for her party's nomination, it also became clear that Obama, as the Democratic nominee, needed to shore up his support among Democratic women voters.

On June 7, 2008, after the last primary was held, Hillary Clinton announced that she would suspend her campaign, thus officially ending her bid for the Democratic nomination. The Obama campaign immediately stepped up efforts to win over women voters who had supported Clinton. Obama's campaign seemingly employed a three-pronged strategy to do so. As the first prong, Obama emphasized his personal narrative – that women in his family had played a critical role in his own personal development. For example, on June 23 in Albuquerque, New Mexico, Obama explained:

> I would not be standing before you today as a candidate for president of the United States if it weren't for working women. I am here because of my mother, a single mom who put herself through school. . . . I am here because of my grandmother, who helped raise me. . . . And I am here because of my wife, Michelle, the rock of the Obama family.[4]

As a second prong of his strategy to win over the women who had supported Clinton, Obama emphasized issue differences between himself and the Republican nominee, John McCain, that he thought would be particularly appealing to key segments of women voters. Obama occasionally highlighted his pro-choice position on the abortion issue in contrast to that of John McCain, who is pro-life. But mostly he tried to appeal to women on the basis of economic issues. Obama talked about the economic struggles working parents face and, in particular, discrimination against women in the workplace. In July, he announced an economic security plan targeted at working women that would "give a tax cut to 71 million working women, guarantee seven days of paid sick leave for 22 million additional women, and make child care more affordable for 7.5 million working mothers."[5] Obama and his campaign also highlighted McCain's opposition to the Fair Pay Restoration Act, a bill (later passed by Congress and signed into law by President Obama in early 2009) to allow women facing pay discrimination to seek back wages and damages at the point that they became aware of the discrimination rather than only within 180 days of their hiring, as a 2007 Supreme Court decision had required. To reinforce this message, the Obama campaign ran ads in several states claiming that McCain opposed equal pay for equal work for women.

The third prong of Obama's effort to win the backing of women voters who supported Hillary Clinton was to have well-known women campaign on his behalf around the country. Of course, the most notable and perhaps the most effective was Clinton herself. Less than one month after she suspended her campaign, Clinton appeared with Obama at a rally in Unity, New Hampshire. She then continued to campaign for Obama throughout the general election, urging her former supporters to throw their support behind Obama. Obama also had other prominent political and nonpolitical women campaigning on his behalf, including Missouri Senator Claire McCaskill, Kansas Governor Kathleen Sebelius, Arizona Governor Janet Napolitano, Caroline Kennedy, Michelle Obama, and even Oprah Winfrey.

As the Republican nominee, John McCain also attempted to appeal to women voters, especially targeting those women who might have been disappointed at Hillary Clinton's defeat. Throughout the summer of 2008, before he was officially nominated, but after he had become the presumptive Republican nominee, McCain began making overtures to women. He and his campaign surrogates praised Hillary Clinton once she was out of the race in an attempt to attract any of her supporters who might have been disaffected with the Obama campaign. McCain appeared on television shows with predominantly female audiences, such as *The View* and *Ellen*. His most prominent female supporter, Carly Fiorina, former chief executive officer of Hewlett-Packard, traveled around the country on his behalf. McCain seemed to focus his efforts most intensively on women who were small-business owners. When asked in July what he would do to win over more women voters, McCain responded:

> I don't have a specific policy at the moment, except... my support of small business and the fact that I will not raise people's taxes. One of the greatest areas of participation of women in America is small business.[6]

McCain's most significant attempt to attract women voters, especially disaffected Hillary Clinton supporters, was his selection of Sarah Palin as his vice presidential nominee. The day after the Democratic National Convention ended, McCain did the unexpected, choosing a woman as his running mate. The hope that Governor Sarah Palin might appeal to women voters was not McCain's only reason for choosing her. Like McCain, Palin had a reputation as a reformer and a maverick, and consequently she could help to underscore those themes of the McCain campaign. She was very popular among social conservatives and thus could help shore up McCain's support with the right wing of his party. Nevertheless, there is little doubt that McCain hoped his vice presidential choice would help to persuade some disaffected Hillary Clinton voters as well as more moderate and independent women voters who had not yet fully made up their minds about how to vote in the November election.

Despite the fact that Palin was subjected to intense media scrutiny and criticism, as Carroll and Dittmar document in Chapter 2 of this volume, the choice of Palin did provide the McCain campaign with a burst of energy and a short-term surge in the polls. A *Washington Post*–ABC News poll, conducted shortly after the Republican convention, found that Obama and McCain were essentially tied.[7] The poll also showed that McCain had made substantial gains among white women, although other polls conducted at about the same time did not show a big shift.[8]

But even if the strategy of putting a woman on the ticket – one who was ideologically to the right of most women voters – to attract women voters worked in the short term, it failed over the longer term. In the end, issues and policy positions mattered more to women voters than did the gender of the vice presidential candidate. As the economy eroded over the course of the fall, so, too, did public support for John McCain and Republican candidates more generally. On Election Day, the majority of women voters opted for Barack Obama and a new direction for the country.

Nevertheless, the 2008 election was one in which the votes of women received more attention than in any previous election. Hillary Clinton came close to winning the Democratic nomination in large part because of the strong support she received from women voters. Her candidacy drew initial attention to women voters and their significance in the 2008 election. And once Clinton exited the race, the two remaining candidates, Obama and McCain, both vied for the support of women who had voted for Clinton in the Democratic primaries as well as the support of other independent and moderate women who had not yet made their choices. In the end, Obama prevailed, winning 56 percent of women's votes, and was elected president by a healthy margin in large part because his message and policy proposals resonated more with women than did McCain's.

THE ORIGINS OF THE GENDER GAP

In Chapter 3 of this volume, Susan A. MacManus describes the suffrage movement that led to the addition of the Nineteenth Amendment to the Constitution in 1920, granting women the right to vote. Over the course of the several decades that it took to win the right to vote, suffragists used a variety of arguments to win support from different segments of the all-male electorate and political structure. Some approaches stressed fundamental similarities between women and men and demanded the vote for women as a matter of simple justice. Suffragists observed that women were human beings just as men were, and therefore women, like men, were created equal and had an inalienable right to political equality and thus the vote.

However, suffragists also used arguments that focused on how women were different from men and would use their votes to help make the world a better place. Suffragists claimed that women's experiences, especially their experiences as mothers and caregivers, gave them special values and perspectives that would be readily apparent in their voting decisions. They argued that women would use their votes to stop wars, promote peace, clean up government, ban the sale of liquor, and bring justice to a corrupt world.

The use of such arguments led some people to eagerly anticipate and others to greatly fear the consequences of women's enfranchisement. Many observers at the time expected women to go to the polls in large numbers and thought that their distinctive impact on politics would be immediately apparent. However, the right to vote, in and of itself, proved insufficient to bring about a distinctive women's vote. Rather, a women's vote would emerge only decades later after other changes in society and women's perceptions of themselves took place. In the elections immediately following women's enfranchisement in 1920, women voted in much lower numbers than men, and there were few signs that women were voting much differently than men were or using their votes to express a distinctive perspective.

As the decades passed after 1920, it seemed that the women's vote, feared by some and longed for by others, would never materialize. However, by the early 1980s, a sufficient number of women finally achieved the social and psychological independence necessary to bring about a divergence in the voting patterns of women and men. In the decades since 1980, the women's vote promised by the suffragists has finally arrived, although with underlying issues and dynamics somewhat different from those anticipated during the suffrage era.

In the decades between 1920 and 1980, the vast majority of women, particularly white women,[9] remained economically dependent on men, not necessarily by choice but because society offered them few options. As a result, women's political interests were very intertwined with, even inseparable from, the political interests of men, and for the most part, women did not make political decisions that differed from those made by men. However, since the 1960s and 1970s, women's dependence on men has begun to unravel, and as this unraveling has taken place, women have started making political choices that are more independent of men's wishes and interests.

At least three critical developments over the past several decades have contributed to the increased independence of women from men and have made possible the emergence of a distinctive women's vote. The first is the fact that, for a variety of reasons, including higher divorce rates and longer life spans, more women are living apart from men, often heading households on their own. The second development is that more women have achieved professional and managerial positions that, even when they live with men, provide them with sufficient incomes to support themselves and allow them a substantial degree of financial independence from men. The third critical development that has contributed to the increased independence of women from men is the contemporary women's movement, which began with the founding of the National Organization for Women (NOW) in 1966 and the development of women's liberation groups around the country in 1967 and 1968. Although even today a majority of women in American society do not call themselves feminists, the women's movement has changed the way most women in the United States see themselves and their life options. Most women now recognize that they have concerns and interests that are not always identical to those of the men in their lives, and they are aware that these concerns can be relevant to their political choices.

Brief glimpses of gender differences in voting had been apparent from time to time before 1980. For example, women were slightly more likely than men to vote for Dwight Eisenhower, the victorious Republican candidate, in the 1952 and 1956 elections. However, these pre-1980 gender differences in voting were not persistent, nor were they accompanied by consistent gender differences in evaluations of presidential performance, party identification, or voting for offices other than president. A textbook on public opinion commonly used in political science courses, published just before the 1980 election, reflected the conventional thinking about gender differences at that time. This 324-page textbook devoted only one-half of a page to women and gender, concluding, "Differences in the political attitudes of men and women are so slight that they deserve only brief mention.... In political attitudes and voting, people are seldom different because of their sex."[10]

Even though women had achieved a substantial degree of independence from men and their attitudes about themselves were changing throughout the 1970s, it was not until 1980 that a political candidate came along who could crystallize political differences between women and men into a gender gap. Governor Ronald Reagan, the Republican who was elected president in 1980 and reelected in 1984, proved to be the catalyst for the gender gap. In contrast to the 1976 presidential campaign, where most positions taken by the Republican and Democratic candidates were not starkly different, the 1980 presidential campaign presented voters with clear alternatives. Reagan offered policy proposals that contrasted sharply with the policies of then-incumbent President Jimmy Carter. Reagan promised to cut back on the size of the federal government, greatly reduce government spending, increase the strength of the U.S. military, and get tough with the Soviet Union. When offered such clear-cut alternatives, the differences in preferences between women and men became apparent.

Although Reagan defeated Carter in 1980 and was elected president, he received notably less support from women than from men. Exit polls, conducted by the major television networks as voters left the polls on Election Day, showed that women were between six and nine percentage points less likely than men to vote for Reagan. For example, an exit poll conducted jointly by CBS and the *New York Times* showed that only 46 percent of women, compared to 54 percent of men, voted for Reagan, resulting in a gender gap of eight percentage points. Clearly, women were less attracted to the candidacy and policies of Reagan than men were. (Alternatively, looking at the gender gap from the flip side, the polls showed that the policies and candidacy of Reagan resonated more with men than with women.)

Many commentators in the early 1980s thought that this gender gap in presidential voting might be short lived and disappear in subsequent presidential elections, much like earlier glimpses of gender differences (e.g., those in the presidential elections of the 1950s), but this time the gender gap was here to stay. As Table 4.1 shows, in every presidential election since 1980, differences have been apparent in the proportions of women and men who voted for the winning candidate, ranging from a low of four percentage points in 1992 to a high of eleven percentage points in 1996. In each of these elections, women have been more likely than men to support the Democratic candidate for president.

If the suffragists who had worked so hard to achieve voting rights for women were able to return today to see the results of their efforts,

TABLE 4.1: A gender gap in voting has been evident in every presidential election since 1980

Election year	Winning presidential candidate	Women voting for winner (%)	Men voting for winner (%)	Gender gap (in percentage points)
2008	Barack Obama (D)	56	49	7
2004	George W. Bush (R)	48	55	7
2000	George W. Bush (R)	43	53	10
1996	Bill Clinton (D)	54	43	11
1992	Bill Clinton (D)	45	41	4
1988	George H. W. Bush (R)	50	57	7
1984	Ronald Reagan (R)	56	62	6
1980	Ronald Reagan (R)	46	54	8

Source: Data are from exit polls conducted by CBS/*New York Times*, 1980, 1984, 1988; Voter News Service, 1992, 1996, 2000; Edison Media Research and Mitofsky International, 2004, 2008.

they would surely say, "I told you so." It may have taken sixty years to arrive, but the women's vote that the suffragists anticipated is now clearly evident and has been influencing the dynamics of presidential elections for almost three decades.

THE BREADTH AND PERSISTENCE OF THE GENDER GAP

The gender gap has become an enduring feature of American politics that is evident across a wide variety of political attitudes, preferences, and behaviors. Since 1980, the gender gap has been apparent not only in voting in presidential elections but also in voting at other levels of office, in party identification, and in the performance ratings of various presidents.

The exit polls conducted on each Election Day have asked voters not only about their voting in the presidential contest but also about their voting choices in U.S. House, U.S. Senate, and gubernatorial elections. In every election since 1982, women have been more likely than men to vote for Democrats in races for the U.S. House of Representatives. For example, according to exit polls conducted by Edison Media Research and Mitofsky International, a majority, 56 percent, of women, compared with a smaller majority, 52 percent, of men voted for the Democratic candidate for Congress in their district in 2008, resulting in a gender gap of four percentage points.[11]

Gender gaps also have been evident in a majority of races for U.S. Senate and gubernatorial seats in recent elections. Thirty-five of the one hundred seats in the U.S. Senate were up for election in 2008, and eleven of the fifty states elected governors. Women and men did not vote differently in all of these contests, but they did have significantly different preferences in about three-fourths of them. In twenty-eight, or 82.4 percent, of the thirty-four races for U.S. Senate seats for which exit polls were conducted, gender gaps ranging from four to nineteen percentage points were evident, according to exit polls conducted by Edison Media Research and Mitofsky International. In seven of the eleven gubernatorial races, or 63.7 percent, there were gender gaps of four to eleven percentage points. In each of the U.S. Senate and gubernatorial elections in which a notable gender gap was present, women were more likely than men to vote for the Democratic candidate.[12]

Not only are women more likely than men to vote for Democratic candidates but also they are more likely than men to identify with the Democratic Party. When asked whether they think of themselves as Democrats, Republicans, or independents, more women than men call themselves Democrats. For example, the Pew Research Center for the People and the Press reported in April 2008 that 56 percent of women among registered voters, compared with 46 percent of men, identified or leaned toward the Democratic Party (a gender gap of ten percentage points). Moreover, men did not have a strong preference for one party over the other. They divided themselves about evenly between the two parties, with 46 percent of men identifying as Democrats and 43 percent as Republicans. However, women showed a clear preference for the Democratic Party over the Republican Party, with 56 percent of women identifying as Democrats and only 33 percent as Republicans.[13]

Some observers have argued that the gender gap is the result of changes in men's, not women's, political behavior, and the data on party identification offer the strongest evidence in support of this point of view. In the 1970s, both women and men were more likely to identify as Democrats than Republicans, and no significant gender gap in party identification was apparent. However, that pattern changed beginning in the early 1980s, following the election of Ronald Reagan. Men shifted in the direction of the Republican Party, becoming more likely to identify as Republicans and less likely to identify as Democrats than they had been in the 1970s. In contrast, women's party identification remained more stable, showing less dramatic changes since the 1970s. Women were more likely to identify as Democrats than as Republicans in the 1970s, and they remained more likely to be Democrats in 2008.

Although the gender gap in party identification apparent today is largely the result of changes among men, this does not mean that the gender gap in party identification is the result of men's behavior alone; the behavior of women has also been critical. Prior to 1980, when shifts occurred in the political environment, women and men generally responded similarly. But with the increasing independence of women from men, the politics of the 1980s produced a different result. When men chose to shift their party identification, women chose not to follow them.

Just as a gender gap has been evident in party identification, a gender gap also has been apparent in evaluations of the performance of presidents who have served since 1980. On surveys conducted throughout the year, the Gallup Poll asks whether people approve or disapprove of the way the incumbent is handling his job as president. Some presidents have had higher approval ratings than others, and the ratings for each president have varied across his tenure in office. For example, although George W. Bush ended his tenure in office as one of the most unpopular presidents in recent history, his approval ratings soared in the months following September 11, 2001, when the World Trade Center was attacked and the American people rallied behind their leader. Even though Bush's approval ratings varied greatly during his eight years in office, women and men differed in their evaluations of his performance across most of his tenure. For example, a Gallup Poll conducted November 11–14, 2007, when Bush's popularity was low, found that 29 percent of women, compared with 35 percent of men, approved of the way Bush was handling his job as president (a six-percentage-point gender gap).[14]

A similar gender gap is apparent in Barack Obama's approval ratings. Shortly after his inauguration in January 2008, when support for Obama was very high, Gallup found that 71 percent of women, compared with 64 percent of men, approved of Obama's performance as president (a seven-percentage-point gender gap).[15]

Gender gaps have been apparent in the performance ratings of all other recent presidents as well. Women have been more critical than men of Republican presidents and more approving than men of the lone Democrat other than Obama who has served as president since 1980. Thus, women were less likely than men to approve of the way Republicans Ronald Reagan and George H. W. Bush handled their jobs as president but more likely than men to evaluate favorably Democrat Bill Clinton's performance.

THE GENDER GAP AND WOMEN CANDIDATES

As other chapters in this volume document, the number of women running for public office has increased over the past several decades. Every election year, women are among the candidates who run for the U.S. House, U.S. Senate, and governor. What happens to the gender gap in the general election when one (or both) of the candidates for one of these offices is a woman?

Unfortunately, there is no straightforward, easy answer to this question. It depends on whether the woman candidate is a Democrat or a Republican, and if she is a Republican, how moderate or conservative she is. The answer may also depend on the state or district in which she runs and the larger context of the election.

Years ago, voter prejudice may have been a major problem for the few women who were brave enough to seek public office. However, bias against women candidates has declined significantly. Since 1937, pollsters have asked voters whether they would be willing to vote for a "qualified" woman for president. In 1937, only about one-third of voters said that they would vote for a woman. In contrast, by the beginning of the twenty-first century, about nine of every ten Americans reported that they would vote for a woman for the nation's highest office (although there is some evidence that this high level of support dipped for a while in the aftermath of the attack on the World Trade Center in 2001).[16] Thus, voter prejudice against women candidates, even for the most powerful office in the United States, has declined considerably, although it has not completely disappeared.

But if there still are voters who are predisposed to vote against women, there also are voters who are predisposed to cast affirmative votes for women candidates. Moreover, research has shown that women are more likely than men to be predisposed to support women candidates.[17] This predisposition on the part of some voters to vote for or against a woman candidate, all other things being equal, becomes an additional factor that can increase or decrease the size of the gender gap when women run for office.

In general, women candidates who are Democrats tend to have gender gaps (with women voters more likely than men to vote for them) that are similar in size to or sometimes larger than those for male Democratic

TABLE 4.2: A gender gap in voting was evident in the races of all women who won election to the U.S. Senate in 2008

	Women voting for winner (%)	Men voting for winner (%)	Gender gap (in percentage points)
U.S. Senate Winners			
Kay Hagen (D-NC)	55	47	8
Mary Landrieu (D-LA)	57	47	10
Jeanne Shaheen (D-NH)	60	45	15
Susan Collins (R-ME)	59	63	4

Source: Edison Media Research and Mitofsky International Exit Polls, 2008.

candidates. In contrast, women candidates who are Republicans tend to have gender gaps (with women voters more likely than men to vote against them) that are similar in size to or sometimes smaller than those for male Republican candidates. An analysis of U.S. House races in three elections in the early 1990s found that the gender gap was, on average, greater in races where the Democratic candidate was a woman candidate than in races where a Democratic man ran against a Republican man. Similarly, on average, the gender gap was smaller in races where the Republican candidate was a woman than in races where a Republican man ran against a Democratic man.[18]

Table 4.2 shows the gender gap in races won by the four women elected to the U.S. Senate in the 2008 elections, and the generalizations presented previously hold up well for these victorious candidates. The average gender gap for the twenty-eight U.S. Senate races in 2008 in which both candidates were men was 6.4 percentage points, with female voters more likely than male voters to vote for the Democratic candidate. As Table 4.2 shows, all three of the Democratic women senators exceeded this norm and had gender gaps greater than the average for races involving two male candidates. Mary Landrieu, an incumbent from Louisiana, and Jeanne Shaheen, who won an open seat in New Hampshire, both had male opponents, and the gender gaps in their races were notably greater than the average for races involving two men. Kay Hagen, a challenger from North Carolina, actually defeated another woman, incumbent Elizabeth Dole, which may help to explain why the gender gap in her race, while still larger than average, was not as large as the gender gaps in Landrieu's and Shaheen's races. Regardless, in 2008, as in previous elections, most female Democratic candidates fared as well as or better than male Democratic candidates in winning support from women voters.

The lone Republican woman elected to the U.S. Senate in 2008, Susan Collins, an incumbent from Maine, had a four-percentage-point gender gap in her race, with women less likely than men to have cast their votes for her (see Table 4.2). The gender gap for Collins was smaller than the 6.4-percentage-point average for U.S. Senate races in which the Republican and Democratic candidates were both men. Collins, who voted with the Christian Coalition only 30 percent of the time in 2007–8 and with the American Conservative Union only 36 percent of the time in 2007,[19] is an example of a moderate Republican woman who was able to appeal to a sufficient number of women voters to reduce the size of the gender gap in her race to smaller than average even though, as a Republican, she attracted fewer votes from women than from men.

Maine is one of three states represented by two women senators, and Maine's other senator, Olympia Snowe, has been one of the rare Republican women who has succeeded in attracting enough votes from women not only to reduce the size of the gender gap as Collins did but also to completely eliminate it. Although Olympia Snowe's seat was not up for reelection in 2008, she was reelected to the U.S. Senate in both 2000 and 2006. In 2000, no gender gap was apparent in Snowe's race; she was reelected with 69 percent of the votes of women and 69 percent of the votes of men in her state. In 2006, Maine's senior Republican senator actually attracted slightly more votes from women than from men; 75 percent of women and 73 percent of men cast their ballots for her.[20] Snowe has a moderate, pro-choice voting record in the U.S. Senate and has been a champion for women during the years she served in both the Senate and the U.S. House. She voted with the Christian Coalition only 20 percent of the time in 2007–8 and with the American Conservative Union only 28 percent of the time in 2007; no other Republican in the U.S. Senate more often voted in opposition to the positions favored by these conservative groups. Moreover, Snowe (like her fellow senator Collins) voted for the positions advocated by NARAL Pro-Choice America 100 percent of the time in 2007.[21] Largely because of her moderate, pro-choice voting record and her advocacy on behalf of women, Snowe has been able to effectively neutralize the gender gap, eliminating the deficit that Republican candidates usually experience with women voters.

TABLE 4.3: A gender gap in voting was evident across a wide range of demographic groups in the 2008 presidential election

Demographic group	Women voting for Obama (%)	Men voting for Obama (%)	Gender gap (in percentage points)
Race or ethnicity			
White	46	41	5
African American	96	95	1
Latino	68	64	4
Age			
18–29	69	62	7
30–44	55	49	6
45–64	53	46	7
65 and older	46	45	1
Marital status			
Married	47	46	1
Unmarried	70	58	12
Parental status			
Children under 18	57	48	9
No children under 18	56	51	5
Employment status			
Employed	60	50	10
Not employed	52	47	5

Source: Edison Media Research and Mitofsky International Exit Polls, 2008.

EXPLANATIONS FOR THE GENDER GAP

One observation about the gender gap can be made with a high degree of certainty: the gender gap is not limited to one or even a few demographic subgroups. In an attempt to undermine women's voting power, political commentators have sometimes claimed that the gender gap is not a broad-based phenomenon but rather one that can be fully explained by the voting behavior of some particular subgroup of women in the electorate – for example, women of color or unmarried voters. Table 4.3 reveals the obvious problem with such claims. When compared with men who shared their demographic characteristics, women of different races and ethnicities, ages, parental statuses, and employment statuses voted for Barack Obama more often than men did (and less often voted for John McCain). In fact, voting differences between women and men are found in most subgroups of the electorate. Consequently, no single demographic category of voters is responsible for the gender gap. Rather, the gender gap is clearly a phenomenon that is evident across many of the various subgroups that comprise the American electorate.

Of course, to say that the gender gap is apparent across many different subgroups does not mean that gender differences are of equal magnitude across all demographic categories. As Table 4.3 also shows, the gender gap is smaller or larger for some demographic groups than for others. The gender gap virtually disappeared in 2008 among African Americans, who voted overwhelmingly for Obama regardless of gender, and among two other groups – senior citizens (voters age sixty-five and older) and married people – who were less supportive of Obama than most other voters. In contrast, gender differences were particularly great among unmarried voters, the employed, and voters with children under the age of eighteen. While voters age eighteen to twenty-nine were more pro-Obama than other age groups, the gender gap among young voters was neither greater nor smaller than the gender gap for those age thirty to forty-four or age forty-five to sixty-four. In contrast to the similarity in the size of the gender gap across all but the oldest age group, the gender gap was greater among parents and the employed than it was among nonparents and the unemployed.

Beyond the fact that the gender gap is not limited to one particular subgroup but rather widespread across the electorate, definitive statements about the gender gap are difficult to make. Indeed, the gender gap appears to be a rather complex phenomenon. Nevertheless, a number of different explanations have been put forward to account for the gender gap in voting. None of these explanations seems sufficient by itself. Moreover, the explanations are not mutually exclusive; in fact, they are somewhat overlapping. However, several of the explanations offered by academic and political analysts do seem to have some validity and are useful in helping to account for the fact that women and men make somewhat different voting choices. Four of the most common explanations – compassion, feminism, economics, and the role of government – are reviewed briefly here.

The compassion explanation focuses on women's roles as mothers and caregivers. Despite recent changes in gender roles, women still bear disproportionate responsibility for the care of children and the elderly in their families and in the greater society. Mothers are still called more often than fathers when children become ill at school, and women are still a large majority of health-care workers, teachers, child-care providers, and social workers. Women's roles as caregivers may lead them to be more sympathetic toward those in need and more concerned with the safety and security of others. Women's caregiving responsibilities may also lead them to put greater emphasis than men on issues such as education and health care.

Consistent with this compassion explanation, education and health care were two of the top issues in the 2000 presidential election, which focused largely on domestic politics rather than foreign affairs. Polls showed that these issues were of greater concern to women voters in the election than they were to men, and both presidential candidates spent a great deal of time talking about these issues. In an obvious attempt to appeal to women voters, the Bush campaign suggested that George W. Bush was not an old-style conservative but rather a "compassionate conservative" who genuinely cared about the well-being of Americans.

While concerns over the economy trumped all other issue concerns for both women and men in 2008, women voters in 2008, as in 2000, continued to express more concern over health care and education than did men. In September 2008, Quinnipiac University Polling Institute asked voters to choose the single most important issue that would influence their vote for president. Health care was the third most frequently mentioned issue among women (after the economy and the war in Iraq), but it ranked fifth for men (behind the economy, the war in Iraq, energy policy, and terrorism). The poll did not list education as a possible response.[22] However, a poll conducted in August 2008 by the Pew Research Center for People and the Press found that women were ten percentage points more likely than men to say that the issue of education would be important to their vote; women were also eleven percentage points more likely to say that the health-care issue would be very important in determining their choice of presidential candidate.[23]

Also consistent with the compassion explanation is the greater reluctance of women than men to use military force to resolve foreign conflicts. In 1980, when the gender gap first became apparent, Americans were being held hostage in Iran, tensions were running high with the Soviet Union, and foreign policy had become a central issue in the presidential campaign. Women reacted more negatively than men to Ronald Reagan's tough posture in dealing with other nations, and women feared more than men that Ronald Reagan might get the country involved in a war. These gender differences were important in explaining why Reagan received stronger support from men than from women.[24] Similarly, in both 2008 and 2004, which was the first presidential election since 1980 where foreign policy was central, a gender difference was evident in women's and men's attitudes toward the war in Iraq. For example, a Rasmussen Reports survey released in June 2008 found that just

26 percent of women, compared with 45 percent of men, believed that troops should stay in Iraq until the mission is finished. Similarly, 67 percent of women, but only 50 percent of men, wanted to see the troops come home within a year.[25] Polls have consistently shown gender gaps on questions such as these, with women having more reservations than men about U.S. involvement in Iraq and other international conflicts. In fact, one of the most persistent and long-standing political differences between women and men is in their attitudes toward the use of military force. For as far back as we have public-opinion polling data, women have been significantly more likely than men to oppose the use of force to resolve international conflicts.

As a second explanation for the gender gap, some observers have suggested the influence of the feminist movement. The discovery of the contemporary gender gap in voting in the aftermath of the 1980 presidential election coincided with intensive efforts by women's organizations, especially NOW, to have the Equal Rights Amendment (ERA) ratified in the necessary thirty-eight states before the June 30, 1982, deadline. In addition, NOW undertook an intensive effort to publicize the gender gap and women's lesser support, relative to men's, for Ronald Reagan. As a result, the ERA and the gender gap became associated in many people's minds, and there was speculation that women were less supportive than men of Ronald Reagan because he opposed the ERA. However, scholarly analyses of voting and public opinion data have consistently shown that so-called women's issues – those issues most closely associated with the organized women's movement, such as the ERA and abortion – do not appear to be central to the gender gap. In part, this may be because women and men in the general electorate have very similar attitudes on these issues, and in part, this may be because candidates for president and other offices seldom choose to campaign on these issues.

However, the fact that women's issues such as the ERA or abortion are not central to the gender gap does not mean that feminism plays no role. As explained earlier in this chapter, the contemporary women's movement has altered the way most women in the United States see themselves and their life options. The movement has provided women with more awareness about their political interests and greater self-confidence about expressing their differences from men. Compelling empirical evidence suggests that women who identify with feminism are more distinctive from men in their political values than are other women, and that for women, a feminist identity may, in fact, foster the expression of the compassion differences described previously. Women influenced by feminism appear more likely than either men or other women to express attitudes sympathetic to those who are disadvantaged and in need, and consequently more predisposed to support the Democratic Party.[26]

Other explanations for the gender gap have focused on economic factors. More women than men live below the poverty line, and women earn only seventy-eight cents for every dollar men earn. Because women on average are poorer than men, they are more dependent on government social services and more vulnerable to cuts in these services. Similarly, women are disproportionately employed in jobs that involve the delivery of human services (health, education, and welfare). Although most women in human services jobs are not directly employed by the government, their employers often receive substantial government funding, and thus their jobs are, to varying degrees, dependent on the continuation of government subsidies. As the principal providers of social welfare services, women are more likely than men to suffer loss of employment when these programs are cut.

Beginning with Ronald Reagan and continuing through the 1990s with the Republican Congress's Contract with America, Republicans at the national level argued that government (with the exception of defense) had grown too large and that cutbacks in domestic spending were necessary. When candidates and politicians propose to cut back on big government or the welfare state, the cuts they propose fall heavily on women who are disproportionately both the providers and the recipients of government-funded services. Consequently, economic self-interest could lead women to favor the Democrats more than the Republicans.

However, women's economic concerns do not appear to be merely self-interested. Evidence shows that women are less likely than men to vote on the basis of economic considerations, but when they do, they are less likely than men to vote on the basis of their own self-interest and more likely to vote on the basis of how well off they perceive the country to be financially.[27] Thus, women are more likely than men to think not just of their own financial situation but also of the economic situation that others are facing. In an election like that of 2008, where polls show that women were very worried about the state of the nation's economy, economic considerations usually work to the disadvantage of the party in power. With a Republican incumbent in the White House, Republican John McCain's chances with women were hurt and Democrat Barack Obama's helped by the dismal state of the economy in the weeks leading up to Election Day.

The final explanation for the gender gap, focusing on the role of government, is clearly related to the economic explanation but extends

beyond economic considerations. In recent years, some of the most consistent and important gender differences in public opinion have shown up
on questions about the role that government should play in Americans'
lives. Both women and men agree that government, especially the federal
government, does not work as effectively as they would like. Beyond that,
however, their attitudes are quite different. Men are more likely than
women to see government as the problem rather than the solution, and
they are considerably more likely than women to favor serious cutbacks
in federal government programs and federal spending on non-defense-
related projects. Men more than women prefer private-sector solutions
to societal problems. In contrast, women are more likely to want to fix
government rather than abandon it. Women are more worried than men
that government cutbacks may go too far; they are more concerned than
men about preserving the social safety net for the people who are most in
need in the United States. The Republican Party, which receives greater
support from men, is commonly perceived as the party that wants to scale
back the size of government, whereas the Democratic Party, which has
more women among its supporters, is more commonly perceived as the
party that defends government programs and works to preserve the social
safety net.

Importantly, gender differences in views about the role of government
are not limited to economics. There is a moral dimension as well, which
offers strong possibilities for Republicans to make inroads with women
voters. Women not only are more likely than men to believe that government should help those who are in economic need but also are more
likely than men to believe that government should play a role in promoting traditional values. In the 1996 presidential election, when the
incumbent Democratic candidate, Bill Clinton, won a convincing victory,
his campaign spent considerable time talking about moral values, focusing
on issues and proposals related to violence in the media, personal responsibility, teen smoking, and drugs. In the 2004 campaign, there was little
discussion by John Kerry and his campaign of proposals to promote moral
values, and most political observers agreed that the Republicans gave
far more attention than did the Democrats to values in their campaign. This lack of attention to moral concerns, which the 1996 Clinton
campaign showed need not be the province of Republican candidates
only, may be one of many reasons why the Kerry campaign did not fare
better with women voters in 2004. In fact, according to the exit polls
conducted by Edison Media Research and Mitofsky International, almost
one-quarter of women voters in 2004 said that the issue that mattered
most in their choice for president was moral values, and of these women,

four out of five voted for George W. Bush. In 2008, moral concerns seem to have played less of a role in the election, with the economic crisis and the war in Iraq taking center stage.

POLITICAL STRATEGIES FOR DEALING WITH THE GENDER GAP AND APPEALING TO WOMEN VOTERS

Given the foregoing explanations for the gender gap, it would appear that the best way for candidates and parties to appeal to women voters is by talking very specifically, concretely, and frequently about issues, whether they be compassion issues (e.g., peace, health care, and education), economic concerns, or moral issues. However, presidential candidates and campaigns often use symbolic appeals in addition to, and sometimes in lieu of, issue-based appeals to win support from women voters.

One of the ways candidates and campaigns have attempted to appeal to women voters symbolically is by showcasing prominent women, as they did in 2008. As noted earlier in this chapter, both Obama and McCain attempted to appeal to women voters by showing that widely admired and accomplished women – for example, Oprah Winfrey, Caroline Kennedy, Carly Fiorina, and Hillary Clinton – supported them. As Barbara Burrell notes in Chapter 8 of this volume, both political parties also featured prominent women at their 2008 presidential nominating conventions.

Beyond the use of well-known women, recent presidential campaigns have used symbolic strategies to appeal to women voters. The presidential campaign of George W. Bush, in particular, was very clever in its use of symbolic appeals to woo women voters. In the 2004 campaign and especially the 2000 campaign, the Bush campaign employed a new term, describing their candidate as a compassionate conservative. Bush himself suggested, "I am a compassionate conservative, because I know my philosophy is full of hope for every American."[28] Although ambiguous as to what concrete policy proposals might flow from this philosophy, the use of the term *compassionate conservative* clearly invoked the image of a candidate who cared about people, and the term undoubtedly was coined, entirely or in part, as a strategy to appeal to women voters. However, the cleverest symbolic strategy of all may have been the name that the Bush campaign chose for its organized effort to win women voters. At Bush campaign events across the country, signs appeared with the slogan "W Stands for Women," a double entendre suggesting that Bush's middle initial and his nickname, "W," indicated his supportive posture toward women.

Another use of symbolic appeals in recent campaigns has focused on the targeting of specific groups of women (and occasionally groups of men, such as NASCAR dads) to the exclusion of large numbers of other women voters. Two examples are the targeting of so-called soccer moms in the 1996 and, to a lesser extent, the 2000 elections, and so-called security moms in the 2004 elections. Both soccer moms and security moms were social constructions – a combination of demographic characteristics, assigned a catchy name by political consultants, with no connection to any existing self-identified group or organizational base. When consultants and the media first started referring to soccer moms in 1996, women did not identify themselves as such, but the term has subsequently entered into popular usage and some women now refer to themselves this way. Similarly, women did not self-identify as security moms before the term was introduced in the context of the 2004 elections.

Although the definition of a soccer mom varied somewhat, she was generally considered a white, married woman with children (presumably of soccer-playing age), living in the suburbs. She also was often described in media coverage as stressed out and driving a minivan. The soccer mom was considered important politically because she was viewed as a swing voter – a voter whose demographics had traditionally led her to vote Republican but who could be persuaded to vote Democratic. One of the most important characteristics of the soccer mom was that she was not primarily concerned about her own self-interest but about her family and, most important, her children. As Kellyanne Fitzpatrick, a Republican pollster, noted, "If you are a soccer mom, the world according to you is seen through the needs of your children."[29]

The security mom, who became a focus of attention during the last several weeks of the 2004 presidential campaign, shared many of the demographic characteristics of the soccer mom. Like the soccer mom, she was considered white and married, with young children. Also like the soccer mom, the security mom did not put her own needs first but rather those of her family and children. She was repeatedly described as preoccupied with keeping her family safe from terrorism. The Republican presidential campaign, in particular, openly campaigned for the votes of these women in 2004. For example, on October 10, 2004, on CNN's *Late Edition with Wolf Blitzer*, Vice President Dick Cheney's daughter, Liz, urged women to vote for the Republican ticket, explaining, "You know, I'm a security mom. I've got four little kids. And what I care about in this election cycle is electing a guy who is going to be a commander-in-chief, who will do whatever it takes to keep those kids safe."[30]

The intensive campaign and media attention devoted to soccer moms in 1996 and 2000 and to security moms in 2004 deflected attention away from the concerns of many other subgroups of women, including feminists, college-age women, older women, women on welfare, women of color, and professional women. Ironically, it even deflected attention away from the concerns of white, middle-class women themselves except in their role as moms. Both the campaigns and the media were able to appear to be responsive to the concerns of women voters by talking about soccer moms and security moms while actually ignoring the vast majority of women. As a result, Clinton was reelected in 1996 and Bush was twice elected to the presidency in 2000 and 2004 without campaigning aggressively on (or, in some cases, even seriously addressing) many of the issues of greatest importance to the majority of women in this country who are not white, middle-class mothers of young children.

CONCLUSION: WHY THE GENDER GAP MATTERS AND A LOOK TOWARD 2012

The gender gap has given women voters increased political influence in recent years. Candidates now must pay attention to women voters to win elections. As Susan A. MacManus observes in Chapter 3 of this volume, in recent elections, women have voted at slightly higher rates than men. Women also are a greater proportion of the population. These two facts combined mean that there have been many more female than male voters in recent elections. In the 2008 election, for example, about 9.7 million more women than men voted.[31] The fact that there are so many more female voters than male voters adds power to the so-called women's vote, and clearly the more women who turn out to vote, the more clout women are likely to have.

Women voters received more attention in 2008 than in any previous presidential election in large part because Hillary Clinton received disproportionate support from women voters throughout the Democratic primary season. Once she was out of the race, both Barack Obama and John McCain sought to win the votes of the millions of women who had supported Clinton in the Democratic primaries as well as the votes of moderate and independent women who had not yet decided between the two candidates. In the end, more women opted for Barack Obama and his message of change, and the gender gap in 2008, with women more likely than men to support the Democratic candidate, looked much like it had in the 2004 election.

Despite the attention to women voters in 2008, the existence of the gender gap, and the larger number of female than male voters, the potential for women voters to influence politics has not yet been fully realized. Too many women still do not vote. In part this is because candidates in recent presidential elections have so frequently relied on symbolic, rather than issue-based, appeals to women voters. In particular, in focusing on specific groups of women such as soccer moms or security moms, presidential candidates have been able to win elections without always addressing in a serious and sustained way the issue-based concerns of greatest importance to the many women who do not fit the demographic profile of these moms.

The more candidates downplay or ignore the issue concerns of various subgroups of women voters (e.g., college-age women, less affluent women, women of color), the more tempting it is for those women to remain uninvolved in politics and to stay away from the polls. However, this is a catch-22. The more uninvolved that certain subgroups of women are, the more likely it is that their interests will be overlooked in the political process. In fact, women whose concerns are not being addressed by candidates need to become more involved in the future and insist that candidates respond to their concerns. Only then will the full potential power of the gender gap be realized.

In the first few months following the 2008 elections, Sarah Palin emerged in polls as one of the leading candidates for the Republican presidential nomination in 2012. Obviously, much can change in the many months before the 2012 election. Sarah Palin may ultimately choose not to run for president in 2012, and other candidates will certainly enter the race for the Republican nomination. But if Palin runs, attention will almost assuredly be paid to how women voters respond to her candidacy. On the Democratic side, Barack Obama will likely seek reelection. Will he be able to maintain the strong backing from women voters that he received in 2008? Will women continue to be more supportive of Obama than men are? Much can change before the next presidential election, but early signs suggest that women voters may play an important and interesting role in the next presidential contest. Meet you at the gender gap in 2012!

NOTES

1 Center for American Women and Politics. 2009. The Gender Gap. <http://www.cawp.rutgers.edu/fast_facts/voters/documents/GGPresVote.pdf> March 1, 2009.

2 Pew Research Center for the People and the Press. December 3, 2007. Democratic Primary Preview: Iowa, New Hampshire, South Carolina. <http://people-press.org/reports/pdf/374.pdf> March 1, 2009.

3 CNNPolitics.com. Election Center 2008. Results: Hillary Clinton. <http://www.cnn.com/ELECTION/2008/primaries/results/candidates/#1746> March 1, 2009.

4 Shailagh Murray and Anne E. Kornblut. June 24, 2008. Clinton to Join Obama as He Courts Female Vote. *Washington Post*.

5 Jason Tuohey. July 9, 2008. Obama Targets Women Voters. *Boston Globe*. <http://www.boston.com/news/politics/politicalintelligence/2008/07/obama_targets_w.html> March 1, 2009.

6 Liz Sidoti and Charles Babington. July 10, 2008. For Obama, McCain, Varied Paths on Women's Issues. *Boston Globe*. <http://www.boston.com/news/politics/2008/articles/2008/07/10/for_obama_mccain_varied_paths_on_womens_issues/> March 1, 2009.

7 Jon Cohen and Dan Balz. September 9, 2008. In Poll, McCain Closes the Gap with Obama. *Washington Post*.

8 See, for example, Frank Newport. Gallup. September 24, 2008. Did Palin Help McCain among White Women? <http://www.gallup.com/poll/110638/Did-Palin-Help-McCain-Among-White-Women.aspx> March 1, 2009.

9 This account applies largely to white women who constituted a large majority of women in the United States throughout these decades. The situation for African American women and other women of color was somewhat different. African American women were less likely than white women to be economically dependent on men because they more often worked outside the home (although usually in low-paying jobs). However, the political interests of African American women and men still were generally intertwined because society offered limited options for African Americans of either gender.

10 Robert S. Erikson, Norman R. Luttbeg, and Kent L. Tedin. 1980. *American Public Opinion: Its Origins, Content, and Impact*, 2nd ed. New York: John Wiley & Sons, 186.

11 CNNPolitics.com. Election Center 2008. Exit Polls. <http://www.cnn.com/ELECTION/2008/results/polls/#USP00p1> March 1, 2009.

12 Ibid.

13 Pew Research Center for the People and the Press. April 28, 2008. Gen Dems: The Party's Advantage among Young Voters Widens. <http://pewresearch.org/pubs/813/gen-dems> February 28, 2009.

14 Gallup. November 20, 2007. Congress' Approval Rating at 20%; Bush's Approval at 32%. <http://www.gallup.com/poll/102829/Congress-Approval-Rating-20-Bushs-Approval-32.aspx#2> February 28, 2008.

15 Gallup. January 6, 2009. Obama's Initial Approval Ratings in Historical Context. <http://www.gallup.com/poll/113968/Obama-Initial-Approval-Ratings-Historical-Context.aspx> February 28, 2008.

16 Jennifer L. Lawless. 2004. Women, War, and Winning Elections: Gender Stereotyping in the Post–September 11th Era. *Political Research Quarterly* 53(3): 479–90.

17 Kira Sanbonmatsu. 2002. Gender Stereotypes and Vote Choice. *American Journal of Political Science* 46: 20–34.

18 Elizabeth Adell Cook. 1998. Voter Reaction to Women Candidates. In *Women and Elective Office: Past, Present, and Future*, ed. Sue Thomas and Clyde Wilcox. New York: Oxford University Press, 56–72.

19 Project Vote Smart. 2009. <http://www.votesmart.org/official_five_categories. php?dist=voting_category.php> March 1, 2009.

20 CNN.com. 2006. AmericaVotes2006 Exit Polls. <http://www.cnn.com/ ELECTION/2006/pages/results/states/ME/S/01/epolls.0.html> March 1, 2009.

21 Project Vote Smart. 2009. <http://www.votesmart.org/official_five_categories .php?dist=voting_category.php> March 1, 2009.

22 Quinnipiac University Polling Institute. 2008. September 18, 2008 – Women, Blacks Give Obama 4-Pt. Lead over McCain, Quinnipiac University National Poll Finds; More Voters Say Dem Tax Plan Helps Middle Class, Poor. <http:// www.quinnipiac.edu/x1295.xml?ReleaseID=1215> March 1, 2009.

23 Pew Research Center for People and the Press. August 21, 2008. More Americans Question Religion's Role in Politics. <http://people-press.org/ report/?pageid=1364> March 1, 2009.

24 Kathleen A. Frankovic. 1982. Sex and Politics: New Alignments, Old Issues. *PS* 15(Summer): 439–48.

25 Rasmussen Reports. June 3, 2008. 59% of Adults Want Troops Home from Iraq within the Year. <http://www.rasmussenreports.com/public_content/ politics/current_events/the_war_in_iraq/59_of_adults_want_troops_home_ from_iraq_within_the_year> March 1, 2009.

26 Pamela Johnston Conover. 1988. Feminists and the Gender Gap. *Journal of Politics* 50(November): 985–1010.

27 Susan J. Welch and John Hibbing. 1992. Financial Conditions, Gender, and Voting in American National Elections. *Journal of Politics* 54(February): 197–213.

28 Joe Conason. September 15, 2003. Where's the Compassion? *The Nation.* <http://www.thenation.com/doc/20030915/conason> July 26, 2009.

29 Neil MacFarquhar. October 20, 1996. Don't Forget Soccer Dads; What's a Soccer Mom Anyway? *New York Times.*

30 CNN. October 10, 2004. Late Edition with Wolf Blitzer. <http://cnnstudent-news.cnn.com/TRANSCRIPTS/0410/10/le.01.html> March 21, 2005.

31 Center for American Women and Politics. 2009. Gender Differences in Voter Turnout. <http://www.cawp.rutgers.edu/fast_facts/voters/documents/ genderdiff.pdf> July 26, 2009.

5 Latinas and Electoral Politics

Movin' on Up

The national campaigns waged by Senators Hillary Clinton and Barack Obama in 2008 for the Democratic Party's nomination for president drew unprecedented attention to the dynamics of gender and race in American politics. The Republican Party's nomination of Alaska's governor, Sarah Palin, for vice president intensified and extended the national discourse on the meaning and impact of gender in national politics. Indeed, scholars and pundits engaged in vigorous debates as to whether racism or sexism was most apparent in media coverage of these candidates and their campaigns, and how a gender bias against women or a racial bias against an African American man might influence voter choice for president.[1]

In a cartoon on the 2008 presidential race, one woman tells another, casually over coffee, "Now all we need is a woman of color in this race – that would really mess with people's minds."[2] Insightfully, the cartoon underscores the complexity of how gender and race – independently and in interaction with each other – complicate American politics. For women of color, gender and race do not involve an either-or proposition when it comes to their identity formation and their lived experiences.[3] But for all the attention the 2008 election showered on gender and racial dynamics in American life, gender and race were largely viewed as independent of or in opposition to each other. Hence, the intersection of gender and race, as lived by women of color, remained little understood or examined. As women of color, Latinas offer a case in point.[4]

Although Latina women figured prominently in the 2008 election, their particular roles and contributions to electoral politics went largely unnoticed. While they were not among the leading candidates on the national stage, they were involved in the election as voters, campaign workers, party elites, national advisers, and top staff. Further, they counted among those seeking public office at the federal, state, and local

144

levels. To be sure, significant media coverage and political punditry commented on the significant role of women or the "Hispanic vote" in the election; however, the particular role of Latina women received little attention. Latina women were subsumed in reports about the women's vote or the Hispanic electorate and did not claim attention in their own right.

The 2008 presidential contest and election revealed how women and people of color are increasingly, if incrementally, ascending to the nation's highest levels of political leadership. Latina women share in this evolving story of America's changing politics. They are expanding their role in the American electorate and among the nation's ranks of political leaders and policy makers. This chapter sheds light on their important, but mostly untold, story. It provides an overview of major aspects of Latina women's involvement in U.S. politics and draws attention to their roles as voters and players in the 2008 presidential election. As increasing numbers of Latina women become engaged in the political process, from grassroots activism to running for public office, their influence will continue to grow – and they will increasingly find a public spotlight on their multifaceted endeavors and accomplishments.

DEMOGRAPHICS AND THE LATINO ELECTORATE

Constituting slightly less than half of the Latino population (48.3 percent), Latina women are part of a rapidly growing ethno-racial population whose increasing numbers imply expanding political power. Having surpassed African Americans as the nation's largest ethno-racial minority population, Latinos now number more than 45.4 million, or 15 percent of the total U.S. population.[5] Demographic growth has brought attention to Latinos' political status, in particular to their potential influence in U.S. elections. However, additional demographic characteristics add complexity or limitations to Latinos' influence in national politics.

The Latino population is quite diverse, encompassing numerous national origin groups with varying histories and political experiences in the United States. According to an adjusted count of the 2000 U.S. Census, the largest country-specific origin groups among Latinos include Mexican Americans (63.4 percent of the total), Puerto Ricans (10 percent), Cuban Americans (3.7 percent), and people from the Dominican Republic (2.8 percent). People from other countries of Central and South America account for the remainder of this population.[6] Commonalities as well as differences underlie their political attitudes and behavior.

This chapter addresses the politics of U.S. Latinas as a group, but we must recognize that national origins, among other factors, mark important distinctions among them. As an example, survey data has shown that Latina women are more highly partisan than Latino men, yet they differ across national origin. Mexican American and Puerto Rican women identify more heavily with the Democratic Party than do men of their own national-origin group. Cuban American women, in contrast, identify at greater levels with the Republican Party than do their male counterparts.[7]

Socioeconomic characteristics such as lower levels of education and income compared to other ethno-racial populations depress Latino levels of political participation. Moreover, age and citizenship requirements for voting lessen Latinos' potential electoral influence. Taylor and Fry note the youthfulness of the Latino population as well as the large number who are noncitizens and, thus, ineligible to vote. In their analysis of 2007 Current Population Survey data, they found that more than one-third of the estimated Latino population was younger than eighteen years of age. Moreover, while about 55 percent of Latino adults, or 16.6 million, were foreign born, only 4.7 million of them, or 28 percent, were naturalized U.S. citizens and, thus, eligible to vote.[8]

Latino voter turnout has historically lagged behind the turnout of other ethno-racial groups. Lopez and Minushkin state, "Since 1974, in presidential and midterm elections, the Latino eligible voter turnout rate has trailed white eligible voters by 13 to 20 percentage points." In the 2004 election, 47 percent of Latino eligible voters reported having voted, in contrast to 67 percent of white eligible voters and 60 percent of black eligible voters. Although the gaps shrink when turnout rates for Latinos are estimated for the adult citizen population, lower rates of voter participation relative to other groups persist. In 2004, U.S. citizen Latinos reported a 58 percent rate of voter registration, compared to rates of 75 percent for whites and 69 percent for blacks.[9]

Notwithstanding lower rates of voter participation relative to other groups, Latinos have expanded their role in elections over time. Table 5.1 shows the increasing pool of eligible Hispanic voters from 1996 to 2007. Politicians and political parties are keenly aware of the expanding voter eligibility pool, for in the end, the raw numbers of votes cast decide elections. To be sure, the total number of votes cast by Latinos has increased over time. In 1996, fewer than 5 million Latinos voted in the general election; however, eight years later, in 2004, 7.6 million reported voting. Accordingly, Latinos increased their share of the total electorate from 4.7 percent in 1996 to 6 percent in 2004.[10] With estimates that the

TABLE 5.1: The proportion of Hispanics among eligible voters has increased over the past decade

Year	Hispanic eligible voters	Hispanic share of total
1996	11,209,000	6.2%
2000	13,940,000	7.4
2004	16,088,000	8.2
2007	18,165,000	8.9

Note: Numbers refer to U.S. citizens age eighteen and older.
Source: Paul Taylor and Richard Fry. December 2007. Hispanics and the 2008 Election: A Swing Vote? Washington, D.C.: Pew Hispanic Center.

eligible Hispanic electorate in 2008 would amount to 18.2 million, the Latino and Latina vote promised to be in great demand.[11]

LATINA POLITICAL BEHAVIOR

In general, Latinas share many political characteristics with their male counterparts. But there are some exceptions. Research on political attitudes has found a gender gap in political knowledge, with Latina women less politically informed than Latino men.[12] But the implications of this finding are unclear, as a gender gap in voter participation between Latino men and Latina women has diminished over time. In fact, recent elections show Latina women outvoting their male counterparts in national elections, a pattern that holds for women overall in American politics.

When examining specific subpopulations, however, gender differences do emerge. In their summary of research on Latina politics, Montoya, Hardy-Fanta, and Garcia report one study that found that Latina heads of household were less likely to vote than their male counterparts. An additional study suggested that predictors of Latina and Latino voting are different. As Montoya and colleagues summarize, "For Latinas alone, the most consistent predictors of turnout across all national origin groups are interest in politics, church attendance, and organizational and school involvement – suggesting that political socialization and institutions have a stronger mobilizing effect on women than on men."[13]

National exit poll data for the 1980, 1984, and 1988 presidential elections showed Latina women to be more liberal and pro-Democratic than Latino men, but the differences were fairly small and somewhat inconsistent.[14] More recent research has confirmed a gender gap in party identification; however, as previously mentioned, differences across national origin appear more salient than differences within specific national-origin groups. Hardy-Fanta and Cardozo found a statistically significant gender difference in Latino voting for president. Although both Latino men and women supported Democrat Bill Clinton's reelection in 1996, Latina support for Clinton was higher.[15]

Research investigating a gender gap between Latino men and Latina women on social and political attitudes shows mixed results. Bedolla, Monforti, and Pantoja found that a gender gap exists "along similar lines to that found among Anglos" on specific issues of public policy. For example, Latina women are less supportive of the death penalty and increases in military spending than Latino men. They believe to a greater degree than Latino men that mothers are responsible for the religious upbringing of children. On a so-called compassion issue, Latina women expressed higher levels of agreement than Latino men on the item "The government in Washington should do everything possible to improve the standard of living for all Americans."[16]

But the authors also draw attention to important attitudinal differences between Latinas and Latinos based on national origin. They note variation and similarities within Latino national-origin groups on the policy issues studied. These authors posit that agreement within national-origin groups suggests common experiences of marginalization among Latina women and Latino men. They state:

> Why is it, for example, that Anglo men and women seem to have significantly different attitudes towards social welfare programs and yet Mexican origin men and women do not? It is possible . . . that the gender differences among whites and those of Mexican origin are the result of experiences of marginalization. White women have had those experiences, as do Mexican origin women *and* Mexican origin men.[17]

They suggest that the lack of gender difference among Latinas and Latinos with regard to certain policy questions means that national origin may operate "as a proxy for marginalization in general" and explain attitudes more than gender.[18]

Further research is required to fully understand the extent to which Latina women's political behavior differs from that of their male counterparts. At this point, the bottom line appears to be that gender differences among Latinos are not necessarily obvious or consistent. Indeed, Latina women are like Latino men on a number of electoral and attitudinal dimensions. Gender differences that do appear may be heavily conditioned by national-origin differences across Latino subgroups.

LATINA WOMEN IN ELECTED OFFICE

Latinos in general are severely underrepresented in U.S. politics. As Garcia and Sanchez state, "Hispanics have lower proportions in virtually every representative body in the United States than is their proportion in their communities."[19] Furthermore, there is a significant gender gap in the number of Latino men and women who hold elected office. But Latino men and women have improved, albeit incrementally, their levels of representation at all levels of government over time. Furthermore, Latina women have enjoyed in recent years relatively higher election rates than Latino men.

According to the National Association of Elected and Appointed Officials (NALEO), between 1996 and 2009, the total number of Hispanic elected officials (HEOs) in the United States grew from 3,743 to 5,670. During this time span, the number of Latina elected officials grew more quickly than the number of Latino male officials. Latinas accounted for 907 of the total number of HEOs in 1996, or 24.2 percent. By 2009, they accounted for 1,814 HEOs, or 32 percent of the total. The total number of Latina officials thus doubled, a 100 percent increase, compared to an increase of 36 percent for Latino men.[20]

Scholars note that, in addition to this rate of increase vis-à-vis Latino men, Latina women also hold office at rates higher than women in general. A case in point is state legislative officeholding. In 2009, Latina women account for 29.4 percent of the state legislative seats held by all Hispanics, a proportion greater than the 24.3 percent of state legislative seats held by women overall.[21]

Most underrepresented are HEOs in national office. In the 111th U.S. Congress, only two Latino men (one Democrat and one Republican) and no Latina women serve in the U.S. Senate. A total of twenty-three HEOs are in the House of Representatives: twenty Democrats and three Republicans, seventeen men and six women. In statewide office, HEOs are even fewer and farther between. In 2009, Bill Richardson (D-NM) is the nation's sole Hispanic governor; six HEOs (three men and three women) hold other statewide offices (see Table 5.2).[22]

TABLE 5.2: Only nine Latinas served in statewide and federal offices in 2009

Statewide Elected Officials
  Susan Castillo (NP-OR), superintendent, public instruction
  Mary Herrera (D-NM), secretary of state
  Catherine Cortez Masto (D-NV), attorney general
Congresswomen, 111th Congress
  Rep. Grace Napolitano (D-CA)
  Rep. Ileana Ros-Lehtinen (R-FL)
  Rep. Lucille Roybal-Allard (D-CA)
  Rep. Linda Sanchez (D-CA)
  Rep. Loretta Sanchez (D-CA)
  Rep. Nydia Velasquez (D-NY)

Note: NP = nonpartisan election.
Source: Center for American Women and Politics. Women of Color in Elective Office 2009. Fact Sheet. <http://www.cawp.rutgers.edu/fast_facts/levels_of_office/documents/color.pdf>.

Local offices are an important entry point for Latina women and Latino men in politics. Although a majority of both sexes serve in local government, there is a gender difference in the type of local office held. Over forty-one percent (41.6 percent) of Latina officeholders serve on school boards, compared to 33.3 percent of Latino male officials. At the same time, more Latino men (32 percent) are found in municipal office than Latina women (26.5 percent).[23] Efforts to increase Latina representation in public office have targeted women in community politics for special trainings on how (and why) to run for public office. Given Latina women's long-established involvement in grassroots community organizing and activism, such recruitment strategies are likely to pay off in the long run.

The profile of Latina officeholders nationwide reveals a relatively fast-growing number of women in the trenches of state and local government. Far fewer Latinas occupy federal or statewide office. Early in the 2008 election cycle, candidates from both major political parties, but especially the Democratic Party, sought endorsements and campaign support from this Latina political infrastructure. However, it was the Latina members of Congress and statewide officials who provided some star power through their roles as political advisers or campaign supporters. In the end, Latina women counted in the 2008 election, as voters, activists, and leaders amid a growing Latino electorate. They would make their presence known throughout the primary and general election, and they would cast deciding votes in key battleground states.

THE LATINO AND LATINA VOTE IN THE 2008 PRESIDENTIAL ELECTION

Several features of the Latino electorate virtually guaranteed that the Latino vote would be heavily sought by candidates from both major political parties in the 2008 presidential election. As mentioned previously, the sheer size of the Latino electorate has continued to grow over the years, as has the proportion of Latinos among the voting electorate. Geopolitics further enhances the attractiveness of the Latino vote. Latinos are concentrated geographically in states with large numbers of electoral votes, a consideration that weighs heavily in presidential campaign strategies. Although Latinos do not vote as one unified bloc, their votes across national-origin groups do cohere around two poles, evident in Mexican American and Puerto Rican support for Democrats and Cuban American support for Republicans.

Furthermore, given the closeness of recent presidential elections, the significant number of Latino voters in battleground states, where the presidential race is highly contested, has elevated the importance of the Latino vote even more. Candidates devote more attention and resources to those states in which the outcome of the race remains fluid; identifiable voting blocs benefit from such attention. Since 1960, a majority of Latinos have supported the Democratic Party's candidate for president. However, the level of Latino support for the party has fluctuated.[24]

When he ran for president in 2000 and 2004, Republican George W. Bush understood that he would be unlikely to capture a majority of the Latino vote. However, the extent to which he could lessen the Democratic vote advantage among Latino voters could serve him well. Indeed, in his 2004 reelection bid, Bush drew an estimated 40 percent of the Latino vote nationwide and attracted sufficient Latino support in selected states, such as New Mexico, to place them in the red column on election night. As a result, the Republican Party aimed to swing the Latino vote to its favor again in 2008 even as the Democratic Party pledged to regain, if not extend, its traditional advantage with Latino voters. Formalizing their overtures to Latino voters, both the Republican and the Democratic parties added the state of Nevada – with a fast-growing Latino electorate – to their early January lineup of presidential primaries and caucuses.

THE PRIMARIES

No candidate would take lessons from previous presidential campaigns to heart more than New York's Senator Hillary Clinton. In seeking the Democratic Party's nomination, Clinton assembled her campaign organization early and included Latinos and Latinas in the mix. She lined up top Hispanic elected officials and other Hispanic leaders for endorsements, hired staff, and put together a strategy by early 2007. She chose Patti Solis Doyle, the daughter of Mexican immigrants, as her campaign manager. Solis Doyle was the first Latina to become a national campaign manager and one of only three Hispanics ever to hold that position. Clinton had known Solis Doyle since 1991, when she began working for the future first lady as her scheduler. According to news reports, the two had developed a close relationship.[25]

Other prominent Latinas joined Clinton's team as personal advisers or major endorsers. Maria Echaveste, who had served in the Clinton administration and White House and worked as a campaign adviser for Al Gore in 2000, campaigned tirelessly for Clinton's nomination.[26] Counted among one of Clinton's most "symbolic endorsements" was Dolores Huerta, cofounder along with Cesar Chavez of the United Farm Workers of America (UFW) and longtime civil rights activist. But as Roberto Suro, former director of the Pew Hispanic Center, observed, Clinton "also scored endorsements from Latino politicians who have the electoral machinery to deliver votes."[27] The Los Angeles county commissioner Gloria Molina and Congresswoman Hilda Solis (D-CA) fit that profile quite well.

Overall, Hillary Clinton locked up an "impressive number and range of Hispanic endorsements" early in the campaign season. It appeared that she had the Latino political establishment on her side.[28] A large proportion of HEOs had come of political age or had been elected to office during President Bill Clinton's two terms in office. Others had first met the Clintons years earlier and had remained friends and political allies. Several Mexican American public officials spoke of first meeting Hillary when, as a young woman, she traveled to South Texas during the early 1970s to work on behalf of George McGovern's presidential campaign and to register Hispanics to vote.

Despite his being the first viable Latino candidate for president, New Mexico's governor Bill Richardson never gained traction in his presidential bid. His popularity with Hispanic voters, in particular, was never really tested, as he dropped out of the race before a significant number of

Latinos (such as in the state of Nevada) had the chance to vote for him. Early in the primary season, Richardson ran a dual strategy of introducing himself to predominantly white electorates in Iowa and New Hampshire and courting Latino voters through his campaign "Mi Familia con Richardson" in Nevada. According to one political scientist, Richardson had more Hispanics in his campaign and targeted Hispanic fund-raisers more than any other candidate. He was the only candidate with a Web site fully "en español" rather than having just portions in Spanish. He also spoke directly to Hispanic issues, such as the need for comprehensive immigration reform.[29] But Richardson's poor finishes in the Iowa caucus (2 percent of the vote) and the New Hampshire primary (less than 5 percent of the vote) drained momentum and money out of his campaign. He withdrew his candidacy for president on January 10, 2008.[30]

Clinton's aggressive outreach to Latinos, which one expert attributed to the role of her campaign manager, Solis Doyle,[31] would prove critically important to sustaining her run through the presidential primary contests. According to Suro, an early goal was "to preempt New Mexico Gov. Bill Richardson from locking up the Latino vote." But after Richardson dropped out of the race and Barack Obama's candidacy gained momentum, "the Clinton campaign started looking to Hispanics as a 'firewall,' the constituency that could hold off Obama's surge."[32]

Latinos primarily participated in the Democratic Party's presidential primaries and caucuses. Polls showed Latinos – men but especially Latina women – to be strong supporters of Clinton over Obama and the other candidates who remained in the race. Numerous media reports surfaced questioning whether Latino and Latina support for Clinton was, in essence, a vote against Obama on the basis of his race. That is, to what extent did racial tensions between Latinos and African Americans – or racist attitudes on the part of Hispanics toward blacks – account for Clinton's popularity with Hispanics?

Clinton pollster Sergio Bendixen triggered the national debate over this question when he stated after the New Hampshire primary, "'The Hispanic voter – and I want to say this very carefully – has not shown a lot of willingness or affinity to support black candidates.'"[33] In New Mexico, the Republican county chair Fernando C de Baca offered his own version of why Obama should not expect the support of Hispanics in New Mexico. In an interview with the BBC, C de Baca asserted even more directly, "'The truth is that Hispanics came here as conquerors. African Americans came here as slaves.... Hispanics consider themselves above blacks. They won't vote for a black president.'"[34]

While acknowledging racial attitudes as a potential issue of concern, experts knowledgeable of the Latino electorate offered more convincing explanations for Clinton's popularity, including her name recognition, their fondness for President Bill Clinton, endorsements from Hispanic elites, and Clinton's successful outreach to and mobilization in Latino communities. At the same time, political analysts pointed to Latinos' lack of familiarity with Barack Obama as a major disadvantage in his courtship of the Latino vote.[35]

As the primary season evolved, the Obama campaign increased its Latino outreach activities and brought to the forefront its own list of prominent Hispanic endorsements. Foremost among them was María Elena Durazo, the head of the Los Angeles County Federation of Labor, an organization of more than eight hundred thousand union members and the biggest regional labor group in California. Among its membership ranks are janitors, teachers, construction and hotel workers, and supermarket and government employees. Although Durazo indicated that her endorsement of Obama was a personal one and that she was taking a leave of absence from her job to work for the campaign, Durazo's ties to the labor movement and its large Latino and Latina constituency provided a considerable boost in visibility and organizing resources to Obama's outreach to Hispanics. Although not as widely identifiable as the personalities with whom she shared the stage, Durazo was part of a celebrity-studded lineup to introduce Michelle Obama at a rally at the University of California, Los Angeles, shortly before the California primary on February 5. Durazo appeared with Caroline Kennedy, Oprah Winfrey, and California's first lady, Maria Shriver, who announced her support for Barack Obama as president.[36]

Hillary Clinton and Barack Obama went the distance in the primary contests for their party's presidential nomination. Their vigorous competition energized the Latino electorate, which "voted in record numbers in some states." NALEO reported that, from 2004 to 2008, Latino voting in Democratic primaries increased in the following states: Arizona (1 percent), California (13 percent), Florida (3 percent), and Texas (10 percent).[37] According to exit poll data analyzed by the Pew Hispanic Center, Latinos voted for Clinton over Obama in the Super Tuesday primaries by 63 percent to 35 percent; in the Texas primary, 66 percent to 32 percent; and in the Puerto Rico primary, 68 percent to 32 percent. Clinton's biggest margin of victory was in her home state of New York, where she claimed 73 percent of the Hispanic vote. Closer contests saw

Clinton winning New Mexico with 56 percent of the Latino vote and capturing Arizona with 55 percent of the Latino vote. Obama won the Latino vote in his home state of Illinois but by a slim margin, 50 percent to Clinton's 49 percent.[38]

A gender gap in Latino voting was evident in both turnout and vote choice. Latina women accounted for approximately 56 percent of the Latino primary electorate; Latino men constituted about 44 percent. Although both Latinos and Latinas favored Clinton, Latina women showed impressive levels of support, voting 67 percent to 32 percent for Clinton over Obama. Among Latino male voters, the gap was not as wide, 58 percent to 40 percent for Clinton over Obama. Age groups also showed a gender gap. Clinton drew two-thirds of support from Latina voters in all age groups; Hispanic women sixty years of age and older heavily favored Clinton, voting for her 75 percent to 24 percent for Obama. In contrast, Latino men between the ages of thirty and forty-four preferred candidate Obama, giving him a majority (53 percent) of their votes. Latino men in the youngest age group (between seventeen and twenty-nine) split their votes between Clinton and Obama (49 percent each).

On the question of whether race or gender was an important influence in voter choice, exit polls on Super Tuesday (February 5) showed that

> Hispanics were more likely than whites to say that race was an important factor in deciding their vote – 28 percent of Hispanics said this compared with 13 percent of whites. However, Hispanics who said that race was important voted for Clinton by about the same percentage (64 percent) as did Hispanics who said race was not important (63 percent). By contrast, whites who said race was important were more likely to vote for Clinton than were other whites.[39]

Hispanics were also more likely than whites to say that a candidate's gender was important in their voting decision. Hispanics for whom gender was important were more likely to vote for Hillary Clinton than were those who said gender was not important.[40]

Latina and Latino voters mobilized in support of Hillary Clinton. In the end, their votes extended Clinton's ability to compete in the Democratic primaries; however, the Latino vote was not sufficient to give her the nomination. Heading into the general election, the media seized on new questions regarding Latino loyalty to Clinton – would Latinos, and especially Latinas, transfer their support for her to Barack Obama? Would they jump ship and vote Republican? Would they sit out the November election?

Perhaps as an example of Clinton support transferring to Obama, the experience of Patti Solis Doyle would prove instructive. In February 2008, as the Obama campaign gained momentum, Clinton reorganized her campaign staff and replaced Solis Doyle, her campaign manager, with Maggie Williams, a longtime aide. Even as the move to replace her was under way, Solis Doyle emphasized "'how personally proud and pleased I am at how greatly the Latino vote delivered for Hillary Clinton on Feb 5th. It means a lot to me as the first Latina campaign manager for a presidential campaign.'"[41] In the months approaching the general election, Solis Doyle went to work for the Obama campaign.

Although far fewer Latino voters participated in the Republican Party's presidential primaries and caucuses, Latino voting proved more critical to the outcome. Exit polling in Florida revealed that former Massachusetts governor Mitt Romney edged out Arizona Senator John McCain in winning white Republican voter support, by 34 percent to 33 percent. At the same time, McCain took the Latino vote decisively. The Latino share of the vote for McCain was 54 percent; for former New York City mayor Rudy Giuliani, 24 percent; and for Mitt Romney, 14 percent. Exit poll data of gender categories was not available. However, given previous patterns of Latina Republican support for the party, it is reasonable to assume that Latina Republicans assisted McCain's efforts to win in Florida.

As a result of the Florida race, Giuliani dropped out and endorsed McCain, and McCain moved on to Super Tuesday contests in the lead and never lost his front-runner status. He rode the momentum, in part provided by Florida's Latino electorate, all the way to his party's nomination. According to some analysts, McCain won support from Latinos largely on the basis of his more moderate stand on immigration.[42]

¡OBÁMANOS! LATINAS AT THE DEMOCRATIC NATIONAL CONVENTION

As delegates, elected officials, and the party faithful gathered at the Democratic National Convention in Denver in late August, a common theme quickly emerged: a historic first would be set when a major political party nominated an African American man as its presidential candidate. Although Obama's nomination had been secured through the

primary process, the convention was not without excitement, anticipation, and some tension over the Clinton-Obama rivalry. Latina women
were clearly present and active at the convention. Indeed, Latinas accounted for more than half (52.3 percent) of all the Hispanic delegates at
the convention. Similarly, African American women constituted a majority (55.6 percent) of black delegates, while white women accounted for
a minority (46.6 percent) of all white delegates.[43] Given how strongly
Latina women supported Hillary Clinton during the primaries, speculation and even suspense ran through various state delegations as to how
they would vote when the roll call of states commenced to decide the
party's nominee.

As an observer at the convention, I witnessed the extreme disappointment that some Hispanic women expressed with Clinton's loss to Obama.
Priscilla Chavez, in the New Mexico delegation, shed tears during Hillary
Clinton's convention speech because she was so moved. Disappointment
with the end of Clinton's campaign ran deep, as Chavez wiped tears away
even as we spoke the morning after. Nevertheless, Chavez pledged to
work for Obama's election in heavily Hispanic areas of southern New
Mexico. She predicted that young voters would be easier to mobilize than
older ones. But she maintained that older voters would show up to vote
for Obama "because so much is at stake."

Another committed Clinton supporter, New Mexico's state senator
Mary Jane Garcia, had rather harsh words for Obama's candidacy dur-
ing the heat of the presidential primary. Her avid support for Hillary
Clinton stretched back to 1992, when the Clintons were in Las Cruces.
She connected with them many times thereafter. Garcia also cried during
Clinton's speech. She marveled at how her candidate was both "gracious"
and "strong" after a bruising primary. Garcia contended that, after all the
Republican attacks, media criticism, and tension with the Obama campaign, "to say what she said, and the way she said it" was impressive. But
she chose the word *closure* to describe her personal feelings at the end
of the day. She found closure in Clinton's endorsement of Obama and
was prepared, as she put it, "to move on" and work for the Democratic
presidential ticket.[44]

Latina women appeared on various stages during the convention.
Congresswoman Loretta Sanchez (D-CA) enthusiastically addressed the
convention's Hispanic Caucus. Linda Chavez-Thompson, former executive vice president of the AFL-CIO, appeared on stage at the Women's
Caucus, as did the television actresses Eva Longoria of *Desperate Housewives*

and America Ferrera of *Ugly Betty*. Numerous Latina elected officials circulated throughout the convention halls in support of their party's ticket.
In leaving Obama's acceptance speech at Denver's Invesco Field, my eye
caught a Latina woman wearing a T-shirt with the slogan "*¡Obámanos!*" a
creative way of signaling – in Spanglish – Hispanic support for Obama.[45]
Latina women appeared to be on board with the Obama-Biden campaign.

THE GENERAL ELECTION

Although no Latinas were among Barack Obama's top campaign staff,
they were present among his top advisers. The former New Mexico attorney general Patricia Madrid (who had endorsed John Edwards in 2004
and early in the 2008 primaries), joined Obama's National Latino Advisory Council. Joining Madrid were ten Latino men and an additional
four Latinas: Congresswomen Linda Sanchez (D-CA), Hilda Solis (D-CA),
and Nydia Velasquez (D-NY), and Geoconda Arguello-Kline, president of
the Culinary Workers Union, Local 226, in Nevada.[46] Maria Echaveste
and Dolores Huerta, who had both worked for Clinton in the primary,
shifted their support to Obama, as did the Latino and Latina political
establishment.

As Bush had done in his 2004 reelection bid, McCain had hoped to
appeal to conservative Latinos, and especially Latina women, by emphasizing family values (i.e., his opposition to abortion and same-sex
marriage). Given the Roman Catholic Church's official pro-life stance,
McCain's campaign felt that Latino men and women, a majority of whom
were Catholic, would be a natural constituency. The Republican Party
in New Mexico went so far as to distribute prayer cards before Mass in
Catholic churches that featured John McCain in front of an image of
the Virgin of Guadalupe, a vastly popular female religious icon throughout Latin America. On the back of the card was a prayer in English and
Spanish for McCain, that he might "continue to defend the right to life of
the unborn and promote peace, justice and freedom for our Nation."[47]

Ana Navarro, McCain's adviser on Hispanic affairs, spoke of McCain's
stand on immigration as a position that should resonate with Hispanics.
She noted, however, that the party had lost support among new Hispanic citizens because of some Republican lawmakers' remarks during
the recent congressional debate over proposed immigration reforms. She
observed that the campaign's Spanish-language ads were designed to convince Hispanics "that he was on their side of that fight and that he has had
a lifelong interest in Latin America."[48]

As the fall election season commenced, preelection polls suggested answers in the affirmative to both the Hillary thesis (Would Latinas move from Clinton to Obama?) and the Barack thesis (Would Hispanics vote for a black man?). A national poll of Hispanic likely voters administered in mid-October found that a majority of Latino men (68 percent) and an even greater majority of Latina women (71 percent) indicated support for Obama.[49] A poll conducted by NALEO in four battleground states where Latinos were concentrated showed Obama performing quite well. Nearly two-thirds of the Latino respondents in New Mexico and Colorado indicated "strong" support for Obama; a majority (55 percent) of the Nevada Latino respondents did the same. Even among Latino respondents in Florida, McCain was only slightly ahead of Obama. The same poll underscored that the state of the economy and job opportunities were of central concern to the Latino electorate.[50]

Election results pointed to an energized and expanding Latino electorate. Latino votes increased from 7.5 million in 2004 to 10 million in 2008. Latinos increased their proportion of the voting electorate to 9 percent, one percentage point higher than in 2004. National exit polls showed that all Latino demographic subgroups voted for Obama by heavy margins. Once again, Latina women showed greater levels of support for the Democratic candidate than their male counterparts: 68 percent of Hispanic women and 64 percent of Hispanic men supported Obama. The Pew Hispanic Center pointed out the remarkable turnaround in Latino voting: "No other major demographic voting group in the country swung so heavily to Obama as Latinos did between the primaries and the general election."[51]

State-level results underscored how Latina women delivered for Barack Obama. According to MSNBC, 78 percent of Hispanic women in Colorado supported Obama, compared to 73 percent of Hispanic men. The gender gap was even greater in New Mexico, with 72 percent of Hispanic women voting for Obama, compared to 65 percent of Hispanic men. And in Texas, where the statewide vote predictably went to McCain, 71 percent of Hispanic women as compared to 55 percent of Hispanic men supported Obama, a gender gap of sixteen points.[52] In Nevada, exit polls showed no gender gap: 76 percent of Latina women and men voted for Obama. However, Latina women accounted for 9 percent of voters while Latino men accounted for 7 percent.[53] Obama took a majority of the Latino vote (57 percent) in Florida, but he won more support from Latino men (60 percent) than from Latina women (55 percent).[54]

CONCLUSION

The November election did not increase the number of Latina women in the U.S. Congress. But all seven female incumbents won reelection. However, the departure of Congresswoman Hilda Solis (D-CA) to become secretary of labor in the Obama administration reduced the number of Latinas in the 111th Congress to six. NALEO reported no change in the number of Latina statewide officials. Latinas increased their number in state senates from twenty-one to twenty-three, but their numbers in state houses decreased, from fifty to forty-nine.[55] The journey to elective office for Latinas continues to be slow and incremental.

But overall, Latino political participation in U.S. politics continues to expand. Over the past several presidential elections, Latinos have voted in greater numbers and constituted a greater proportion of the general electorate. Although they have yet to vote the strength of their numbers in the population, their rates of voter registration and turnout are on the rise. They can wield considerable influence in U.S. elections, especially in closely contested races. In 2008, the Latino vote proved significant in electing Barack Obama as the forty-fourth president of the United States. Latina women were an intrinsic part of the victorious electoral coalition in this historic election. While their roles as voters, party activists, and elected leaders became evident as the election progressed, for the most part, their contributions did not command the public recognition that they deserved.

The particular conditions present in the 2008 presidential election brought to the forefront gender and race as major dimensions to be examined and understood in American politics. Yet public discourse in the election framed important issues regarding gender and race too simplistically, as gender or race. Latinas' contributions would receive more attention if gender and race were recognized as interactive features of American politics. To be sure, greater availability of data that examine gender within the Latino electorate would enhance our understanding of Latina political behavior. Latina women fall through the cracks when only the women's vote or the Hispanic vote commands public attention and analysis.

In 2008, Latinas helped to swing the Latino vote back toward the Democratic Party. The extent to which the Latino vote will remain comfortably in the Democrats' winning coalition is unclear. Just as speculation that Latino support for George W. Bush in 2004 heralded a possible electoral realignment, results from the 2008 election have sparked discussion of shifting coalitions in the opposite direction. What is known is that Latinas will help provide the answers in the future.

NOTES

1 See, for example, Sally Kohn and Gloria Steinem. January 11, 2008. Gloria Steinem Debates Racism and Sexism in the '08 Election. AlterNet. <http://www.alternet.org/story/73545/> Accessed March 4, 2008.

2 Ann Telnaes. Obmama and Hillary. February 5, 2008. Commentoon, Women's eNews. <http://www.womensenews.org/article.cfm/dyn/aid/3483/context/archive> February 12, 2008.

3 Questions of race and gender also pertain to whites and to men. But the 2008 election focused on Hillary Clinton's gender as a woman and Barack Obama's race as a black person, not on Clinton's race as a white person or Obama's gender as a man.

4 In this article, the terms *Latino* and *Hispanic* are used interchangeably. In general, these terms refer to those persons living in the United States who come from or who trace their ancestry to the Spanish-speaking countries of Latin America and the Caribbean. The term *Latina* refers to women of Latino or Hispanic origin.

5 U.S. Census Bureau. 2007. American Community Survey 1-Year Estimates. S0201. Selected Population Profile of the United States: Hispanic or Latino. American FactFinder. <http://www.factfinder.census.gov> April 10, 2009.

6 F. Chris Garcia and Gabriel R. Sanchez. 2008. *Hispanics and the U.S. Political System: Moving into the Mainstream.* Upper Saddle River, NJ: Pearson Prentice-Hall, 8.

7 Lisa J. Montoya, Carol Hardy-Fanta, and Sonia Garcia. 2000. Latina Politics: Gender, Participation, and Leadership. *PS: Political Science & Politics* 33 (3): 555–61.

8 Paul Taylor and Richard Fry. December 2007. Hispanics and the 2008 Election: A Swing Vote? Washington, D.C.: Pew Hispanic Center, 14.

9 Mark Hugo Lopez and Susan Minushkin. October 23, 2008. Hispanic Voter Attitudes and the 2008 U.S. Elections. Migration Information Source, 3–4. <http://www.migrationinformation.org/feature/print.cfm?ID=699> October 27, 2008.

10 National Association of Latino Elected and Appointed Officials (NALEO). 2008. 2008 Latino Election Handbook. Los Angeles: NALEO Educational Fund, 12.

11 Taylor and Fry 2007, 15.

12 Lisa Garcia Bedolla, Jessica L. Lavariega Monforti, and Adrian D. Pantoja. 2006. "A Second Look: Is There a Latina/o Gender Gap?" In *Intersectionality and Politics: Recent Research on Gender, Race, and Political Representation in the United States*, ed. Carol Hardy-Fanta. New York: Haworth Press, 147–71.

13 Montoya, Hardy-Fanta, and Garcia 2000, 556.

14 Christine Marie Sierra and Adaljiza Sosa-Riddell. 1994. Chicanas as Political Actors: Rare Literature, Complex Practice. *National Political Science Review* 4:297–317.

15 Carol Hardy-Fanta and Carol Cardozo. 1997. Beyond the Gender Gap: Women of Color in the 1996 Election, paper delivered at the Annual Meeting

of the American Political Science Association, Washington, D.C., August 28–31.

16 Bedolla, Monforti, and Pantoja 2006, 152.

17 Ibid. at 166, original emphasis.

18 Ibid.

19 Garcia and Sanchez 2008, 202.

20 National Association of Latino Elected and Appointed Officials. 2005 NALEO Fact Sheet; and The NALEO 2009 National Directory of Latino Elected Officials. Los Angeles: NALEO Educational Fund.

21 NALEO 2009. The NALEO 2009 National Directory of Latino Elected Officials; and Center for American Women and Politics (CAWP). 2009. Facts on Women in State Legislatures. <http://www.cawp.rutgers.edu/fast_facts/levels_of_office/StateLeg-CurrentFacts.php> March 4, 2009.

22 NALEO 2009. The NALEO 2009 National Directory of Latino Elected Officials.

23 Ibid.

24 Garcia and Sanchez 2008, 130 (see their Table 6.3).

25 CandidatoUSA. February 11, 2008, 2 (6). <http://www.CandidatoUSA.com> March 4, 2008.

26 Echaveste and her husband, Christopher Edley, the dean of Boalt Law School at the University of California, Berkeley, formed one of the "mixed marriages" to emerge during the election. Edley, an African American man, was an early supporter of Barack Obama for president.

27 Roberto Suro. February 11, 2008. Does Education Explain the Latino Gap between Clinton and Obama? CandidatoUSA. 2 (6), 8 <http://www.CandidatoUSA.com> March 4, 2008.

28 Valerie Martinez-Ebers. February 13, 2009. Latinos in Presidential Politics. Public lecture. National Hispanic Cultural Center, Albuquerque, New Mexico.

29 Martinez-Ebers 2009.

30 Leslie Wayne. January 10, 2008. Richardson Is Expected to Drop Out of Primaries. *New York Times*, A22.

31 Martinez-Ebers 2009.

32 Suro 2008, 8.

33 Gregory Rodriguez. January 26, 2008. The Black-Brown Divide. Time.com, quoting Bendixen. <http://www.time.com/time/magazine/article/0,9171,1707221,00.html> February 5, 2008.

34 Trip Jennings. September 19, 2008. BBC: N.M. GOP Leader Says Hispanics 'Won't Vote for a Black President'. *New Mexico Independent*, quoting C de Baca. <http://newmexicoindependent.com/5/bbc-nm-gop-leader-says-hispanics-wont-vote-for-a-black-president> March 18, 2009.

35 CandidatoUSA. February 11, 2008, 2 (6). <http://www.CandidatoUSA.com> March 4, 2008; Martinez-Ebers 2009; and Suro 2008. In numerous interviews with the national media on the 2008 election, I and my department colleague, Gabriel Sanchez, had to respond to questions that focused on racial tension between Hispanics and Blacks. Perhaps an implicit gender bias was

also embedded in this line of questioning (i.e., that a white woman in her own right could not attract the support of people of color).

36 Robin Abcarian. January 16, 2008. Obama Gets Major Labor Endorsement. *Los Angeles Times*.<http://theenvelope.latimes.com/la-na-labor16jan16, 0,1465411.story> March 4, 2008; and Maria Shriver Endorses Obama at UCLA Rally. February 3, 2008. LAist. <http://laist.com/2008/02/03/maria_shriver_e.php> March 4, 2008.

37 National Association of Latino Elected and Appointed Officials. 2008. 2008 Latino Election Handbook, 3.

38 CandidatoUSA. February 11, 2008; and Susan Minushkin and Mark Hugo Lopez. June 2008. The Hispanic Vote in the 2008 Democratic Presidential Primaries. Washington, D.C.: Pew Hispanic Center.

39 Minushkin and Lopez 2008, 3.

40 Ibid.

41 CandidatoUSA. February 11, 2008, 1, quoting Solis Doyle.

42 National Association of Latino Elected and Appointed Officials. 2008. 2008 Latino Election Handbook.

43 Carol Hardy-Fanta. October 28, 2008. Latina Women in the 2008 Election. Panel presentation for the Center for American Progress, Washington, D.C.

44 Christine Marie Sierra. August 28, 2008. From Hillary to Barack. Blog for KNME TV-5, Albuquerque, New Mexico.

45 See Christine Marie Sierra. August 31, 2008. *¡Obámanos!* Blog for KNME TV-5, Albuquerque, New Mexico.

46 Patricia Madrid Named to Obama's National Latino Advisory Council. August 22, 2008. Democracy for New Mexico. <http://www.democracy-fornewmexico.com/democracy_for_new_mexico/2008/08/patricia-madr-2.html> March 18, 2009.

47 Prayer card. Distributed by the Republican Party of New Mexico, 2008. On file with author.

48 Associated Press. October 6, 2008. Campaigns Woo New Hispanic Citizens as Key Bloc. <http://kob.com/article/stories/S607863.shtml> October 6, 2008.

49 Zogby Poll: Hispanic Likely Voters Support Obama over McCain, 70%–21%. October 20, 2008. Posted on Latino-Caucus LISTSERV (LATINO-C@LISTSERVE.ilstu.edu).

50 National Association of Latino Elected and Appointed Officials. 2008. 2008 Latino Vote Survey in Key Battleground States. Los Angeles: NALEO Educational Fund.

51 Mark Hugo Lopez. November 2008. The Hispanic Vote in the 2008 Election. Washington, D.C.: Pew Hispanic Center. <http://www.pewhispanic.org> March 4, 2009.

52 JoNel Aleccia. November 5, 2008. Hispanic Women Swell Ranks of Obama Support. Politics: Decision '08 Archive. MSNBC. <http://www.msnbc.com/id/27557684/> November 6, 2008.

53 Institute for Women's Policy Research. November 6, 2008. Women's Vote Clinches Election Victory: 8 Million More Women Than Men Voted for Obama. <http://www.iwpr.org/pdf/08ElectionRelease.pdf> March 4, 2009.

54 CNN.com. 2008. Election results. <http://www.cnn.com/Election/2008/results/polls> March 4, 2009.

55 National Association of Latino Elected and Appointed Officials. 2008. 2008 National Directory of Latino Elected Officials. Los Angeles: NALEO Educational Fund; and The NALEO 2009 National Directory of Latino Elected Officials.

6 African American Women and Electoral Politics

A Challenge to the Post-Race Rhetoric of the Obama Moment

The election of President Barack Obama as America's first African American president has prompted many commentators and pundits to assert that America is entering into a post-race moment in which race and racial politics are no longer a part of America's political tapestry. Obama enjoyed widespread support from across the electorate, winning even in states that had not supported Democratic presidential candidates in recent years, the so-called red states. Defying the Democratic Party's declining support among white voters, Obama fared quite well with many white voters. Not since the election of Lyndon B. Johnson in 1964 has the Democratic Party carried a majority of white voters, and winning the white vote has been a challenge for Democrats since that time. Jimmy Carter lost the white vote by four percentage points in 1976, and Bill Clinton lost the white vote by two percentage points in 1992 and in 1996. Obama lost white voters by twelve percentage points, improving on the records of Senator John Kerry, who lost white voters by seventeen points in 2004, and Vice President Al Gore, who lost among whites by thirteen points in 2000.

Obama's successful run for the presidency and relative success across broad and diverse groups of Americans has prompted suggestions that America is now a post-race society in which race and racial politics are a thing of the past. This is certainly an exciting moment for a country haunted by such a sordid racial history and with staggering disparities among whites, African Americans, Latinos, and Native Americans in housing, health care, earnings, and incarceration rates. The prospect of setting aside both the country's racial history and the current socioeconomic disparities that divide racial groups is quite appealing. Yet the political realities of people of color in America offer stark reminders that,

165

while we are moving toward a post-racial reality, we are far from attaining that goal.

Beyond President Obama's victory, the 2008 elections stand as a strong reminder that we still have far to go to achieve racial and gender parity in American politics. When we examine the political fortunes of candidates of color seeking other offices, we see that they are still underrepresented at all levels. In this chapter, I focus on African American women in politics, noting that both structural barriers and Americans' race and gender preferences still affect the success of women of color in securing political office. I chart how African American women are faring in electoral politics at the national, state, and local levels, illustrating the considerable challenges they continue to face. Traditional measures and indicators of political participation suggest that African American women would be among the least likely to participate in politics, yet they are heavily engaged in a range of political activities. After identifying what I term the *paradox of participation*, I trace African American women's participation in formal electoral politics from Shirley Chisholm's 1972 presidential campaign to the present day. African American women are still experiencing a number of firsts in electoral politics, which signifies that their journey from the shadows to the spotlight in American politics is not yet complete. In response to the many barriers they encounter, African American women are organizing and exploring new strategies to ensure their future leadership in American politics. By focusing on their experiences, we can examine the extent of America's progress toward political inclusiveness along both race and gender lines and toward a society in which race and gender are less significant as determinants of electoral success.

AFRICAN AMERICAN WOMEN AND THE PARADOX OF PARTICIPATION

African American women have consistently participated in American politics despite formidable barriers to their participation in formal electoral roles as voters and candidates. At its inception in 1787, the U.S. Constitution limited the citizenship rights of African Americans, both women and men, regarding each one as only three-fifths of a person. Later, as Mamie Locke argues, African American women would move from three-fifths of a person under the Constitution to total exclusion from constitutional protections with the passage of the Fifteenth Amendment in

1870, which extended the right to vote to African American men only.[1] When women earned the right to vote in 1920 with the passage of the Nineteenth Amendment, large numbers of African American women remained restricted from the franchise through the cultural norms of the Jim Crow South. African Americans were disenfranchised through literacy tests, poll taxes, grandfather clauses, and all-white primaries. It was not until the passage of the Voting Rights Act of 1965 that African American women secured the right to freely practice the franchise.

The impact of the Voting Rights Act was keenly apparent in the states of the Deep South. African American voter registration in Mississippi, for example, increased from 6.7 percent in 1964 to 64 percent in 1980.[2] The Voting Rights Act of 1965 was arguably the single most important piece of legislation in securing the franchise for African American voters and realizing political empowerment. The rapid growth in the numbers of African American elected officials is further evidence of the Act's impact. At the time the Voting Rights Act passed, fewer than five hundred African American elected officials held office nationwide. Today the number of African American elected officials has grown to more than nine thousand.[3]

Studies of American politics have defined political participation narrowly in terms of electoral participation. As Cathy Cohen argues, such a limited definition of political participation has hindered the development of research on African American women's political activism because their political participation tends to extend beyond electoral politics to community organizing and civic engagement.[4] Because African American women were excluded from participation in formal politics until the passage of the Voting Rights Act of 1965, first by the condition of their enslavement and then by equally oppressive systems of exclusion, their nontraditional political activism developed outside the electoral system and was informed by their political, economic, and social conditions.[5]

Defining political participation beyond the narrow framework of voting and holding elected office allows us to see the consistent levels of African American women's political participation across history. By asking new questions and examining the nontraditional spaces of women's activism, such as churches, private women's clubs, and volunteer organizations, feminist historians have uncovered countless activities of women of color involved in social movements. African American women have been central to every effort toward greater political empowerment for both African Americans and women. As the historian Paula Giddings

Figure 6.1: **The number of African American women elected officials has increased in recent elections while the number of African American men has leveled off.**

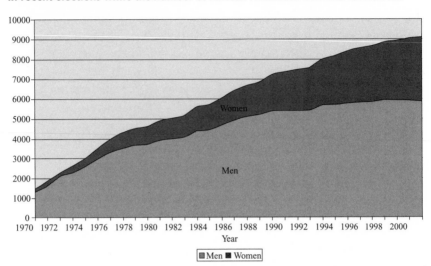

Source: Compiled by author from David Bositis, *Black Elected Officials: A Statistical Summary*, Washington, D.C.: Joint Center for Political and Economic Studies, 2001.

attests, African American women were the linchpin in struggles against racism and sexism. They understood that the fates of women's rights and black rights were inextricably linked and that one would be meaningless without the other.[6]

In spite of this rich legacy of activism, African American women's political participation represents a puzzle of sorts. African American women appear to be overrepresented in elective office while simultaneously holding the characteristics that would make them least likely to be politically engaged. African American women account for a greater proportion of black elected officials than white women do of white elected officials.[7] In the 111th Congress (2009–10), 29 percent of African Americans in the House were women, compared with only 17 percent of all members of the House who were women. Further, as Figure 6.1 illustrates, since the early 1990s, there has been a steady increase in the number of African American women elected officials, which has not been the case for African American men. In fact, over the past decade, all of the growth in the number of black elected officials can be attributed to African American women. This reverses the trends of the 1970s immediately following the passage of the Voting Rights Act, when 82 percent of the growth in black elected officials was attributed to African American men.[8]

Scholars who study the intersection of race and gender argue that African American women suffer from a "double disadvantage" in politics, in that they are forced to overcome the ills of both sexism and racism.[9] Darcy and Hadley, however, conclude that African American women defied expectations, proving more politically ambitious than their white counterparts and enjoying greater success in election to mayoral, state legislative, and congressional office in comparison with white women throughout the 1970s and 1980s. These authors link the puzzle of African American women's achievement to their activism in the civil rights movement and the skills developed during the movement, which African American women quickly translated into formal politics once passage of the Voting Rights Act opened opportunities.[10]

Studies of political participation have consistently concluded that the affluent and the educated are more likely to participate in politics at higher rates.[11] However, for African American women, the usual determinants of political participation – education and income – are not strong predictors of their participation.[12] African American women's high level of officeholding contrasts with their material conditions, which suggest that they would be far less politically active. As of the 2000 U.S. Census, 43 percent of black families were headed by a single mother, and the poverty rate among African American women was more than twice that of non-Hispanic white women.[13] Regardless of their socioeconomic status, African American women are far more likely than African American men to engage in both traditional forms of political participation (including voting and holding office) and nontraditional forms of participation (such as belonging to organizations and clubs, attending church, and talking to people about politics). For example, the proportion of voters who were African American increased from 11 percent in 2004 to 13 percent in 2008. African American women were 58 percent of the black vote, in comparison with African American men's 42 percent.[14] Social scientists do not fully understand these inconsistencies in African American women's political participation.[15] The 2008 elections present an opportunity to better understand their political participation by focusing on their experiences as candidates for elected office.

AFRICAN AMERICAN WOMEN AND THE PRESIDENCY

African American women have a long established history of seeking political inclusion via the highest office in the land, the presidency. Across history, at least seven African American women have had their names on the

TABLE 6.1: Six African American women have appeared on general election ballots for president

Candidate	Political party	Year
Charlene Mitchell	Communist Party	1968
Lenora Fulani	New Alliance Party	1988 and 1992
Margaret Wright	Peoples' Party	1976
Isabel Masters	Looking Back Party	1992 and 1996
Monica Morehead	Worker's World Party	1996 and 2000
Cynthia McKinney	Green Party	2008

Source: Compiled by author using data from http://www.jofreeman.com.

general election ballot for the presidency, including Cynthia McKinney, who ran in 2008 representing the Green Party (see Table 6.1).[16] As was the case with McKinney in this most recent election, most of these candidates represented fringe or third parties. Two African American women have run for the presidency seeking to represent the Democratic Party. Shirley Chisholm ran in 1972, and more than thirty years later, Carol Moseley Braun ran in 2004. Both Chisholm and Braun's candidacies were declared nonviable from the onset, but in both of these cases, these women offered serious challenges to the status quo that suggests that presidential politics is not the domain of women of color. In this section, I highlight the candidacies of Chisholm, Braun, and McKinney, showing the differences among their campaigns and the challenges that mark women of color's ascension to the highest political office.

In 1972, Congresswoman Shirley Chisholm broke barriers as the first African American woman to make a serious bid for the presidency.[17] Chisholm was well positioned to run for president, with political experience at the community, state, and national levels. She served in the New York General Assembly before becoming the first African American woman elected to Congress. As the lone African American woman in Congress, she joined her twelve African American male colleagues in founding the Congressional Black Caucus (CBC).[18]

After two terms in the House of Representatives, Chisholm decided to run for president. Her run came at a point when the civil rights leadership was calling for greater political engagement and the women's movement was at its height. In running for president, Chisholm hoped to bring the concerns of these communities to the forefront of national politics. She spoke out for the rights of African Americans, women, and gays. She was quickly dismissed, perceived as not a serious candidate.

Chisholm faced a 1970s America that was just becoming accustomed to women in the workforce and in politics. She challenged notions of women's proper place. On the campaign trail, she routinely encountered hecklers who were happy to tell her the proper place for a woman. She told the story of a man at a campaign stop who questioned whether she had "cleaned her house" and "cared for her husband" before coming there.[19] Chisholm often faced such blatant sexism and, in other encounters, racism in her campaign, but she continued to press toward the Democratic National Convention.

Although Chisholm fashioned herself as both the "black candidate" and the "woman candidate," she found herself shunned by both black leaders in Congress and the feminist community. Far from supporting her, members of the CBC, an organization she had helped to found, charged that her run was detrimental to the black community, dividing it along gender lines at a time when the black community could not afford such divisive politics. Chisholm, a founder of the National Organization for Women (NOW), was dealt an equally devastating blow when prominent feminists such as the cofounder of NOW, Gloria Steinem, and fellow U.S. Congresswoman Bella Abzug decided not to endorse her candidacy publicly. Instead, they opted to protect their political leverage by supporting Senator George McGovern, who was considered at that time the more viable candidate of the Democratic contenders and the candidate most capable of defeating then president Nixon.[20]

Deserted by both the leaders of the CBC and the feminist community, Chisholm survived the primaries and remained a candidate at the outset of the Democratic National Convention. She received 151 delegate votes on the first ballot, far short of the roughly 2,000 needed to secure the nomination. In the end, Chisholm acknowledged that her bid for the White House was less about winning and more about demanding full inclusion for African Americans and women. By waging a national presidential campaign, her candidacy had shown the world what was possible for women and men of color with increased access to political empowerment in a more democratized America. Indeed, Chisholm blazed the trail that would eventually lead to the election of Barack Obama.

More than three decades later, there was no doubt that Carol Moseley Braun benefited from Chisholm's pioneering candidacy. The differences between the two experiences signify some progress for African

American women as high-profile candidates, even as they bring to light enduring problems African American women face in achieving greater political empowerment.

Carol Moseley Braun's treatment in the 2004 election cycle symbolizes some progress from the blatant, overt sexism and racism that Shirley Chisholm encountered in 1972. Moseley Braun experienced more subversive, structurally embedded sexism and racism, which are more difficult to recognize. Her experiences reflect the extent to which the office of the president is consistently associated with white men, a pattern Georgia Duerst-Lahti documents in Chapter 1 of this volume. There is an understanding that the president of the United States will be a man and white, and this sentiment has dominated thinking about the presidency.[21] Because Moseley Braun was neither a man nor white, she struggled constantly to convince the public that her candidacy was, in fact, viable. The doubts surrounding the feasibility of her candidacy affected all aspects of her campaign, but they were most devastating to her fund-raising efforts. The negligible and trivializing media coverage she received reinforced doubts and further stymied her campaign. Such struggles are reflective of the remaining institutional racism and sexism that continue to impede qualified candidates who differ from societal expectations about who should serve as president. Moseley Braun campaigned promising to "take the 'men only' sign off the White House door," but this seemed to be a challenge America was not ready to accept.

By objective measures, Moseley Braun was well positioned to run for the presidency. Once questioned as to why she was running, Moseley Braun quickly responded, "Why not?" adding, "If I were not a woman – if I were a guy – with my credentials and my experience and what I bring to the table, there would be no reason why I wouldn't think about running for president."[22] In the field of Democratic contenders, Moseley Braun's political record was among the most stellar. She was the only candidate to have experience at the local, state, national, and international levels of government.

Despite the energetic responses Moseley Braun drew from crowds at campaign stops, political pundits remained dismissive of her campaign. According to her, this was nothing new, "Nobody ever expected me to get elected to anything. For one thing, I'm black, I'm a woman and I'm out of the working class. So the notion that someone from my background would have anything to say about the leadership of this country is challenging to some."[23] Like Shirley Chisholm, she also faced charges of running a purely symbolic campaign to establish that women are capable of running for the country's top executive office.

Campaign fund-raising plagued Moseley Braun's campaign from the onset, and her fund-raising efforts continuously lagged behind those of most other candidates, even after she gained impressive endorsements from the National Women's Political Caucus (NWPC) and NOW, two of the leading feminist organizations. Notable white feminists, including the legendary Gloria Steinem and Marie Wilson, director of the White House Project, a nonprofit organization dedicated to getting a woman into the White House, publicly supported the campaign. Black women's organizations, including the National Political Congress of Black Women, invested in Moseley Braun's campaign, and she enjoyed public endorsements from notable African American women from Coretta Scott King to Dr. Dorothy Height, president emerita of the National Council of Negro Women. Receiving such ardent support from the women's community and black women's organizations, Braun's candidacy represented progress over the struggles faced by Shirley Chisholm's campaign.

Garnering media attention proved to be an equally challenging problem for Moseley Braun's campaign, creating a circular effect; without media visibility, her ability to raise funds was limited, and with minimal funding, her campaign drew less media attention. She had extreme difficulty getting her message to the voters. When she received any coverage at all, it most often referred to her as "improbable," "nonviable," a "long-shot" candidate, or at worst an "also-ran."

Whatever its challenges, Moseley Braun's campaign was certainly not confronted with the overt sexism and racism that Chisholm had experienced. Instead, a much more subtle, indirect brand of racism and sexism plagued her campaign, characterized by the outright dismissal of her candidacy as a serious bid for the White House. Consistent slights affected all facets of her campaign. The failure to garner media attention, along with fund-raising challenges, forced Carol Moseley Braun to formally pull out of the race in January 2004, even before the first primary.

David Bositis of the Joint Center for Political and Economic Studies may have best captured her predicament when he argued, "Part of Carol Moseley Braun's problem is that she is a black woman." Bositis observed that Democratic voters were looking for a candidate who could beat George H. W. Bush, and unfortunately, she was not perceived as a candidate who could do that.[24] Further, the political scientist Paula McClain argues that Moseley Braun was disadvantaged from the onset in crafting a name for herself in this campaign, given the Democratic Party leadership's preference that candidates forgo more leftist politics. As she argues, Moseley Braun's identity as an African American woman positioned her clearly as a "left-of-center candidate" and subsequently constrained her ability to establish an alternative identity as a candidate in the minds of voters.[25]

The 2008 presidential election is considered by all accounts as one of the most memorable presidential contests in modern history. The election will certainly be remembered for electing the first African American man, Senator Barack Obama, to the presidency. It will also be historicized for Senator Hillary Clinton's remarkable run, during which she won more than 18 million votes. Moreover, this presidential election cycle will be noted for giving rise to the vice presidential candidacy of Alaska Governor Sarah Palin, only the second woman to be named to a major party's presidential ticket. Buried among all the historic firsts of this election cycle, few will note that the 2008 presidential election cycle also marked the first time two women of color ran on a political party's ticket as the presidential and vice presidential candidates.

The former congresswoman Cynthia McKinney, an African American, was tapped as the Green Party's presidential candidate. McKinney selected Rosa Clemente, a Latina, New York–based hip-hop community activist, as her vice presidential running mate. McKinney and Clemente appeared on the ballot in thirty-one states and the District of Columbia, ultimately receiving 157,759 votes to finish sixth among all tickets. During their campaign, they raised a range of social justice–based issues, including an end to racial disparities in health, housing, education, and incarceration. They supported a right-of-return policy for New Orleans residents displaced by Hurricane Katrina; greater access to reproductive choice, including the right to bear children for poor women and women of color; and an end to Social Security policies that disproportionately harm women. Their platform pushed beyond the Green Party's more familiar stances on the environment to include a broad, progressive social justice–based platform.

Like most third-party candidates, McKinney and Clemente struggled to gain attention from media outlets and raise critical campaign dollars to execute a robust campaign. With so much attention focused on the major party candidates, this election cycle was especially hard for third-party candidates. As a progressive, McKinney was particularly pressed to articulate a rationale for posing even the potential of a threat to Obama's campaign success. McKinney and her supporters were challenged to make an argument for supporting their ticket in the face of Obama's historic run. The Green Party advocated a strategy of supporting Obama in critical states, even campaigning on his behalf, but in Democratic Party strongholds or states in which polls showed Obama well ahead of McCain (such as California, Illinois, and New Jersey), Green Party activists urged voters to open the dialogue to the Green Party by supporting their candidates. With a dismal showing in the polls, the Green Party failed to obtain the 5 percent of the national vote that would make it eligible to obtain federal matching funds for the 2012 election.

Although McKinney is a former member of the Democratic Party and a six-term congresswoman (serving from 1993 to 2003 and again from 2005 to 2007) by most accounts, McKinney's run for the presidency was a long shot. Not only her third-party candidate status but also her own reputation in politics placed her outside the mainstream. McKinney has long articulated a politics to the left of most members of the Democratic Party. She garnered national attention for her outspoken support of Palestine and for one of her final acts as a member of Congress – the filing of impeachment charges against President Bush on the grounds that he misled the American people in going to war in Iraq. Many argue that her extreme leftist politics and brazen approach accounted for the loss of her congressional seat in 2003.[26] After an altercation with a congressional security guard who failed to recognize her as a member of Congress and attempted to detain her, McKinney's reputation was further tarnished.

McKinney's fate was sealed in many ways by running as a third-party candidate in a two-party electoral system. Yet even in coverage of those who "also ran" during the 2008 presidential race, McKinney hardly garnered a mention from most press outlets, particularly in comparison to Ralph Nader, who ran as an independent, or even the former congressman Bob Barr, who ran on the Libertarian Party ticket. Green Party activists launched a strong critique of mainstream and even progressive media outlets for their refusal to recognize the historic nature of the McKinney-Clemente ticket, even in the midst of an election cycle marked by a continuous nod to history.

McKinney's experiences in 2008 are somewhat reminiscent of those of Chisholm and Braun, who were treated as nonviable candidates, thus diminishing their chances of reaching the American people. Although the 2008 presidential election is heralded for all the ways it disrupted the status quo in politics, on some level, this election cycle continues the legacies of past elections by reaffirming the belief that African American women are not appropriate, viable contenders for the presidency.

AFRICAN AMERICAN WOMEN AND ELECTED OFFICE: ON THE PATH TO HIGHER OFFICE?

The presidential candidacies of Chisholm, Moseley Braun, McKinney, and the other African American women who have sought the presidency across history compel us to ask whether there are African American women poised to run for the presidency in future elections. Women and politics scholars and activists discuss increasing the numbers of women elected to public office at lower levels as the first step toward moving women into higher offices.[27] Feeding the political pipeline has become a critical strategy in preparing women to successfully seek the highest offices, including the presidency. Are African American women moving through that pipeline? Are they securing offices at the local, state, and national levels in preparation for the highest political offices? Are they poised to run for the presidency in future elections?

To date, African American women's engagement in electoral politics as a means of securing greater political empowerment and placing their concerns on the political agenda has produced mixed results. On the one hand, they are gaining increased access to political offices, now outpacing African American men in winning elections. On the other hand, they continue to face considerable obstacles to securing high-profile offices at both the state and the national levels.

AFRICAN AMERICAN WOMEN IN STATE AND LOCAL POLITICS

Of the more than three thousand African American women elected officials, most are elected to sub-state-level offices, such as regional offices, county boards, city councils, judicial offices, and local school boards. African American women have gained increasing access to leadership positions at the local level. As of 2008, forty-eight African American mayors led cities with populations of fifty thousand or more, and twelve of those were women (see Table 6.2).[28] Three African American women – Shelia Dixon (Baltimore), Shirley Franklin (Atlanta), and Yvonne Johnson (Greensboro, North Carolina) – lead large cities with populations of more than two hundred thousand. Still, few scholars have devoted attention to women of color in sub-state-level offices, largely because variations among localities make comparisons difficult.

As African American women move beyond the local level, they face greater challenges in winning office. In many ways, statewide offices are

TABLE 6.2: Twelve African American women were mayors of cities with populations of more than fifty thousand in 2008

Mayor	City	Population
Sheila Dixon	Baltimore, Maryland	651,154
Shirley Franklin	Atlanta, Georgia	416,474
Yvonne J. Johnson	Greensboro, North Carolina	240,955
Rhine McLin	Dayton, Ohio	166,179
Shirley Gibson	Miami Gardens, Florida	105,457
Gwendolyn Faison	Camden, New Jersey	79,904
Brenda L. Lawrence	Southfield, Michigan	78,296
Lorraine H. Morton	Evanston, Illinois	74,239
Patricia A. Vance	Evanston Township, Illinois	74,239
Terry Bellamy	Ashville, North Carolina	68,889
Yvonne Scarlett-Golden	Daytona Beach, Florida	64,112
Joyce Seals	Saginaw, Michigan	61,799

Source: Compiled by author from the Joint Center for Political and Economic Studies (http://www.jointcenter.org) and the Center for American Women and Politics.

more difficult for African American candidates to secure, especially for African American women. No state has ever elected an African American woman as governor, and only three African American women currently hold statewide offices. Democrat Denise Nappier of Connecticut made history in 1998 as the first African American woman elected as state treasurer, and in 2009, she continues to serve in that capacity. Sandra Kennedy was elected in 2008 to serve as corporation commissioner in Arizona. In January 2009, Velda Jones-Potter was appointed as Delaware's state treasurer to complete the remaining term of Jack Markell, who was elected governor.[29]

In running for statewide offices, African American candidates do not have the benefit of African American majority electorates, as they often do when they run in smaller districts. As a result, they must depend on the support of white majorities for election. Because African Americans are generally significantly more supportive of African American candidates than whites are, attracting white voters is a significant challenge. African American candidates, who must depend on racially tolerant whites to win,[30] face the dual challenge of offering strong crossover appeal for white voters while maintaining a connection to communities of color to ensure their high voter turnout.

In state legislatures, African American women are steadily increasing their numbers, yet their gains still appear minuscule, especially relative to the number of available legislative seats. As of 2009, there were 7,382 state legislators, of whom only 349 were women of color. African American women led women of color in holding state legislative seats with 230, followed by 73 Latinas, 32 Asian American–Pacific Islander women, and 14 Native American women.[31] Although the numbers of women of color in state legislatures remain small, they have increased steadily, while the overall numbers of women in state legislatures, as reported in Kira Sanbonmatsu's Chapter 10 in this volume, seems to have reached a plateau. In 1998, for example, only 168 African American women served as state legislators. Over the past ten years, their numbers have increased by sixty-two.[32] Similar trends hold for Asian American–Pacific Islander, Latina, and Native American women.

African American women's influence in state legislatures is concentrated in a limited number of states (see Table 6.3). Only thirty-eight state legislatures have African American women currently serving. Maryland leads the states, with twenty African American women serving in its legislature, followed by Georgia (sixteen), Alabama and Mississippi (thirteen each) and Florida, New York, and Illinois (twelve each).[33] Overall, women have traditionally fared poorly in southern and border-state legislatures, yet the trend is different for African American women, who have experienced some of their greatest successes in these states. This is largely a result of the significant concentrations of African American voters in these states.

AFRICAN AMERICAN WOMEN IN CONGRESSIONAL POLITICS

In the aftermath of the 2008 elections, the 111th Congress opened with fourteen African American women members. The 2008 elections produced a first for African American women at the national level: the election of the first African American congresswoman from the state of Maryland, Donna Edwards.[34] Edwards accomplished an unlikely success in defeating an eight-term incumbent, Albert Wynn, in the Democratic primary. With her primary victory, Edwards was ensured a win in the general election, given the overwhelming Democratic Party advantage in the Fourth Congressional District. Most often, women candidates, like candidates in general, are most successful when running for open seats rather than when challenging incumbents. This major upset

TABLE 6.3: The proportion of African American women among state legislators varies across the states

	No African American women in state legislature	0.1%–4% African American women in state legislature	>4% African American women in state legislature
States with African American population of less than 5%	Minnesota Colorado Hawaii Maine South Dakota Utah North Dakota Montana Vermont Wyoming Idaho	Nebraska Alaska Arizona Washington West Virginia Iowa New Mexico Oregon New Hampshire	
States with African American population of 5%–15%	Kentucky	Michigan Pennsylvania Connecticut Indiana Oklahoma Nevada California Massachusetts Wisconsin Kansas Rhode Island	New Jersey Ohio Texas Missouri
States with African American population of 15.1%–20%		Arkansas	Virginia Tennessee New York Illinois Florida
States with African American population greater than 20%		South Carolina Delaware	Mississippi Louisiana Georgia Maryland Alabama North Carolina

Note: In each cell, states are listed in descending order by African American population. Maryland has the highest proportion of African American women in its state legislature (10.6 percent), followed by Louisiana (7.6 percent), Mississippi (7.5 percent), and Georgia (7.2 percent).

Source: Center for American Women and Politics, 2009 Fact Sheets. State percentage of African American population is drawn from 2007 U.S. Census data.

TABLE 6.4: Fourteen African American women were serving in the U.S.
House of Representatives in 2009

Congresswoman	Party	District	Major city in the district	Year first elected to Congress
Rep. Corrine Brown	D	3rd	Jacksonville, FL	1992
Rep. Donna Christensen[a]	D	–	U.S. Virgin Islands	1996
Rep. Yvette Clark	D	11th	New York, NY	2006
Rep. Donna Edwards	D	4th	Ft. Washington, MD	2008
Rep. Marcia Fudge	D	11th	Cleveland, OH	2008
Rep. Eddie Bernice Johnson	D	30th	Dallas, TX	1992
Rep. Carolyn Cheeks Kilpatrick	D	15th	Detroit, MI	1996
Rep. Barbara Lee	D	9th	Oakland, CA	1997
Rep. Sheila Jackson Lee	D	18th	Houston, TX	1994
Rep. Laura Richardson	D	37th	Compton, CA	1996
Rep. Gwen Moore	D	4th	Milwaukee, WI	2004
Del. Eleanor Holmes Norton[a]	D	–	Washington, D.C.	1991
Rep. Maxine Waters	D	35th	Los Angeles, CA	1990
Rep. Diane E. Watson	D	32nd	Los Angeles, CA	2000

[a] Donna Christensen is a nonvoting delegate representing the U.S. Virgin Islands and
  Eleanor Holmes Norton is a nonvoting delegate representing the District of Columbia.
Source: Compiled by author from Center for American Women and Politics, 2009 Fact
Sheets; David Bositis, *Black Elected Officials: A Statistical Summary*, Washington, D.C.:
Joint Center for Political and Economic Studies, 2001.

symbolizes the growing possibilities for African American women in
national politics (see Table 6.4).

Donna Edwards capitalized on the sweeping demand for change
expressed by American voters across the United States in 2008. In positioning herself as an outsider, she offered an alternative to the more cen-
trist Democratic style of the incumbent. Edwards aligned herself closely
with Barack Obama, who enjoyed widespread appeal in the mostly
African American district. Standing in opposition to the Iraq War, Edwards presented a stark contrast to the incumbent, whom she successfully constructed as too moderate and too entrenched in Washington
politics for the district. Her roots in social justice activism solidified her
position as the public interest candidate, while she artfully highlighted
Wynn's associations with corporate interests.[35]

Although the Edwards campaign was nontraditional in the sense that she unseated an incumbent, her 2008 bid was typical in the sense that it was not her first run for Congress. In 2006, Edwards had gained far-reaching name recognition in the district and attracted the attention of national women's organizations and other social justice–based groups whose support helped to build her financial coffers for the 2008 campaign. After losing to Wynn by only three points in 2006, Edwards never stopped campaigning.

In 2008, the intersections of Edwards's identity and her politics allowed her to draw on groups across the progressive spectrum. Liberal groups across the country supported her stance as an antiwar candidate; Moveon.org spent $150,000 to expose the incumbent's vote on the Iraq War. Edwards's national supporters included labor unions and women's groups such as EMILY's List and the NOW Political Action Committee. As a cofounder of the National Network to End Domestic Violence, Edwards gained national prominence through her work on the 1994 Violence Against Women Act and had strong ties with the domestic violence advocacy community, which proved valuable in her congressional bid. Likewise, she benefited from connections with African American organizations, campaign finance reform groups, and antiwar groups.

With the excitement of the contest between front-runners Hillary Clinton and Barack Obama for the presidential nomination, turnout for Democrats was higher than expected. Edwards's similarity to Obama was not lost on voters who were drawn to the antiwar message of both candidates.

Edwards's success is also related to the district in which she competed. Most African American candidates are still elected from districts in which African Americans are in the majority. Majority-minority districts resulted from provisions in the Voting Rights Act of 1965 and its subsequent extensions, which allowed for the formation of new districts where African Americans consisted of a plurality or majority of the electorate. In these new districts, African Americans could run for open seats, which not only alleviated the incumbency advantage but also freed them from dependence on white voters. Many scholars concede that historically, it has been nearly impossible for African American candidates to win in districts without black majorities, as some whites continue to resist voting for African American candidates.[36]

The number of African American women serving in Congress today is largely a result of the creation of majority-minority districts. Although 1992 was widely proclaimed the "Year of the Woman" in politics, reflecting the phenomenal success of women candidates for Congress, for African American women, 1992 was also the "Year of Redistricting." A number of open seats were created nationally as a result of redistricting following the 1990 Census, and most were majority-minority districts. African American women (including Cynthia McKinney) claimed five additional seats in the U.S. House of Representatives in 1992, more than doubling their numbers.[37] Four of the five African American women won in newly created majority-minority districts. The fifth African American woman elected in 1992, Eva Clayton of North Carolina, won a special election for a seat that was vacant because of the death of the incumbent, also in a majority-minority district.

While majority-minority districts have helped to secure African American women's place in Congress, these districts have been challenged in the courts as a means of increasing black representation. As a result of a string of cases in the 1990s from Georgia, Louisiana, North Carolina, and Texas, the future of majority-minority districts is now in question. Many scholars insist that African Americans' continued success in winning elective office, particularly congressional seats, is dependent on the preservation of majority-minority districts. Because of the precarious future of such districts, the number of African American women elected to Congress is likely to grow at a considerably slower pace than it did in the 1990s. To the extent that the number of African American women does grow in future years, the increase in their numbers will likely come largely at the expense of African American men who must compete with them for the limited number of seats available in majority-minority districts.[38]

THE FUTURE OF AFRICAN AMERICAN WOMEN IN POLITICS

African American female elected officials are enduring symbols of the long fight for political inclusion in U.S. electoral politics. Although legal barriers preventing their participation in politics have been removed, African American women continue to confront considerable barriers when seeking political office. The higher profile the office, the more formidable barriers they face to being considered viable candidates.

In light of the formidable challenges as they seek higher-profile offices, African American women are not leaving their political futures to chance. They are forming political action committees to address serious barriers to fund-raising. One group, Women Building for the Future (Future PAC), formed in 2002 to capitalize on the growing voting power of African American women. Future PAC's major objective is to increase the numbers of African American women elected at every level of government by supporting candidates financially and identifying women to run for office. In describing the purpose of the group, Donna Brazile, a strategist for the Democratic Party, argues that African American women face three major hurdles in seeking office: achieving name recognition, overcoming the tendency of the "old-boy network" to endorse other men, and garnering financial support. Brazile adds, "Our objective is to try to help women overcome one of the major barriers – financial – which will hopefully break down the other two."[39] Future PAC endorses African American women who have proven records in their communities and who share the group's views on a range of issues from education to health care.[40]

This type of organizing is essential if African American women are to continue increasing their representation. Such organizing efforts hold the promise of translating African American women's high voting rates into increased officeholding. Other national groups, such as the Black Women's Roundtable, established by the National Coalition on Black Civic Participation, are also working to increase political participation by mobilizing African American organizations, including Greek-letter fraternities and sororities, around voter education and civic empowerment.[41] These groups are invested in the important work of empowering citizens, mobilizing voters, and identifying likely candidates.

The most difficult work, however, remains in transforming American society to fully embrace African American women as political leaders. This issue must be addressed both inside the African American community and in the greater American society. The public's willingness to regard these well-prepared women as viable, appropriate political leaders is essential. The political parties, in particular the Democratic Party, which is the party affiliation of most African American women, must end their practice of assuming that African American women are left of center by virtue of their intersecting identities as both African Americans and women. Donna Edwards's congressional campaign illustrates that an intersecting identity is a strength that attracts voters from multiple communities. Not until such core cultural issues are addressed will the journey toward a post-race America truly begin. The election of the first African American president certainly represents progress toward an America in which race is less a defining feature of American politics. When well-qualified women of color successfully move through the political pipeline to hold elected offices at the local, state, and federal levels, we will be even closer to the post-race America hoped for by millions of Americans.

NOTES

1 Mamie Locke. 1997. From Three Fifths to Zero. In *Women Transforming Politics*, ed. Cathy Cohen, Kathleen B. Jones, and Joan Tronto. New York: New York University Press 377–386.

2 Frank R. Parker. 1990. *Black Votes: Count Political Empowerment in Mississippi after 1965*. Chapel Hill: University of North Carolina Press.

3 Linda F. Williams. 2001. The Civil Rights-Black Power Legacy: Black Women Elected Officials at the Local, State, and National Levels. In *Sisters in the Struggle: African American Women in the Civil Rights-Black Power Movement*, ed. Bettye Collier-Thomas and V. P. Franklin. New York: New York University Press 306–332.

4 Cathy J. Cohen. 2003. A Portrait of Continuing Marginality: The Study of Women of Color in American Politics. In *Women and American Politics: New Questions, New Directions*, ed. Susan J. Carroll. New York: Oxford University Press 190–213.

5 See Paula Giddings. 1984. *When and Where I Enter: The Impact of Black Women on Race and Sex in America*. New York: Bantam Books; Darlene Clark Hine and Kathleen Thompson. 1998. *A Shining Thread of Hope: The History of Black Women in America*. New York: Broadway Books; Dorothy Sterling. 1997. *We Are Your Sisters: Black Women in the Nineteenth Century*. New York: W. W. Norton.

6 Giddings 1984.

7 Williams 2001.

8 David A. Bositis. 2001. Black Elected Officials: A Statistical Summary 2001. Washington, D.C.: Joint Center for Political and Economic Studies.

9 See Robert Darcy and Charles Hadley. 1988. Black Women in Politics: The Puzzle of Success. *Social Science Quarterly* 77: 888–98; Gary Moncrief, Joel Thompson, and Robert Schuhmann. 1991. Gender, Race and the Double Disadvantage Hypothesis. *Social Science Journal* 28: 481–7.

10 Darcy and Hadley 1988.

11 See Andrea Y. Simpson. 1999. Taking Over or Taking a Back Seat? Political Activism of African American Women. Paper delivered at the annual meeting of the American Political Science Association, Atlanta, September 1–5. For an extensive discussion of political participation, see Sidney Verba, Kay Lehman Scholzman, and Henry E. Brady. 1995. *Voice and Equality: Civic Volunteerism in American Politics*. Cambridge, MA: Harvard University Press.

12 Sandra Baxter and Marjorie Lansing. 1980. *Women and Politics: The Invisible Majority*. Ann Arbor: University of Michigan Press.

13 U.S. Bureau of the Census. 2003. U.S. Census. The Black Population in the United States. <http://www.census.gov/prod/2003pubs/pg20–541.pdf> February 23, 2005.

14 David A. Bositis. 2008. Blacks and the 2008 Elections: A Preliminary Analysis. Washington, D.C.: Joint Center for Political and Economic Studies.

15 Simpson 1999.

16 Jo Freeman. The Women Who Ran for President. <http://jofreeman.com> January 15, 2009.

17 Although Shirley Chisholm's 1972 run for the White House is most often cited, there is a long legacy of African Americans running for the presidency, largely as third-party candidates. For a full discussion, see Hanes Walton Jr. 1994. Black Female Presidential Candidates: Bass, Mitchell, Chisholm, Wright, Reid, Davis, and Fulani. In *Black Politics and Black Political Behavior: A Linkage Analysis*, ed. Hanes Walton Jr. Westport, CT: Praeger 251–276.

18 Katherine Tate. 2003. *Black Faces in the Mirror: African Americans and Their Representatives in the U.S. Congress*. Princeton, NJ: Princeton University Press.

19 Shirley Chisholm. 1973. *The Good Fight*. New York: Harper & Row.

20 For a more elaborate discussion of Chisholm's supporters and detractors during the 1972 presidential campaign, view "Chisholm '72 Unbought and Unbossed," a documentary by the filmmaker Shola Lynch.

21 Georgia Duerst-Lahti and Rita Mae Kelly, eds. 1995. *Gender Power, Leadership, and Governance*. Ann Arbor: University of Michigan Press.

22 Monica Davey. December 18, 2003. In Seeking Presidency, Braun Could Win Back Reputation. *New York Times*.

23 Nedra Pickler. May 2, 2003. Washington Today: Braun Appears with the Presidential Candidates, but Isn't Running Like One. Associated Press State and Local Wire.

24 Adam Reilly. December 12–18, 2003. Hitting with Her Best Shot. *Portland Phoenix*. <http://www.portlandphoenix.com> March 15, 2005.

25 Paula McClain. 2004. Gender and Black Presidential Politics: From Chisholm to Moseley Braun Revisited. Comments made at Roundtable on Black and Presidential Politics, American Political Science Association meeting, September 1–5, Chicago.

26 See Wendy Smooth. 2005. African American Women in Electoral Politics: Journeying from the Shadows to the Spotlight. In *Gender and Elections*, ed. Susan J. Carroll and Richard L. Fox. New York: Cambridge University Press 117–142.

27 For a full discussion on getting women into the political pipeline, see Jennifer Lawless and Richard L. Fox. 2005. *It Takes a Candidate*. New York: Cambridge University Press.

28 For a complete listing, see the Web page of the Joint Center for Political and Economic Research, <http://www.jointcenter.org> July 31, 2009.

29 Center for American Women and Politics. 2009. Fact Sheet. Women of Color in Elective Office 2009. <http://www.cawp.rutgers.edu/fast_facts/levels_of_office/documents/color.pdf> July 31, 2009.

30 See Lee Sigelman and Susan Welch. 1984. Race, Gender, and Opinion toward Black and Female Candidates. *Public Opinion Quarterly* 48: 467–75; Ruth Ann Strickland and Marcia Lynn Whicker. 1992. Comparing the Wilder and Gantt

Campaigns: A Model of Black Candidate Success in Statewide Elections. *PS: Political Science and Politics* 25: 204–12.

31 Center for American Women and Politics. 2009. Fact Sheet. Women of Color in Elective Office 2009. <http://www.cawp.rutgers.edu/fast_facts/levels_of_office/documents/color.pdf> July 31, 2009.

32 See Center for American Women and Politics. Women of Color in Elected Office Fact Sheets for 1998 and 2009. <http://www.cawp.rutgers.edu/fast_facts/levels_of_office/documents/color.pdf> July 31, 2009.

33 See Center for American Women and Politics. African American Women in Electoral Politics. <http://www.cawp.rutgers.edu/fast_facts/women_of_color/FastFacts_AfricanAmericanWomeninOffice.php> July 31, 2009.

34 Donna Edwards was elected in a special election in June 2008 to complete the term of the incumbent, Albert Wynn. Wynn resigned to accept a position as a lobbyist following his defeat by Edwards during the February Democratic Party primary. Edwards went on to win her first full congressional term during the November general election.

35 Rosaland Helderman, William Wann, and Ovetta Wiggins. February 14, 2008. Rare Dual Losses in Maryland Put Incumbents on Notice. *Washington Post*.

36 Bernard Grofman and Chandler Davidson, eds. 1992. *Controversies in Minority Voting: The Voting Rights Act*. New York: Cambridge University Press.

37 Tate 2003.

38 Irwin N. Gertzog. 2002. Women's Changing Pathways to the U.S. House of Representatives: Widows, Elites, and Strategic Politicians. In *Women Transforming Congress*, ed. Cindy Simon Rosenthal. Norman: Oklahoma University Press 95–118.

39 Joyce Jones. January 2004. The Future PAC. *Black Enterprise*.

40 Robin M. Bennefield. July/August 2004. Women Join Forces to Support Black Female Politicians. *Crisis* (The New) 111:12.

41 See the Black Women's Roundtable (BWR), a part of the National Coalition on Black Civic Participation at <http://www.bigvote.org/bwr.htm> February 20, 2005.

RICHARD L. FOX*

7 Congressional Elections

Women's Candidacies and the Road to Gender Parity

After losing in the midterm congressional elections in 2002, Democratic Party House Minority Leader Richard Gephardt announced that he would be stepping down. Immediately thereafter, California Congresswoman Nancy Pelosi, who had been in Congress since 1987 and was serving as the Democratic whip, announced her candidacy. Pelosi quickly dispatched with two male rivals for the position and was elected to the post of minority leader. After Pelosi officially assumed the position, the *Christian Science Monitor* proclaimed in a headline: "Pelosi Shatters a Marble Ceiling."[1] The selection of Pelosi was truly historic, as she was the first woman in the 216-year history of the U.S. Congress to head one of the major parties. Although Pelosi was well known on Capitol Hill, an NBC News/*Wall Street Journal* poll released right after her election found that 61 percent of the public was not sure who she was.[2] But women's rights advocates were generally thrilled with the selection of Pelosi. Peg Yorkin, cofounder of the Feminist Majority Foundation noted, "Suddenly, in the midst of all those essentially gray, white men in the Republican leadership, you've got a friendly, intelligent, warm woman who doesn't stand on ceremony.... It's going to be something."[3] Pelosi continued as minority leader after the 2004 elections, which saw the Republicans retain control of the White House and both houses of Congress.

The political winds shifted mightily in the 2006 midterm elections as the public, having lost patience with the war in Iraq and expressing concerns about the direction of the country, returned the Democrats to power in both the House and Senate for the first time since 1994. With this election, Nancy Pelosi was elevated to the position of Speaker of the House, becoming the highest-ranking woman elected official in

* I would like to thank Ellen Hou for assistance in data collection.

U.S. history. The public face of Congress was no longer only that of men. Pelosi herself, in a speech right before the election, commented on her rise to be Speaker: "It says to women everywhere that...anything is possible."[4]

After 2008, the Democrats increased their numbers in both houses, and Pelosi appears to have a potentially long run as House speaker ahead. It is, of course, much too soon to determine how successful a trailblazer Pelosi will be as speaker. She has been a controversial figure, castigated by Republicans as a San Francisco liberal out of touch with the values of the country. In a Gallup Poll right after the 2008 election, 42 percent of the public had a favorable view of her, and 41 percent had a negative view.[5] Regardless, Pelosi's ascension to the top congressional leadership role marks a dramatic breakthrough and the dismantling of one more glass ceiling in U.S. politics.

Despite the success of Nancy Pelosi, women's journey toward gender parity in the U.S. Congress remains a slow process. In fact, recent elections can be viewed as a disappointment in terms of the progress of women candidates. Gains in Congress have been in very small increments, and one of the major political parties has actually been putting forward fewer and fewer women candidates. Further, the 2006 election reveals that electoral environments and strategies can still be very gendered enterprises.

After disappointing losses in the 2002 and 2004 elections, the Democrats made a push to recruit and run more military veterans, responding to the perceived advantage Republicans had in claiming they could keep Americans safe in the post-9/11 era. The *New York Times* reporters James Dao and Adam Nagourney summarized the strategy: "For Democrats struggling to win back Congress,... [this was] the most obvious of election strategies: erase the Republican advantage on national security by running real-life combat veterans as candidates."[6] In the end, fifty-three veterans, forty from the Iraq and Afghanistan wars, emerged as Democratic challengers to run for open seats or to take on Republican incumbents. Out of this group, only two were women.[7]

The recruitment of military veterans to demonstrate the image of toughness is a strategy that precludes many women from running, because only 15 percent of active-duty personnel are women and only 6 percent of veterans are women.[8] Further, this strategy plays into gender stereotypes that masculinity and aggressiveness are the best symbols to exude toughness in times of military conflict.

Did the strategy to run war veterans work? The results were mixed, but many women candidates, including the Iraq War veteran Tammy

Duckworth, running in Illinois' Sixth District, lost close races. Many were predicting big gains for women House candidates in the 2006 elections, with the veteran political forecaster Larry Sabato asserting that women would gain a minimum of nine seats in the House, making it the best single-year gain for women since 1992.[9] Sabato was wrong, as women lost close races around the country and netted only four new seats. A number of analysts pointed to the masculine "get tough" electoral atmosphere as among the reasons women underperformed.

As the stories of Nancy Pelosi's rise to the House speakership and the use of veterans in the 2006 midterm elections illustrate, the opportunities and difficulties facing women candidates are multifaceted. Women are making tremendous strides in electoral politics, but they continue to face many challenges that have plagued women's candidacies throughout modern U.S. electoral history. This chapter examines the evolution of women's candidacies for Congress and the role gender continues to play in congressional elections. Ultimately, I focus on one fundamental question: why are there still so few women serving in the House and Senate? In exploring the persistence of gender as a factor in congressional elections, I divide the chapter into three sections. In the first section, I offer a brief historical overview of the role of gender in congressional elections. The second section compares male and female candidates' electoral performance and success in House and Senate races through the 2008 elections. The results of this analysis confirm that, when considered in the aggregate, the electoral playing field has become largely level for women and men. In the final section of the chapter, I provide some answers as to why, in that case, so few women are in Congress. Here, I turn to the subtler ways that gender continues to affect congressional elections. The combination of gendered geographic trends, women's presence in different types of congressional races, the lack of women running as Republicans, and the gender gap in political ambition suggests that gender is playing an important role in congressional elections.

THE HISTORICAL EVOLUTION OF WOMEN'S CANDIDACIES FOR CONGRESS

Throughout the 1990s, women made significant strides competing for and winning seats in the U.S. Congress. The 1992 elections, often referred to as the "Year of the Woman," resulted not only in an historic increase in the number of women in both the House and the Senate but also in the promise of movement toward some semblance of gender parity in our political institutions (see Table 7.1). After all, in the history of the

TABLE 7.1: Over time, more Democratic women than Republican women have emerged as House candidates and winners

	1970	1980	1990	1992	2000	2004	2006	2008
General election candidates								
Democratic women	15	27	39	70	80	88	95	95
Republican women	10	25	30	36	42	53	42	38
Total women	25	52	69	106	122	141	137	133
General election winners								
Democratic women	10	11	19	35	41	43	50	58
Percentage of all Democratic winners	3.9	4.5	7.1	13.6	19.4	21.4	21.5	22.6
Republican women	3	10	9	12	18	23	21	17
Percentage of all Republican winners	1.7	5.2	5.4	6.8	8.1	9.9	10.4	9.6

Note: Except where noted, entries represent the raw number of women candidates and winners for each year.
Source: Center for American Women and Politics, 2008 Fact Sheets, http://www.cawp .rutgers.edu/fast_facts/index.php.

U.S. Congress, there have been more than 11,600 male representatives but only 255 female representatives (see Figure 7.1). Only thirty-eight women have ever served in the U.S. Senate, nineteen of whom either were appointed or won special elections.

However, the gains of 1992 were not repeated at a steady pace. Currently, 83 percent of the members of the U.S. Senate and 83 percent of the members of the U.S. House are male. This places the United States eighty-fifth worldwide in terms of the proportion of women serving in the national legislature, a ranking far behind that of many other democratic governments.[10] Further, the overwhelming majority of the women elected to Congress have been white. Of the 75 (out of 435) women elected to the U.S. House in the 2008 election, there are 12 African Americans, 7 Latinas, and 2 Asian Pacific–Pacific Islander Americans. There are no women of color among the seventeen women currently serving in the U.S. Senate.

The continued dearth of women in Congress suggests that a masculine ethos, ever present across the history of Congress, still permeates the congressional electoral environment. A host of interrelated factors – money, familiarity with power brokers, political experience, and support from

Figure 7.1: **Historical gender disparities in congressional representation.**

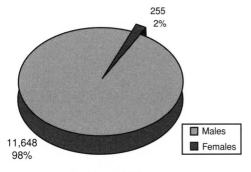

Since 1789 only 2% of members
of Congress have been women.

255
2%

11,648
98%

☐ Males
■ Females

(as of January 2009)

Note: Figure includes both House and Senate members.
Source: Center for American Women and Politics, 2009 Fact Sheet.

the political parties – all contribute to a winning campaign. Traditional
candidates are members of the political or economic elite. Most emerge
from lower-level elected offices or work in their communities, typically
in law or business. They tend to receive encouragement to run for office
from influential members of the community, party officials, or outgo-
ing incumbents. And these same elites who encourage candidacies also
contribute money to campaigns and hold fund-raisers. This process has
been in place for most of the recent history of congressional candidacies and, for obvious reasons, has served men well and women very
poorly.

Because they have been excluded from their communities' economic
and political elites throughout much of the twentieth century, women's
paths to Congress often take different forms. Widows of congressmen
who died in office dominated the first wave of successful female candidates. Between 1916 and 1964, twenty-eight of the thirty-two widows
nominated to fill their husbands' seats won their elections, for a victory
rate of 88 percent. Across the same time period, only 32 of the 199 non-
widows who garnered their parties' nominations were elected (a 14 percent victory rate).[11] Overall, roughly half the women who served in the
House in this time period were widows. Congressional widows were the
one type of woman candidate who was readily acceptable to party leaders
at this time.

The 1960s and 1970s marked the emergence of a second type of woman candidate – one who turned her attention from civic volunteerism to politics. A few women involved in grassroots community politics rode their activism to Washington. Notable figures who pursued this path include Patsy Mink in Hawaii, elected in 1964; Shirley Chisholm in New York, elected in 1968; Bella Abzug in New York, elected in 1970; and Pat Schroeder in Colorado and Barbara Jordan in Texas, both elected in 1972.

We are currently in the third and possibly final stage of the evolution of women's candidacies. The prevailing model of running for Congress is far less rigid. The combination of decreased political party power and growing media influence facilitates the emergence of a more diverse array of candidates competing successfully for their parties' nominations. Converging with this less rigid path is an increase in the number of women who now fit the profile of a "traditional" candidate. Women's presence in the fields of business and law has dramatically increased. Further, the number of women serving in state legislatures, a springboard to Congress, has roughly tripled since 1975 (although it is important to note that women's presence in the state governments has stalled in recent elections; for more on this, see Kira Sanbonmatsu's Chapter 10 in this volume). Together, these developments help to explain why the eligibility pool of prospective women candidates grew substantially throughout the 1990s.

Despite the growth in the number of eligible women who could run for Congress, the most recent congressional election cycles indicate that women's progress has continued only in fits and starts. The 2002 elections marked the first time since 1994 that women did not increase their presence in the House. Women had a relatively good year in the 2004 elections, gaining eight House seats. In 2006 and 2008, there were more modest gains for women, with net increases of four and three new House members, respectively. In the Senate, the rate of increase has been just as slow, with a net increase of four women over the past five election cycles. Perhaps more important, though, there has not been a steady increase in the number of women filing to run for Congress. In 2006 and 2008, slightly more than two hundred women filed to run for the U.S. House of Representatives; more women sought office in the 1992 and 1996 House elections. Similar patterns exist for U.S. Senate races. A record twelve women won their party's U.S. Senate nominations in 2006, but the number dropped to a mere seven candidates in 2008. Table 7.1 presents the number of women candidates who won their party nominations and ran in House general elections from 1970 through 2008. Although there has been steady, albeit slow, growth in the number of women running in general election races over the past thirty years, the only dramatic single-year jump occurred in 1992. The 2004 election did set a record, with 141 women candidates winning their party nominations for House seats. But to put this number into perspective, it is helpful to recognize that more than 675 male candidates garnered their parties' nominations. The number of major-party nominees has actually come down a little bit in the past two election cycles. An important factor illustrated in Table 7.1 is the divergent paths of the Democratic and Republican parties. The Democrats have been on a slow and steady path, continually increasing the number of women candidates and winners. The Republicans, in contrast, have put forward significantly fewer women over the past two election cycles, and the percentage of women in the Republican House delegation has declined in the past two electoral cycles.

Overall, the historical evolution of women's candidacies demonstrates that we are in a period of increasing opportunities for women candidates, yet progress is very slow. From this point, we turn our attention to examining the potential challenges that are facing women candidates, focusing on the question of why there continue to be so few women elected to the U.S. Congress.

MEN AND WOMEN RUNNING FOR CONGRESS: THE GENERAL INDICATORS

In assessing why so few women serve in Congress, most researchers have turned to key election statistics and compared female and male congressional candidates. Turning first to overt voter bias against women candidates, the research is mixed. In a series of experimental studies in which participants are presented with a hypothetical match-up between men and women candidates, researchers have identified bias against women.[12] But studies that focus on actual vote totals fail to uncover evidence of bias.[13] Barbara Burrell, a contributor to this volume, concluded in an earlier study that candidates' sex accounts for less than 1 percent of the variation in the vote for House candidates from 1968 to 1992. Kathy Dolan, who carried out a comprehensive 2004 study of patterns in gender and voting, concluded that candidates' sex is a relevant factor only in rare electoral circumstances.[14] Jennifer Lawless and Kathryn Pearson, in an analysis of congressional primary elections between 1958 and 2004, found that women candidates are more likely to face more crowded

TABLE 7.2: Women and men House candidates have similar vote shares for 2006 and 2008

	2006		2008	
	Women %	Men %	Women %	Men %
Democrats				
Incumbents	74	75	72*	67
	(44)	(146)	(43)	(143)
Challengers	41	38	40*	37
	(45)	(154)	(35)	(122)
Open seats	62*	50	51	49
	(12)	(25)	(10)	(26)
Republicans				
Incumbents	56*	61	58	60
	(23)	(182)	(17)	(140)
Challengers	29	29	31	30
	(16)	(134)	(19)	(167)
Open seats	45	49	47	47
	(7)	(30)	(2)	(34)

Notes: Candidates running unopposed are omitted from these results. Entries indicate mean vote share won. Parentheses indicate the total number of candidates for each category. Significance levels: *$p < .05$; difference of means test.

Source: Compiled from *New York Times* listing of election results.

and competitive primaries, though they did not find evidence of voter bias.[15]

If we look at the performance of men and women in House elections in 2006 and 2008, we arrive at a similar conclusion. The data presented in Table 7.2 confirm that there is no widespread voter bias against women candidates. In the most recent House races, women and men fared similarly in terms of raw vote totals. In fact, Democratic women running for open seats in 2006 and as incumbents and challengers in 2008 appeared to have a slight advantage over their male counterparts. Conversely, incumbent Republican women fared a little worse in 2006 than did male incumbents. In the Senate, with no more than twelve female general election candidates running in any year, and as few as six in some elections (such as 1996), statistical comparisons are not useful. The general trends, however, reveal no general bias for or against women Senate candidates from 2006 or 2008.

Turning to the second most important indicator of electoral success – fund-raising – we see similar results. In the 1970s and 1980s, because so few women ran for office, many scholars assumed that women in electoral politics simply could not raise the amount of money necessary to mount competitive campaigns. Indeed, older research that focused mostly on anecdotal studies concluded that women ran campaigns with lower levels of funding than did men. More systematic examinations of campaign receipts, however, have uncovered little evidence of sex differences in fund-raising for similarly situated candidates. An early study of congressional candidates from 1972 to 1982 found only a "very weak" relationship between gender and the ability to raise campaign funds.[16] More recent research indicates that, by the 1988 House elections, the disparity between men and women in campaign fund-raising had completely disappeared.[17] In cases where women raised less money than men, the differences were accounted for by incumbency status: male incumbents generally held positions of greater political power and thus attracted larger contributions.[18] Since 1992, political action committees such as EMILY's List have worked to make certain that viable women candidates suffer no disadvantage in fund-raising. (See Chapter 8, by Barbara Burrell, in this volume for a discussion of EMILY's List.)

If we examine fund-raising totals of male and female general election House candidates in 2006 and 2008, we see few gender differences (see Table 7.3). In fact, the discrepancies that do exist reveal an advantage for women candidates in several instances. Women challengers in both parties, for instance, substantially outraised their male counterparts in 2008. The number of women Senate candidates is too small for meaningful statistical comparisons with men. If we look at the three most competitive Senate races in which women ran against men, the results do not suggest any clear gender patterns in fund-raising. In the 2006 open-seat race in Minnesota, Republican Mark Kennedy raised $9,741,224, compared to Democrat Amy Klobuchar's $9,202,052. Klobuchar ultimately won the race handily. In the hotly contested race for Missouri's U.S. Senate seat, Republican incumbent Jim Talent outspent his Democratic opponent Claire McCaskill $23,765,577 to $11,412,117. Despite the financial edge for Talent, McCaskill pulled out the race with a three-point victory. The Democratic tide in 2006 overwhelmed Talent's financial advantage. In 2008, Democratic challenger Jeanne Shaheen in New Hampshire and Republican incumbent John Sununu had similar fund-raising totals, with $8,333,838 and $8,879,301, respectively. In a year of many Democratic success stories, Shaheen won fairly easily. Overall, though, no clear

TABLE 7.3: Women and men House candidates have similar fund-raising patterns for 2006 and 2008

	2006		2008	
	Women	Men	Women	Men
Democrats				
Incumbents	$1,036,889	$1,183,077	$1,305,944	$1,459,846
	(42)	(146)	(50)	(178)
Challengers	1,056,608	477,711	914,181*	528,420
	(41)	(154)	(35)	(122)
Open seats	1,450,498	1,253,155	1,635,608	1,776,123
	(12)	(24)	(10)	(26)
Republicans				
Incumbents	1,904,349	1,417,444	1,597,852	1,414,514
	(23)	(184)	(17)	(154)
Challengers	265,111	289,508	629,246	342,182
	(12)	(134)	(19)	(167)
Open seats	1,175,896	1,570580	600,709	984,990
	(7)	(26)	(2)	(34)

Notes: Candidates running unopposed are omitted from these results. Entries indicate total money raised. Parentheses indicate the total number of candidates in each category. Significance levels: *$p < .10$ in difference of means test.
Source: Compiled from 2008 Federal Election Commission (FEC) reports.

gender differences emerge in House or Senate competition for funds. As Barbara Burrell suggests in her chapter on party organizations and interest groups, women and men may turn to different fund-raising sources, but the net results appear to be similar levels of financial success.

On the basis of general indicators, we see what appears to be a gender-neutral electoral environment. Women are slowly increasing their numbers in Congress, and men and women perform similarly in terms of vote totals and fund-raising. The data certainly suggest that men have lost their stranglehold over the congressional election process and that women can now find excellent political opportunities. But these broad statistical comparisons tell only part of the story.

ARE WOMEN MAKING GAINS EVERYWHERE? STATE AND REGIONAL VARIATION

Women have not been equally successful running for elective office in all parts of the United States. Some regions and states appear to be far more amenable to the election of women than others. But across the 2006 and 2008 congressional elections, women made some significant breakthroughs, with none more apparent than in Oklahoma. The only woman ever to serve in the U.S. Congress from Oklahoma was Alice Mary Robertson, who was elected for one term in 1920. It would take eighty-six years before Oklahoma would elect its next female House member. Republican Mary Fallin had already made history in Oklahoma by becoming the first woman lieutenant governor in 1995. When she decided to run for the open seat in Oklahoma's Fifth District, she was joined in a crowded Republican primary by five other candidates contesting the election. Fallin won the primary, but she did not receive enough votes to avoid a runoff with Oklahoma City mayor Mick Cornett. She ultimately won the runoff and cruised to victory in the general election against a little-known Democrat in the heavily Republican district.

While Fallin was breaking the glass ceiling in Oklahoma in 2006, women challengers running in recent elections in other states with poor records of electing women, such as Iowa, Mississippi, and Alabama, have not been as successful. In Alabama, for instance, the former lieutenant governor Lucy Baxley noted that women have done better in local elections and that "there has been a line" drawn at federal office. The University of Alabama political science professor William H. Stewart simply observed regarding a recently defeated woman candidate, "A good conservative man is the ideal candidate" in that district.[19] After the June 2008 primary in Iowa, John Deeth, writing for the *Iowa Independent*, commented that 2008 might be the year that the "Iowa-Mississippi jinx" was broken.[20] In the primary, the Democrats nominated Becky Greenwald to run against seven-term incumbent Tom Latham in the Fourth District, and Republicans nominated Mariannette Miller-Meeks in the Second District to run against the first-term congressman Dave Loebsack. While there was some initial enthusiasm about the prospects of these candidates, both were defeated handily in the general election.

As the results of recent elections in places like Iowa and Alabama suggest, women may face disadvantages when running for office in some parts of the United States. If we examine the prevalence of male and female House candidates by region and state, we see that the broader inclusion of women in high-level politics has not extended to all regions of the country equally. Table 7.4 tracks women's electoral success in House races since 1970 but breaks the data down by four geographic regions. Before 1990, the Northeast saw two and three times as many women candidates as any other region in the country. The situation changed dramatically with the Year of the Woman elections in 1992.

TABLE 7.4: Sharp regional differences exist in the proportion of U.S. representatives who are women

	West %	South %	Midwest %	Northeast %
1970	3.9	0.0	2.5	4.9
1980	2.6	1.6	3.3	8.1
1990	8.2	2.3	6.2	9.6
1992	17.2	7.9	6.7	12.4
2000	25.8	9.2	10.9	11.3
2002	25.5	8.7	11.5	9.8
2004	26.5	11.0	14.0	10.9
2006	28.6	9.9	18.0	11.6
2008	28.6	9.2	18.0	14.7
Net percentage change (1970 to 2008)	**24.7**	**9.2**	**15.5**	**9.8**

Notes: Percentages reflect the proportion of House members who are women. The ratio for the West is heavily skewed by California; without California, the percentage for the West delegation after the 2008 elections is 20 percent women.
Source: Compiled by author from Center for American Women and Politics, 2008 Fact Sheets.

The number of women winning election to Congress from western states more than doubled; and in the South, the number more than tripled. Gains were much more modest in the Midwest and the Northeast. Since the late 1990s, only the West continues to show clear gains for women. A lot of the gains in the West can be attributed to the high number of women holding House seats from California, but women have a strong record of success in other western states, such as Wyoming, Nevada, and Washington. The geographic breakdown in Table 7.4 puts the 1992 elections, as well as the modest increases of women's elections to Congress since that time, into perspective. The 1992 Year of the Woman gains were largely in the West and the South.

More specific than region, there are also several striking differences among individual states. Consider, for example, that heading into the 2008 elections, nineteen states had no women representatives in Washington. Further, twenty-seven states had never been represented by a woman in the U.S. Senate. Table 7.5 identifies the states with the best and worst records in sending women to serve in the House of Representatives following the 2008 elections. In the 2006 and 2008 elections, women made breakthroughs in a number of states where they had been having

TABLE 7.5: More than one-third of the states had no women serving in the U.S. House of Representatives in 2008

States with no women representatives	States with high percentage of women representatives
Georgia (13)	Nevada (3) – 67%
New Jersey (13)	Hawaii (2) – 50%
Virginia (11)	Maine (2) – 50%
Indiana (9)	New Hampshire (2) – 50%
Alabama (7)	California (53) – 36%
Louisiana (7)	West Virginia (3) – 33%
Kentucky (6)	Colorado (7) – 29%
South Carolina (6)	Ohio (18) – 28%
Iowa (5)[a]	Arizona (8) – 25%
Oregon (5)	Kansas (4) – 25%
Arkansas (4)	Minnesota (8) – 25%
Mississippi (4)[a]	Wisconsin (8) – 25%
Nebraska (3)	Florida (25) – 24%
Utah (3)	Illinois (19) – 21%
Idaho (2)	New York (29) – 21%
Rhode Island (2)	Connecticut (5) – 20%
Alaska (1)	Oklahoma (5) – 20%
Delaware (1)[a]	
Montana (1)	
North Dakota (1)	
Vermont (1)[a]	

[a] Indicates states that have never sent a woman to either the House or Senate.

Notes: Three states – Alaska, Arkansas, and Louisiana – that have no women House members, do have women serving in the U.S. Senate. Two states, each with only one House seat, Wyoming and South Dakota, both have a woman serving. Number in parentheses is the number of House seats in the state as of 2008.

Source: Compiled by author from Center for American Women and Politics, 2008 Fact Sheets.

trouble getting elected. Prior to 2006, some states with relatively large House delegations, including Massachusetts (ten members) and Maryland and Arizona (eight members each), had sent no women to the House for some time, but women candidates were successful in these states in recent elections. Still, several larger states continue to lag behind in electing women to Congress. Georgia and New Jersey, with thirteen House seats each, and Virginia, with eleven, have no women representatives. Also, among some of the largest states women are still scarce – only two of Pennsylvania's nineteen House members are women, and only three of the thirty-two House members from Texas are women.

Table 7.5 also demonstrates that women congressional candidates have succeeded in a number of high-population states, like California, Florida, and New York. Why have women done well in these states and not others? California, New York, and Florida are among those states with the biggest delegations, so perhaps we can assume that more political opportunities for women drive the candidacies. But this would not explain women's lack of success in large states like Texas and Pennsylvania. Moreover, what explains women's success in states like Missouri, where, for much of the 1990s, three of the state's nine House members were women? Missouri borders Iowa, which has never elected a woman House candidate. By the same token, why has Connecticut historically elected so many more women than neighboring Massachusetts?

Some political scientists argue that state political culture serves as an important determinant of women's ability to win elective office. The researchers Barbara Norrander and Clyde Wilcox have found considerable disparities in the progress of women's election to state legislatures across various states and regions. They explain the disparities by pointing to differences in state ideology and state culture.[21] States with a conservative ideology and a "traditionalist or moralist" culture are less likely to elect women.[22] A strong correlation between the percentage of women in the state legislature and the number of women in Congress, however, does not always exist. Massachusetts and New Jersey, for example, are better than average in terms of the number of women serving in the state legislature, yet each has a very poor record of electing women to the House of Representatives.

Barbara Palmer and Dennis Simon, in their book *Breaking the Political Glass Ceiling: Women and Congressional Elections*, propose a diagnosis for the specific causes of regional and state differences in electing women U.S. House members. Examining all congressional elections between 1972 and 2000, Palmer and Simon introduce the idea of women-friendly districts. They find that several district characteristics are important predictors of the emergence and success of women candidates. For example, U.S. House districts that are not heavily conservative, are urban, are not in the South, have higher levels of racial minorities, and have higher levels of education are much more likely to have a record of electing women candidates. Palmer and Simon's findings suggest that the manner in which gender manifests itself in the political systems and environments of individual states is an important part of the explanation for why so few women are in Congress.[23]

ARE WOMEN RUNNING FOR BOTH PARTIES AND UNDER THE BEST CIRCUMSTANCES?

Most congressional elections are dominated by hopeless challengers running against safely entrenched incumbents. Reporters for *Congressional Quarterly* completed an analysis of all 435 U.S. House races in June 2004, five months before the 2004 elections, and concluded that only 21 (out of 404) races with incumbents running were competitive.[24] Even in the more tumultuous elections of 2006 and 2008, fewer than 20 percent of House races were rated as competitive by the parties and experts. In 2006, with the political environment dramatically shifting, one expert projected that 60 of the 435 House races could be considered competitive.[25] The political environment stayed relatively fluid in 2008, when the noted political analyst Charlie Cook rated 77 of 435 House elections as competitive, but with only 27 as true "toss-ups."[26]

Expectedly, political scientists often identify the incumbency advantage as one of the leading explanations for women's slow entry into electoral politics. Low turnover, a direct result of incumbency, provides few opportunities for women to increase their numbers in male-dominated legislative bodies. Between 1946 and 2002, only 8 percent of all challengers defeated incumbent members of the U.S. House of Representatives.[27] In most races, the incumbent cruised to reelection with well more than 60 percent of the vote. Accordingly, as the congressional elections scholars Ronald Keith Gaddie and Charles Bullock state, "Open seats, not the defeat of incumbents, are the portal through which most legislators enter Congress."[28]

In the 2008 general elections, only 36 of the 435 seats in the House of Representatives did not have an incumbent running. Of the thirty-five seats up for reelection in the Senate, only five were open. Ninety-six percent of the 399 House incumbents who ran in the general election won their races. Moreover, because open-seat races tend to attract the largest number of qualified and experienced candidates, particularly those with experience serving in local and state government offices, they also tend to be better funded.

To begin to assess whether women are as likely as men to take advantage of the dynamics associated with an open-seat race, we can examine the presence and performance of women in open-seat House contests. Table 7.6 compares women's presence in House elections by time period, party affiliation, and type of seat. In this analysis, I divide the data into two time periods and the two most recent elections to more clearly examine the evolution of women's candidacies. As expected, women were

TABLE 7.6: Types of seats contested by women candidates in the U.S. House vary by years and party

Type of seat	1980–90		1992–2004		2006		2008	
	Democrat %	Republican %	Democrat %	Republican %	Democrat %	Republican %	Democrat %	Republican %
Open seat	11	8	25	15	32	19	28	6
	(24)	(16)	(88)	(49)	(12)	(7)	(10)	(2)
Challengers	10	9	21	12	21	8	22	10
	(80)	(98)	(230)	(153)	(41)	(12)	(35)	(19)
Incumbents	4	5	14	8	22	11	22	10
	(59)	(52)	(224)	(101)	(42)	(23)	(50)	(17)

Note: Entries indicate the percentage of all candidates for that electoral category who were women. The number of candidates for each category is in parentheses.

Source: Compiled by author from Center for American Women and Politics, 2008 Fact Sheets and *New York Times* listing of election results.

significantly more likely to run for office in the later eras, although the increase in women candidates is not constant across parties. In the 1980s, the parties were very similar in terms of the types of races women ran in. Between the first and second time period, however, the number of women Democrats running in all types of races more than doubled, whereas the increases among the Republicans were quite small. The disparities between the parties became even starker in the most recent elections. In both 2006 and 2008, roughly 30 percent of the Democratic open-seat candidates were women. The Republicans had their highest share of women open-seat candidates in 2006, at almost 20 percent, but in 2008, the Republicans nominated only two women to run for open-seat races. With open-seat races usually providing some of the best opportunities for electoral pickups, Democrats are nominating women to run for these seats but Republicans are not.

Aside from open-seat races in 2006 and 2008, the Democrats have been much more likely than the Republicans to nominate women to run for all seats (see also Table 7.1). This carries serious long-term implications for the number of women serving in Congress. For women to achieve full parity in U.S. political institutions, women must be represented fully in both parties.

ARE MEN AND WOMEN EQUALLY AMBITIOUS TO RUN FOR CONGRESS?

The decision to run for office and ultimately seek a seat in Congress is a critical area of inquiry for those interested in the role of gender in electoral politics. Examples abound from women politicians who expressed some difficulty in taking the plunge. The current Wisconsin congresswoman Gwen Moore never thought of herself as someone who would run for office until she was coaxed to run for a state legislative seat in the 1990s.[29] Even Nancy Pelosi claims that she had never thought of running for office until she was encouraged to do so in 1987.[30]

Until recently, very little empirical research had explored the initial decision to run for office. But if the general election playing field is largely level, then gender differences in political ambition likely provide a crucial explanation for women's underrepresentation in Congress. In 2001 and 2008, Jennifer Lawless and I conducted the Citizen Political Ambition Panel Study. This is a series of surveys that ask women and men working in the three professions (law, business, and education) most likely to precede a career in Congress about their ambition to someday run for

TABLE 7.7: Among potential candidates, women are less interested than men in seeking elective office

	2001		2008	
	Women %	Men %	Women %	Men %
Has thought about running for office	36	55	36	53
Discussed running with party leaders	4	8	7	12
Discussed running with friends and family	17	29	20	28
Discussed running with community leaders	6	12	8	12
Solicited or discussed financial contributions with potential supporters	2	4	3	6
Investigated how to place your name on the ballot	4	10	6	11
Sample size	1,248	1,454	689	848

Notes: Sample is composed of lawyers, business leaders and executives, and educators. Entries indicate percentage responding "yes." All differences between women and men are significant at $p < .05$.

Sources: Adapted from the Citizen Political Ambition Study. For 2001, see Richard L. Fox and Jennifer L. Lawless, "Entering the Arena: Gender and the Decision to Run for Office," *American Journal of Political Science*, 2004, 48(2): 264–80. For 2008, see Jennifer L. Lawless and Richard L. Fox, "Why Are Women Still Not Running for Public Office?" *Brookings Institute Issues in Governance Studies* 16, May 2008.

elective office. Table 7.7 shows some of the results of the survey, focusing on whether women and men have ever thought about running for office and whether they have ever taken any of the steps that usually precede a candidacy, such as speaking with party officials and community leaders. On the critical question of interest in running for office, the results of the study highlighted a substantial gender gap in political ambition. The results of the most recent survey in 2008 reveal that there has been almost no change in the gap across the past decade. In 2001, there was a 19 percent gap, with men more likely than women to have thought about running for office. In 2008, the gap stood at 17 percent, virtually unchanged. In terms of the concrete steps that a potential candidate might take before running for office, the gender gaps on all of those measures were roughly unchanged across the time period. Even though all of the empirical evidence shows that women who run for office are just as likely as men to be victorious, a much smaller number of women than men are

TABLE 7.8: Among potential candidates, women are less interested than men in running for the U.S. House or Senate

	2001		2008	
	Women %	Men %	Women %	Men %
First office you would likely run for . . .				
U.S. House of Representatives	5	10	3	7
U.S. Senate	2	4	0	3
Interested in someday running for . . .				
U.S. House of Representatives	15	27	11	21
U.S. Senate	13	20	9	16
Sample size	816	1,022	689	848

Notes: Sample is composed of lawyers, business leaders and executives, and educators who indicated some degree of interest in running for office. Entries indicate percentage responding "yes." All differences between women and men are significant at $p < .05$.

Sources: Adapted from the Citizen Political Ambition Study. See Richard L. Fox and Jennifer L. Lawless, "Entering the Arena: Gender and the Decision to Run for Office," *American Journal of Political Science*, 2004, 48(2): 264–80. For 2008, see Jennifer L. Lawless and Richard L. Fox, "Why Are Women Still Not Running for Public Office?" *Brookings Institute Issues in Governance Studies* 16, May 2008.

likely to emerge as candidates, because women are far less likely than men to consider running for office.

Further, when we consider male and female potential candidates' interest in running for Congress, the gender gap in political ambition is amplified. Table 7.8 shows the interest of potential candidates in running for the U.S. House and Senate in both waves of the survey. Potential candidates were asked to identify what offices they would be most likely to seek first. They were also asked to identify which offices they might ever be interested in running for. For both questions, men were significantly more likely than women to demonstrate an interest in running for Congress. Men were twice as likely as women to name the U.S. House and U.S. Senate as the first offices they would run for. Again, the gender gap in interest in congressional offices persisted across both time periods. The one change between 2001 and 2008 was that both women and men expressed less interest in running for Congress overall, likely a result of the increasingly negative and partisan view of politics in Washington.

Ultimately, three critical factors uncovered in the Citizen Political Ambition Panel Study explain the gender gap in ambition. First, women are significantly less likely than men to receive encouragement to run for office. This difference is very important, because potential candidates are twice as likely to think about running for office when a party leader, elected official, or political activist attempts to recruit them as candidates. Second, women are significantly less likely than men to view themselves as qualified to run for office. In other words, women, even in the top tier of professional accomplishment, tend not to consider themselves qualified to run for political office, even when they have the same objective credentials and experiences as men. Third, even among this group of professionals, women were much more likely to state that they were responsible for the majority of child care and household duties. Even though many of the women in the study had blazed trails in the formerly male professions of law and business, they were still serving as the primary caretakers of their homes. As a result, many women noted that they simply did not have the time to even think about running for office.[31]

CONCLUSION AND DISCUSSION

When researchers and political scientists in the late 1970s and early 1980s began to study the role of gender in electoral politics, concerns about basic fairness and political representation motivated many of their investigations. For many scholars, the notion of governing bodies overwhelmingly dominated by men offends a sense of simple justice. In this vein, some researchers argue that the reality of a male-dominated government suggests to women citizens that the political system is not fully open to them. These concerns are as pertinent today as they were in the past. As Susan J. Carroll and I noted in the introduction to this volume, a growing body of empirical research finds that a political system that does not allow for women's full inclusion in positions of political power increases the possibility that gender-salient issues will be overlooked. Evidence based on the behavior of public officials clearly demonstrates that women are more likely than men to promote legislation geared toward ameliorating women's economic and social status, especially concerning issues of health care, poverty, education, and gender equity.[32] Despite the substantive and symbolic importance of women's full inclusion in the electoral arena, the number of women serving in elected bodies remains low. This chapter's overview of women's performance in congressional elections makes it clear that we need to adopt a more nuanced approach if we are to understand gender's evolving role in the electoral arena.

As to answering this chapter's central question of why there are still so few women in Congress, two broad findings emerge from the analysis.

First, on a more optimistic note, women now compete in U.S. House and Senate races more successfully than at any previous time in history. There are almost no gender differences in terms of the major indicators of electoral success – vote totals and fund-raising. The evidence presented in this chapter continues to show that women and men general election candidates performed similarly in the 2006 and 2008 elections. On the basis of the results of recent congressional elections, I confirm, as a number of other studies have found, that there is no evidence of widespread gender bias among voters and financial contributors.

The second broad finding to emerge from this chapter, however, is that gender continues to play an important role in the electoral arena and in some cases works to keep the number of women running for Congress low. Notably, there are sharp state and regional differences in electing men and women to Congress. Women cannot emerge in greater numbers until the candidacies of women are embraced throughout the entire United States and by both parties. Women's full inclusion will not be possible if the overwhelming majority of women candidates continue to identify with the Democratic Party. Recent declines in the number of women running as Republicans bode very poorly for the future, at least in the short term. Further, the almost impenetrable incumbency advantage and the dearth of open-seat opportunities make the prospect for any sharp increase in the number of women serving in Congress dim. Finally, and perhaps most important, gender differences in political ambition – particularly in the ambition to run for the U.S. Congress – suggest that gender is exerting its strongest impact at the earliest stages of the electoral process. Many women who would make ideal candidates never actually consider running for office. The notion of entering politics still appears not to be a socialized norm for women. As these findings suggest, gender permeates the electoral environment in subtle and nuanced ways. Broad empirical analyses tend to overlook these dynamics, yet the reality is that these dynamics help explain why so few women occupy positions on Capitol Hill.

NOTES

1 Gail Russell Chaddock and Mark Sappenfield. November 14, 2002. Pelosi Shatters a Marble Ceiling. *Christian Science Monitor*, 1.
2 NBC News/*Wall Street Journal* Poll. December 2002. <http://www.polling report.com> October 4, 2004.
3 Chaddock and Sappenfield, 1.

4 Margaret Talev. November 8, 2006. Pelosi Likely Next Speaker; Other Top Jobs up for Grabs. *Seattle Times*.

5 *USA Today*/Gallup Poll. November 7–9, 2008. <http://www.pollingreport .com> December 1, 2009.

6 James Dao and Adam Nagourney. February 19, 2006. They Served, and Now They're Running. *New York Times*, section 4, 1.

7 Bryan Bender. February 9, 2006. Band of Democrats Touts Military Values; 40 Veterans Launch Bid to Serve Nation Again – In Congress. *Boston Globe*, A2.

8 Shauna Curphey. March 22, 2003. 1 in 7 U.S. Military Personnel in Iraq is Female. Women's eNews.

9 Anushka Asthana. October 7, 2006. A Political Opportunity for Women; Advocates Predict Gains in Congress and Push for More Participation. *Washington Post*, A9.

10 Inter-Parliamentary Union. 2009. Women in National Parliaments. <http://www.ipu.org/wmn-e/classif.htm> June 30, 2009.

11 Irwin Gertzog. 1984. *Congressional Women*. New York: Praeger, 18.

12 For examples of experimental designs that identify voter bias, see Leonie Huddy and Nadya Terkildsen. 1993. Gender Stereotypes and the Perception of Male and Female Candidates. *American Journal of Political Science* 37: 119–47; Leonie Huddy and Nadya Terkildsen. 1993. The Consequences of Gender Stereotypes for Women Candidates at Different Levels and Types of Office. *Political Research Quarterly* 46: 503–25; and Richard L. Fox and Eric R. A. N. Smith. 1998. The Role of Candidate Sex in Voter Decision-Making. *Political Psychology* 19: 405–19.

13 For a comprehensive examination of vote totals through the mid-1990s, see Richard A. Seltzer, Jody Newman, and M. Voorhees Leighton. 1997. *Sex as a Political Variable*. Boulder, CO: Lynne Reinner.

14 Kathleen A. Dolan. 2004. *Voting for Women*. Boulder, CO: Westview.

15 Jennifer Lawless and Kathryn Pearson. 2008. The Primary Reason for Women's Under-Representation: Re-evaluating the Conventional Wisdom. *Journal of Politics* 70(1): 67–82.

16 Barbara Burrell. 1985. Women and Men's Campaigns for the U.S. House of Representatives, 1972–1982: A Finance Gap? *American Political Quarterly* 13: 251–72.

17 Barbara Burrell. 1994. *A Woman's Place Is in the House*. Ann Arbor: University of Michigan Press, 105.

18 Carole Jean Uhlaner and Kay Lehman Schlozman. 1986. Candidate Gender and Congressional Campaign Receipts. *Journal of Politics* 52: 391–409.

19 Lauren Shepherd. February 18, 2004. Belk Hoping to Break through Glass Ceiling in Conservative Ala. *The Hill*.

20 John Deeth. May 12, 2008. Miller-Meeks seeks to Break Iowa-Mississippi Jinx. *Iowa Independent*.

21 Barbara Norrander and Clyde Wilcox. 1998. The Geography of Gender Power: Women in State Legislatures. In *Women and Elective Office*, ed. Sue Thomas and Clyde Wilcox. New York: Oxford University Press.

22 Kira Sanbonmatsu. 2002. Political Parties and the Recruitment of Women to State Legislatures. *Journal of Politics* 64(3): 791–809.

23 Barbara Palmer and Dennis Simon. 2008. *The Political Glass Ceiling: Women and Congressional Elections*, 2nd ed. New York: Routledge.

24 Republicans Maintain a Clear Edge in House Contests. June 4, 2004. *CQ Weekly*.

25 Larry J. Sabato and David Wasserman. Crystal Ball 2006: The Predictions. Center for Politics, November 2, 2006. <http://www.centerforpolitics.org/crystalball/article.php?id=LJS2006110201> November 2008.

26 Charlie Cook. 2008. Cook Political Report. <http://www.cookpolitical.com/node/1774> February 15, 2009.

27 Gary C. Jacobsen. 2004. *The Politics of Congressional Elections*, 6th ed. New York: Longman, 23.

28 Ronald Keith Gaddie and Charles S. Bullock. 2000. *Elections to Open Seats in the U.S. House*. Lanham: Rowman and Littlefield, 1.

29 Reluctant to Take the Plunge. May 29, 2008. *USA Today*, 10A.

30 Dana Wilkey. November 13, 2002. From Political Roots to Political Leader, Pelosi Is the Real Thing. Copley News Service.

31 Jennifer L. Lawless and Richard L. Fox. 2005. *It Takes a Candidate: Why Women Don't Run for Office*. New York: Cambridge University Press.

32 For one of the most recent analyses of how women in Congress address different policy issues from those that men address, see Michele L. Swers. 2002. *The Difference Women Make*. Chicago: University of Chicago Press.

8 Political Parties and Women's Organizations
Bringing Women into the Electoral Arena

Contemporary U.S. elections tend to be candidate centered, but political parties and other political organizations also help candidates gain public office, particularly at the national level. They are especially significant for newcomers to the campaign process, and they played key roles in the campaigns of women in the 2008 election.

Democratic women candidates in particular have benefited from party organizational and women's groups activities in recent electoral cycles. A substantial national growth in party resources in the 2006 and 2008 elections favored Democrats, and thus female Democratic candidates. Republican women, particularly those who are pro-choice (a minority position within the activist base of the Republican Party) have access to training and some recruitment activities on the part of their national party organizations and women's groups, but in general they have been much less advantaged. Few Republican women have entered primaries for national elective office, whether through strategic decisions of their own (realizing that the political atmosphere was not conducive to ultimate Republican victories) or from anemic recruitment efforts by party leaders in districts or states leaning favorably toward their party.

At the end of the 2008 election, the gap at the national level between the numbers of Democratic and Republican women officeholders was wider than ever. The defeat of U.S. Senator Elizabeth Dole by Democrat Kay Hagan in North Carolina meant that only four Republican women senators would serve in the 111th Congress (2009–10), compared to thirteen Democratic women.[1] Women would be 22 percent of all Senate Democrats, but just 10 percent of Senate Republicans. In the U.S. House of Representatives, fifty-eight Democratic and seventeen Republican women were elected, respectively 23 percent and 10 percent of their parties' caucuses. Only two Republican women were newly elected to the

House, while eight new Democratic women were elected. In addition, four Democratic women had won special elections to the House during the 110th Congress, making for a twelve-to-two Democratic advantage in seating new women. At the state legislative level, while the numbers of women elected overall increased in 2008, the numbers of Republican women declined to levels not seen since 1988.[2]

Organizational activity targeting officeholding from the local level to the highest levels and across generations should certainly be considered a major characteristic of the U.S. women's movement at the beginning of the new millennium. To understand the contemporary picture, this chapter will review the historical development of women's engagement in the political party organizations, party efforts to elect women to national office, and the development of women's campaign organizations. The chapter touches on several interrelated topics:

The relationships of national political parties and women's organizations with women running for national legislative office

The efforts of women's groups to recruit, train, and support women candidates for state- and local-level public offices

Activities to promote a sense of political efficacy and interest among girls and young women to stimulate them to think about political careers

WOMEN WITHIN THE PARTIES: HISTORICAL BACKGROUND

Beginning with the suffragists, women have a long and complex history of working within party organizations to become voters, attain political influence, and help other women to win electoral office. Table 8.1 presents a chronology of important dates in the history of parties, women's organizations, and women's candidacies for public office from suffrage to the contemporary period.

Suffragists lobbied party organizations to include planks supporting the women's vote in their platforms. By their account, they undertook 277 such campaigns in the seventy-two-year effort to secure the right to vote.[3]

In the years immediately preceding the passage of the Nineteenth Amendment, party leaders feared the entrance of women onto the voter rolls. The major political parties worried that women, armed with the vote, might form their own parties and act independently in the political process, undermining the capacity of major parties to control elections

TABLE 8.1: Important dates in the history of parties, women's organizations, and women's candidacies for public office

1918	Republican Women's National Executive Committee established.
1919	Democratic National Committee passes a resolution recommending that the Democratic State Committees "take such practical action as will provide the women of their respective states with representation, both as officers and as members thereof;" also passes a resolution calling for equal representation of the sexes on the Executive Committee of the Democratic National Committee.
	Republican National Committee urges state and country committees to select "one man and one woman member" as "the principle of representation."
1920	Delegates to the Democratic National Convention vote to double the size of their national committee and "one man and one woman hereafter should be selected from each state."
1924	Republican National Committee votes for one male and one female representative from each state.
1940	The Republican Party endorses an Equal Rights Amendment to the Constitution in its party platform for the first time.
1944	The Democratic Party includes a plank endorsing the Equal Rights Amendment in its platform for the first time.
1966	The National Organization for Women (NOW) is founded.
1971	The National Women's Political Caucus (NWPC) is founded, with the major aim of increasing the number of women in public office.
1972	U.S. Representative Shirley Chisholm seeks the Democratic nomination for president.
	Frances "Sissy" Farenthold's name is placed in nomination for vice president at the Democratic National Convention. She receives 420 votes.
	Jean Westwood is appointed chair of the Democratic National Committee.
1974	The Women's Campaign Fund is founded, the first women's PAC. Mary Louise Smith is appointed chair of the Republican National Committee.
1975	NOW forms a PAC to fund feminist candidates.
1976	Democrats mandate equal division between men and women in their national convention delegations, effective in 1980.
1977	The NWPC forms a PAC, the Campaign Support Committee.
1979	The NWPC forms a second PAC, the Victory Fund.
1980	The Republican Party removes support for the Equal Rights Amendment from its platform.

1984   Democrats nominate U.S. Representative Geraldine Ferraro for vice president.

The National Political Congress of Black Women is founded.

1985   EMILY's List is founded on the principle that "Early Money Is Like Yeast – it makes the dough rise."

1991   Clarence Thomas, a nominee for associate justice of the U.S. Supreme Court, is accused of sexual harassment by former staffer Anita Hill. Many women are disturbed by the absence of women senators and the dismissive attitude toward Hill during Thomas's confirmation hearings, and one result is a record number of women seeking office.

1992   The WISH List is founded.

The NWPC sponsors the Showcase of Pro-Choice Republican Women Candidates at the Republican convention, with thirteen GOP candidates.

NOW adopts the Elect Women for a Change campaign and raises about $500,000 for women candidates.

NOW also initiates the formation of a national third party, the 21st Century Party.

1999   Elizabeth Dole enters the Republican race for president but drops out before the first caucuses and primaries.

2003   Former U.S Senator Carol Moseley Braun enters the Democratic race for president but drops out before the first caucuses and primaries.

2006   U.S. Representative Nancy Pelosi is chosen by her Democratic colleagues to be Speaker of the House, putting her second in line for the presidency and making her the highest female constitutional officer ever in the United States.

2007   U.S. Senator Hillary Clinton enters the Democratic primary for president of the United States.

2008   In June 2008, at the end of the primary season, Hillary Clinton drops out, conceding the race to Barack Obama after putting "18 million cracks into the political glass ceiling."

U.S. Senator John McCain, Republican nominee for president, chooses Alaska Governor Sarah Palin as his vice presidential running mate, making her the first Republican female nominee for that position.

Source: Compiled by author.

and the spoils of victory. William Chafe notes that parties were concerned about the creation of a "petticoat hierarchy which may at will upset all orderly slates and commit undreamed of executions at the polls" and viewed the formation of the nonpartisan League of Women Voters as threatening to their hegemony in the electoral process.[4]

For these reasons, as Kristi Andersen notes:

> The national party organizations, sensitive to the demands and the
> potential influence of a new element in the electorate, responded
> to the imminent granting of suffrage with organizational changes
> designed to give women nominally equal roles in the party hierarchy
> and to allow for the efficient mobilization of women voters by women
> leaders.[5]

Fearing the independence of women voters, the parties undertook a dual
effort, establishing distinct organizations led by women to work with
women voters and making efforts to integrate women into their leadership committees through expansion of those organizations.

The Democratic Party acted first, creating in 1916 a Women's Bureau
to mobilize women voters in the western states where they had already
gained the right to vote. In 1917, the Democratic National Committee
(DNC), the main governing body of the party, created a women's version
of itself, staffed by appointed female members from the states that had
already granted women full suffrage.[6] In 1919, they adopted a plan for an
Associate National Committee of Women. The DNC also agreed that year
to appoint a woman associate member from each state based on the nomination of the state committeeman. In addition, the DNC recommended
that Democratic state committees provide women with similar representation at the state and local levels and equal representation of men and
women on the executive committee. At their 1920 national convention,
delegates voted to double the size of their national committee and stipu-
lated that "one man and one woman hereafter should be selected from
each state."[7]

In 1918, the Republicans created the Republican Women's National
Executive Committee. The next year, they adopted a plan calling for state
chairmen to appoint "a State Executive Committee of women numbering
from five to fifteen members to act with the State Central Committee"
and established a women's division.[8] But in 1920, they rejected equal
representation for women on the Republican National Committee (RNC),
although eight women were appointed to its twenty-one-member Executive Committee. In 1924, Republican leaders agreed to the enlargement
of the RNC and the election of male and female members from each state.

Women came to represent about 10–15 percent of the delegates to
the parties' national conventions in the years after they won the vote.
Although they gained some measure of formal equality in the party
organizations in those days, women activists struggled for many years

to gain respect and influence within the parties, in part because women did not vote differently than men or in large numbers.

By the latter part of the 1960s, women were still only marginally represented within the ranks of party leadership. Party organizations had not made any particular effort to promote women as candidates for public office, and women were encouraged to run primarily in situations where the party had little chance of winning.

As the second women's rights movement took off, however, activists adopted the strategy of engaging in partisan politics. The National Women's Political Caucus (NWPC), established in 1971 to "help elect women and also men who declare themselves ready to fight for the needs and rights of women and all underrepresented groups," pressured both parties to increase their representation of women as national convention delegates in 1972. The caucus created Democratic and Republican party task forces and challenged both parties to help women achieve positions of public leadership.

The Democratic Party undertook a reform effort in the wake of the debacle of its 1968 national convention and its subsequent loss in the presidential election, establishing the McGovern-Fraser Commission to spearhead the changes. The commission included in its 1971 report a recommendation that racial minorities, youths, and women be represented in state delegations "in reasonable relationship to their presence in the population of the state." The NWPC pushed the Democratic Party to interpret "reasonable representation" as meaning matching the proportions in a state's population. As a result, they were successful in substantially increasing the percentage of women as convention delegates. Prior to the reform effort, at the 1968 Democratic National Convention, only 13 percent of the delegates had been women; in 1972, women constituted 40 percent of the delegates. The push for greater representation of women among delegates continued throughout the 1970s, and since 1980, Democratic Party rules have mandated gender equity within all state delegations to its national conventions.

While the Republicans have not followed the Democrats in mandating equal numbers of men and women in convention delegations, in the 1970s, the GOP, under pressure from the delegates, adopted affirmative steps to encourage state parties to elect more women as convention delegates. The percentage of female Republican delegates increased from 17 percent in 1968 to 30 percent in 1972.

Jo Freeman, one of the founders of the women's liberation movement in the United States and an astute observer of U.S. political parties, describes the parties as having become completely polarized around feminism and their reaction to it. In her view, "On feminist issues and concerns the parties are not following the traditional pattern of presenting different versions of the same thing, or following each other's lead into new territory. They are presenting two different and conflicting visions of how Americans should engage in everyday life."[9] The Republican Party has become more hospitable to antifeminism, while the Democratic Party is perceived as the more pro-feminist party.[10] But both parties want to appear to promote women in political leadership positions. Thus, in an example Freeman cites, the 1992 national conventions emphasized showcasing women candidates and raising money to elect more women far more than discussing polarizing issues.

National party conventions have changed dramatically in recent decades; although once they were occasions for political power struggles and ideological battles with uncertain outcomes fought before the public on television, they have become staged media events to spotlight candidates and promote a favorable impression of the party among the general public. Party platforms and party nominees have already been decided before the convention convenes, requiring only formal ratification. In this new style of convention, one function is to highlight party support for women in political leadership positions, presumably in an effort to attract the support of women voters.

THE 2008 NATIONAL PARTY CONVENTIONS AND WOMEN'S POLITICAL LEADERSHIP

The 2008 conventions targeted women voters as never before, with the longer-term goal of one day cracking the ultimate political glass ceiling by electing women to the presidency and vice presidency. The speeches by potential first lady Michelle Obama, Senator Hillary Clinton, and Republican vice presidential nominee Alaska Governor Sarah Palin were among the highlights of the two parties' national conventions in 2008 as far as "women's events" were concerned and second only to the presidential candidates' acceptance speeches in attracting attention. Indeed, Sarah Palin's acceptance speech drew the highest national audience of all. Many other women shared the podiums during these meetings. And for the first time, all four of the Democratic Party's convention chairs were women: Atlanta's mayor Shirley Franklin, Kansas's governor Kathleen Sebelius, Texas's state senator Leticia Van de Putte, and U.S. House Speaker Nancy Pelosi. Arizona's governor Janet Napolitano headed the

Democratic Platform Committee. And, as Women's eNews reported, the 2008 Democratic platform included "an enhanced section on women's rights that states, 'We believe that standing up for our country means standing up against sexism and all intolerance. . . . Responsibility lies with us all.'"[11]

Following its party rule regarding equal representation of male and female delegates, 50 percent of the Democratic delegates were women. The Republican rules ask only that each state "take positive action to achieve the broadest possible participation by men and women" without any kind of quota. According to a *New York Times*/CBS survey, 68 percent of the 2008 Republican national convention delegates were men (up from 57 percent in 2004).[12]

At the conventions, the parties showcased their women leaders in a number of ways. For example, the Democratic National Convention made Tuesday, August 26 Women's Equality Day, commemorating the eighty-eighth anniversary of women winning the right to vote. The day included a gala fund-raiser sponsored by EMILY's List, a presentation of a "checklist for change" by women senators from the convention hall's podium, and a prime-time address by Senator Hillary Clinton.[13] Marches and protests for women's rights also took place outside the convention hall.

Both conventions sponsored events featuring screenings of *14 Women*, a documentary film about the female members of the U.S. Senate during the 109th Congress (2005–6). The Democratic National Convention showcased a prominent speech by Lilly Ledbetter, the Goodyear employee who had lost a Supreme Court case for the right to sue employers for wage discrimination.[14]

The Republican National Convention was shortened by Hurricane Gustav, which devastated the Texas coast as the convention was about to commence. First Lady Laura Bush and Cindy McCain, the wife of Republican presidential candidate John McCain, appeared on Monday night to appeal to the American public to contribute aid to states affected by the hurricane. Other prominently featured women included Carly Fiorina, former head of Hewlett-Packard and economic adviser to the McCain campaign, and officeholders Governor Linda Lingle of Hawaii, U.S. Senator Kay Bailey Hutchison of Texas, and U.S. Representatives Michele Bachmann (MN), Mary Fallin (OK), Marsha Blackburn (TN), and Thelma Drake (VA). The marquee event was Sarah Palin's Wednesday-night acceptance speech, after which Palin was described by CNN anchor Wolf Blitzer as "hitting the ball out of the park." Conservative columnist Kathleen Parker illustrated the rave reviews with her commentary,

"What she showed was strength, conviction, determination, confidence, a willingness to rumble and fearlessness. No caribou caught in the headlights, she."[15]

PARTY EFFORTS TO ELECT MORE WOMEN

Several steps are required to increase the number of women in elective office. Women willing to run in winnable districts must be identified; some will initiate the process themselves, while others may need encouragement and training. Candidates may require assistance in securing resources to win their party's nomination and in financing their campaigns once they become nominees.

The Democratic Party's distinct culture made it the site of early action to recruit and promote women.[16] Feminists, as an accepted organized group within the party, had the attention of leadership and gained a sympathetic ear within the party's liberal wing. As early as 1974, the Democratic Party sponsored the Campaign Conference for Democratic Women aimed at electing more women to political office.[17] The 1,200 women who attended the workshop passed resolutions urging their party to do more for potential women candidates. Most of the female members of the U.S. House of Representatives in the 1970s were Democrats, including a number who won their seats not because they were championed within their local party organizations but because they challenged local party structures and beat them.

The Republican Party did not begin to hold similar women's conferences until nearly a decade later. This later start by the Republicans does not mean that their party has been less receptive to female candidacies, however. Indeed, at one time, the feminist leaders Eleanor Smeal, former chair of the National Organization for Women (NOW), and the former congresswoman Bella Abzug argued just the opposite.[18] Republican women in the 1980s tended to credit men for bringing them into the organization.[19] However, the Republicans have not kept pace in the recruitment and promotion of women's candidacies.

Wanting to appear supportive of women in the face of an emerging gender gap in the 1980s, the parties saw it as expedient to champion women candidates. Republican leaders, in particular, publicly acknowledged this fact. The Republican Senatorial Campaign Committee (RSCC) chair Senator Richard Lugar issued a press statement in 1982 declaring:

A concerted drive by the Republican Party to stamp itself as the party of the woman elected official would serve our nation as well as it serves our own political interests. The full political participation of women is a moral imperative for our society and intelligent political goal for the Republican Party.

He pledged to

commit the RSCC to the maximum legal funding and support for any Republican woman who is nominated next year, regardless of how Democratic the state or apparently formidable the Democratic candidate. I am prepared to consider direct assistance to women candidates even prior to their nomination, a sharp departure from our usual policy.[20]

The Democrats in 1984 included a section in their party platform on political empowerment for minorities and women. This section stated:

We will recruit women and minorities to run for governorships and all state and local offices. The Democratic Party (through its campaign committees) will commit to spending maximum resources to elect women and minority candidates and offer these candidates in-kind services, including political organizing and strategic advice. And the bulk of all voter registration funds will be spent on targeted efforts to register minorities and women.

In 1988, both national party platforms included statements recommending support for women's candidacies. The Democrats endorsed "full and equal access of women and minorities to elective office and party endorsement," while the Republicans called for "strong support for the efforts of women in seeking an equal role in government and [commitment] to the vigorous recruitment, training and campaign support for women candidates at all levels." However, these pledges did not include any action plans for implementation. Prior to 1990, the calls for increasing the number of women candidates were only rhetoric, as there were few substantive actions to ensure that women were nominated in favorable electoral circumstances.

Then, for a variety of reasons, 1992 emerged as the "Year of the Woman" in American politics. With the end of the Cold War, attention was increasingly turning away from foreign policy and defense and toward domestic issues where women were perceived as having expertise. The confirmation hearings for Clarence Thomas's nomination to the U.S. Supreme Court shone a spotlight on the absence of women in the Senate and upset women who thought that Anita Hill's charges of sexual harassment against Thomas were trivialized. And the reapportionment and redistricting process resulted in more open seats than usual, creating new electoral opportunities. All of these forces stimulated the parties to direct an even greater share of their recruitment activity toward women than in previous years. The leadership of both parties' congressional campaign committees made special efforts to seek out qualified women House candidates. The Democratic Senatorial Campaign Committee (DSCC) formed a women's council that raised approximately $1.5 million for Democratic women running for the Senate. These affirmative steps did not, however, spur the parties to clear the field of primary competition for women or discourage anyone, male or female, from running against women.[21]

Specific efforts by Republican women in their party to recruit and train women as political and public leaders include the work of the National Federation of Republican Women (NFRW) and the Republican National Committee's Excellence in Public Service Series. The NFRW has provided training for potential Republican women candidates. As early as 1976, it published the booklet *Consider Yourself for Public Office: Guidelines for Women Candidates*. The Excellence in Public Service Series is a political leadership development program offered by groups of Republican women in a number of states; most of the programs are named for prominent Republicans. First was the Lugar Series in Indiana, initiated in 1989; now there are programs in nineteen additional states, although not all are offered every year. Typically, a yearlong series of programs, with eight monthly sessions and a three-day leadership seminar in Washington, D.C., is offered to selected women willing to make a commitment to play an active role in the political arena. Classes are designed to encourage, prepare, and inspire women leaders to seek new levels of involvement in government and politics. The extra edge afforded by these programs is very much needed, because research has shown that the biggest hurdle for Republican women has been winning their party's primaries.

CONGRESSIONAL CAMPAIGN COMMITTEES AND WOMEN'S CANDIDACIES

The parties' congressional campaign committees – the Democratic Congressional Campaign Committee (DCCC), the National Republican Congressional Committee (NRCC), the Democratic Senatorial Campaign Committee (DSCC), and the Republican Senatorial Campaign Committee (RSCC) – have achieved significant roles in the contemporary campaign era. They participate in recruiting candidates in opportune races, whether by taking on vulnerable incumbents of the opposite party or by winning open seats. They are also major sources of campaign money, services, and advice for congressional candidates.[22] In recent election cycles, both parties have promoted women into leadership positions within their campaign committees and have established subgroups to promote the candidacies of women.

By federal law, these groups may contribute directly to any one candidate's campaign only $5,000 for a primary race and $5,000 for the general election. Beyond these funds, these organizations can contribute much larger amounts in coordinated expenditures (e.g., financing a public opinion poll for several candidates), and in independent expenditures (e.g., buying television ads supported by the party committee and shown "independently" of the candidates' campaigns).

Such expenditures have taken on new prominence since the passage of the McCain-Feingold Bipartisan Campaign Reform Act in 2002, but important questions remain regarding whether the party leaders see women and men as viable candidates to the same degree and assist them in winning to the same extent. When it comes to pouring money into races in the final weeks of the election, it would be important to know whether the same bundles of cash are spent on advertising for female candidates and against their opponents as for their male counterparts.

Women as Leaders in the Party Campaign Committees

In the 107th Congress (2001–2), Congresswoman Nita Lowey of New York chaired the Democratic Congressional Campaign Committee and Senator Patty Murray chaired the Democratic Senatorial Campaign Committee. In 1999, Lowey had founded Women Lead, a fund-raising subsidiary of the DCCC to target women donors and contributors to women candidates. When Lowey became chair of the DCCC, she appointed Congresswoman Jan Schakowsky of Illinois to head Women Lead. In the 2001–2 election cycle, that committee raised approximately $25 million for women candidates. Lowey had admired Schakowsky's fund-raising prowess in her initial run for an open House seat in 1997. Schakowsky had approached all the female law partners in the greater Chicago area asking for donations in what she called "an untapped constituency" of women contributors. "The strategy paid off.... Schakowsky raised 57 percent of her campaign funds from women donors that year – a higher percentage than any other congressional candidate in the 1998 election cycle."[23]

Prior to being appointed to chair the DSCC, Murray had launched a similar program in 1999 called Women on the Road to the Senate, which helped elect four women senators in 2000. In 2002, the program, renamed the Women's Senate Network and now headed by Senator Debbie Stabenow of Michigan, raised $1.3 million on top of some $2 million collected through separate events early in that election cycle. Fundraising activities included $1,000-per-person issue conferences that showcased Senators Hillary Clinton, Dianne Feinstein, and other "prominent senators who happen to be women" in a series of seminar discussions on topics such as terrorism, national security, and the economy. Stabenow noted that it irked her that her female colleagues are so rarely interviewed on such topics.[24] In 2004, this group held a similar event in California, netting $200,000 for Senator Barbara Boxer's campaign for reelection.

The election of Congresswoman Nancy Pelosi to the position of House minority leader in 2003 further encouraged party recruitment of women candidates. Pelosi, a longtime party activist before her election to Congress, was sensitive to the importance of recruiting women candidates and proactive in that effort. Now she, rather than the old-boys network, would be directing decisions about the types of people who should be recruited to run in viable districts to maintain and expand the number of seats the Democratic Party held. In 2006, she became Speaker of the House when Democrats won back their majority after twelve years out of power. Her prowess at raising money and distributing it strategically among Democratic candidates was an important factor in her developing a strong base of supporters in the U.S. House.

In 2004, Democrats in the U.S. House initiated the Red to Blue campaign in which they would mount major efforts to recruit and support strong Democratic candidates in normally Republican districts. Twenty-seven Democratic House candidates benefited from Red to Blue at an average rate of $250,000 per campaign in 2004. In the 2006 election cycle, the DCCC credited Red to Blue with raising $22.6 million for fifty-six campaigns. In that cycle, the first-term congresswoman Debbie Wasserman Schultz of Florida was put in charge of the DCCC's Frontline campaign, which aimed to provide assistance to the party's ten most vulnerable incumbents. Representative Wasserman Schultz had garnered attention as an open-seat candidate in 2004 when she strategically donated $100,000 to the DCCC from her campaign's finances. In 2008, she was appointed a cochair of the Red to Blue campaign, and in the 111th Congress (2009–10), she was named a vice chair of the DCCC. Representative Van Hollen, who chaired the committee in the 110th Congress, maintained that role for the 2009–10 session, but Wasserman Schultz would be a leading contender for chair of the DCCC in the next Congress.

Through the 108th Congress (2003–4), no woman had chaired a corresponding Republican campaign committee, although Representative Anne Northup of Kentucky headed recruitment for the National Republican Congressional Committee. However, for the 109th Congress (2005–6), Republicans elected Senator Elizabeth Dole of North Carolina to head the Republican Senatorial Campaign Committee (RSCC). She won the position by defeating Senator Norman Coleman of Minnesota by one vote in the Senate Republican caucus. Dole had campaigned for the presidency in the early stages of the 2000 election before winning her Senate seat in 2002. She had also served in two cabinet positions in earlier Republican presidential administrations. Described as "about as close to a rock star as the Republican Senate has," she is considered to be a celebrity within the party.[25] She helped raise more than $16 million for the RSCC in the 2004 election cycle.[26] In addition, "Dole's supporters argued that she would help Republicans win over female and minority voters by putting a 'different face on the party.'"[27]

Dole's leadership of the RSCC proved otherwise. The committee fell $30 million behind the Democratic Senatorial Campaign Committee. Dole and her committee were blamed by some of the losing Republican Senate candidates for a lack of support and for making bad decisions regarding advertising in support of their campaigns and against their opponents. The Associated Press reported:

> President Bush's low approval ratings, the unpopular war on Iraq, voter concern about corruption and Democratic fundraising all figured in the GOP loss of Senate control in last month's elections. But among Republicans, long-hidden tensions are spilling into view, with numerous critics venting their anger at the GOP Senate campaign committee headed by North Carolina Sen. Elizabeth Dole.[28]

The Republican National Committee set up outside checks on the Senate committee.[29] But given GOP defeats in both Senate and House races and President Bush's low approval ratings, the RSCC could be counted as only one of many factors in the Republican loss of control of the Senate.

In 2007, the RCCC chair Tom Cole tapped Representative Candice Miller of Michigan to lead an effort to recruit women as candidates for the House.[30] Little appeared in the media after this announcement about any follow-up recruitment activities, and the miniscule number of Republican women who mounted candidacies for House seats in the 2008 election, especially in the twenty-six House districts vacated by Republican incumbents, suggests that this effort was anemic at best.

Party Campaign Committee Support for Women Candidates

Women candidates in contemporary elections have been

> strategic politicians... experienced, highly motivated career public servants who carefully calculate the personal and political benefits of running for higher office, assess the probability of their winning, and determine the personal and political costs of defeat before deciding to risk the positions they hold to secure a more valued office.[31]

Referring to the field of women candidates in 2004, Karen White of EMILY's List, a top player in recruiting and promoting women's candidacies, described the women who were running as "tough as nails." She continued, "These are women who know how to raise the money, put together the campaign operation, and have the political and constituent bases."[32] The women running in these recent elections would seem to be well positioned to compete for party resources and women's political action committee support.

Analyses of campaign contributions in recent elections show that the parties have provided comparable direct financial support (limited by federal law) to similarly situated female and male Congressional nominees.[33] And looking at the larger base of funding, including coordinated and independent expenditures, the national party committees appear to have poured significant resources into the campaigns of female candidates. This support has important implications, not only for encouraging women to enter the electoral arena but also for increasing the likelihood of their success.

Independent expenditures have become central to winning, and anecdotal data from previous elections suggest that female nominees in competitive districts and states are not disadvantaged in this regard.[34] Analysis of party organizational independent expenditures in congressional races in the 2006 election has showed:

> [O]n average, the parties' congressional committees were more generous with their female nominees with major party opponents than with their male nominees. The NRCC supplied an average of $410,553 to its women nominees and $195,042 to its male nominees while the DCCC provided an average of $238,715 to its female nominees and $153,140 to its male nominees. Nine Democratic female candidates (9% of female nominees with opponents) and eight Republican female candidates (19% of female nominees with opponents) received $1 million or more. These figures compare with 6 percent of the Democratic male nominees and 7 percent of the 60 Republican male nominees.[35]

Moving forward to 2008, the parties' national organizations in total each raised more than $900 million; according to Opensecrets.org December 2008 reports, the DCCC raised more than $171 million, the NRCC almost $118 million, the DSCC nearly $156 million, and the RSCC more than $93 million. Final figures may be even higher.

The DSCC poured $7.5 million into the New Hampshire Senate race between challenger Jeanne Shaheen and Republican incumbent John Sununu. It also gave more than $7 million to Kay Hagan in her successful race challenging Senator Elizabeth Dole in North Carolina. These expenditures were exceeded only by the $9 million spent in the Oregon senatorial race won by Democratic challenger John Merkley.

On the other side, the RSCC spent $4.3 million against Jeanne Shaheen in New Hampshire and $3.7 million against Kay Hagan in North Carolina. (On her own, Senator Dole vastly outraised Hagan, by $19.5 million to $8.5 million.)

In 2008, the DCCC's Red to Blue campaign identified twenty-two open seats being vacated by Republican incumbents as having strong Democratic candidates eligible for support. In addition, forty-one Republican incumbents were targeted as vulnerable to strong Democratic challengers. Women were the Democratic nominees in seven of the twenty-two open seats targeted for financial, communications, and strategic support from the Red to Blue campaign (32 percent), and women were also fifteen of the forty-one challengers supported by the program.

In contrast, the Republican Party has exhibited less effort in recent years to diversify its congressional representation along gender lines or to recruit women as candidates. However, the unexpected decision by 2008 Republican presidential nominee John McCain to name Alaska Governor Sarah Palin as his running mate electrified the party and, at least to a degree, countered the party's antiwoman image.

WOMEN'S PACS, WOMEN'S ORGANIZATIONS, AND WOMEN'S CANDIDACIES

For candidates – female or male – to be considered viable and worthy of party support, they must display sufficient resources and credentials from the outset. Women's political organizations can play a pivotal role in this process, especially in primary campaigns, where party organizations may hold off while waiting for nominees to emerge with early money and person power. Running for open seats, women candidates have tended to equal or surpass their male counterparts in acquiring early war chests to finance their campaigns.[36] Women's groups, integral in prodding the parties to advance women's candidacies, have also taken matters into their own hands, undertaking recruitment, training, and development of resource bases for women candidates. The formation of women's political action committees (PACs) has been especially significant.

Political action committees are set up to provide financial contributions to political candidates. Women's PACs that raise money primarily or exclusively for female candidates stand "at the nexus of political change and politics as usual: bringing women into positions of power by mastering the political money game."[37] They have encouraged women to run, trained them in campaign tactics and strategy, raised vital early money to start their campaigns, and provided a network of supportive organizations that can sustain a campaign during the final weeks of an election.[38]

The activities of Linden Rhoads Amadon and Tracy Newman in Seattle illustrate this kind of effort. In 2001, they were angry over the defeat of Al Gore in the 2000 presidential election and worried about the implications of a Bush administration for abortion rights. In their view, men had dominated Democratic fund-raising events, while liberal women had not been paying attention to politics. They decided to find a way for pro-choice women to wield greater influence on politics. Recognizing that senators vote on Supreme Court nominations, they launched a women-only political committee, Washington Women for Choice, with the singular mission of supporting pro-choice U.S. Senate candidates. During the 2004 election, seventy contributors pledged at least $1,000 per year to the group. According to a *Boston Globe* article, "The movers and shakers in liberal Democratic politics quickly added this PAC to their Seattle fund-raising schedule, eager to make a connection with such a high-profile group of women."[39] Washington Women for Choice contributed $119,000 to Democratic pro-choice candidates who ran for the U.S. Senate across the country in 2004. One female senatorial nominee received $5,000 from the group, and six candidates received $10,000, the maximum allowed by federal law. In 2008, the group contributed $140,000 to U.S. House and Senate candidates; Senate candidates Jeanne Shaheen, Mary Landrieu, and Kay Hagan all received the maximum allowable contribution of $10,000 from Washington Women for Choice.[40]

The Center for American Women and Politics lists forty-seven women's PACs or donor networks that either give money predominantly to women candidates or have a predominantly female donor base, not including issue PACs.[41] This list includes fourteen national women's PACs or donor networks and thirty-three state or local PAC or donor networks.[42]

Donor networks collect checks from individuals written directly to candidates and package them in "bundles" to present to endorsed candidates, a concept originated by EMILY's List in the 1980s. Members of the organization are encouraged – and in some cases committed – to support endorsed candidates in this fashion. While PACs themselves are limited to a total of $10,000 in direct contributions to candidates for national office, bundling greatly expands a PAC's clout by allowing it to deliver larger sums made up of individual contributions – a $20,000 package consisting of two hundred $100 checks, for example. Employing this strategy made EMILY's List one of the nation's most prominent campaign funders but also generated controversy as the donor list became increasingly powerful.

A 2004 election example illustrates the influence of EMILY's List. Three candidates sought the Democratic Party nomination for the open U.S. Senate seat in Florida: U.S. Representative Peter Deutsch, Miami-Dade County mayor Alex Penelas, and University of South Florida president Betty Castor. Deutsch, trailing in the polls but having raised $4.2 million, accused EMILY's List of trying to buy the Senate seat for Castor. EMILY's List contributors had donated more than $1 million to her campaign, and the organization was spending $800,000 on televised advertising praising her health agenda. In a televised debate, Deutsch complained that, although all three candidates had the same pro-choice views, the men in the race had a problem. "No matter what we do, unless we go through a sex-change operation, we're not getting EMILY's List's endorsement," quipped Deutsch. A Deutsch supporter filed a complaint with the Federal Election Commission (FEC), claiming that the political organization and Castor were coordinating a campaign strategy in violation of FEC rules. Castor went on to win the primary handily but lost the general election. Even so, it was an ironic twist that a women's group had become powerful enough to cause a male candidate to complain of discrimination.

In contemporary elections, EMILY's List, the WISH List, the National Women's Political Caucus (NWPC), and the Women's Campaign Fund (which became the Women's Campaign Forum in 2006) have been the most prominent national women's groups recruiting, training, and providing resources to women candidates. Table 8.2 profiles these four organizations. The NWPC is the oldest of the four groups, while the Women's

TABLE 8.2: Description of four major women's PACs

Year founded	Mission statement	2008 election activity		
		Endorsed	Raised	Contributed
National Women's Political Caucus				
1971	The National Women's Political Caucus is a multicultural, intergenerational, and multi-issue grassroots organization dedicated to increasing women's participation in the political process and creating a true women's political power base to achieve equality for all women. NWPC recruits, trains and supports pro-choice women candidates for elected and appointed offices at all levels of government regardless of party affiliation. In addition to financial donations, the Caucus offers campaign training for candidates and campaign managers, as well as technical assistance and advice. State and local chapters provide support to candidates running for all levels of office by helping raise money and providing crucial hands-on volunteer assistance.	2 U.S. Senate and 22 U.S. House candidates	$19,421	$16,250 (to federal candidates)
The Women's Campaign Forum PAC (Women's Campaign Fund before 2006)				
1974	The Women's Campaign Forum PAC (WCF PAC) is dedicated to electing pro-choice women candidates of all parties by providing them with the financial contributions and supplemental support they need to win.	11 U.S. Senate, 70 U.S. House, 2 gubernatorial, and 41 state legislative candidates	$1,532,696	$84,450 (to federal candidates)
EMILY's List				
1985	EMILY's List members are dedicated to building a progressive America by electing pro-choice Democratic women to office.	1 presidential, 2 U.S. Senate, 26 U.S. House, and 2 gubernatorial candidates	$33,401,859	$161,778 (to federal candidates), $2,735,374 (independent expenditures)
WISH List				
1992	The WISH List raises funds to identify train and elect pro-choice Republican women at all levels of government – local, state, and national.	1 U.S. Senate and 8 U.S. House candidates	$587,880	$34,761 (to federal candidates)

Source: Compiled by author from Opensecrets.org, December 17, 2008.

Figure 8.1: EMILY's List contributions increased dramatically from 1986 to 2006.

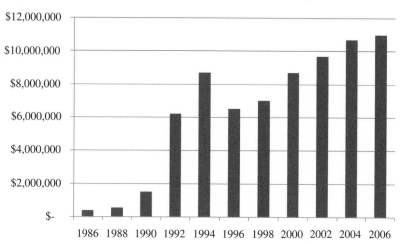

Source: EMILY's List, http://www.emilyslist.org/about/where-from.html.

Campaign Fund, founded in 1974, was the first to establish a PAC to provide resources for women candidates. These two groups are bipartisan, supporting both Democratic and Republican candidates who are pro-choice, but the vast majority of their money has gone to Democratic candidates, who are more likely to support reproductive rights. The leadership of the NWPC in recruiting and providing resources for women candidates has faded in recent years as the two intraparty groups, EMILY's List and the WISH List, have become key players. Created as a Republican counterpart to EMILY's List supporting pro-choice Republican female candidates, WISH List has grown over the years, but it faces an uphill climb within the Republican Party. In 2008, only one nonincumbent candidate at the federal level, Lynn Jenkins in the Second District of Kansas, met its endorsement criteria; she emerged victorious.

EMILY's List has come to wield considerable power within Democratic circles because of its accumulated financial clout and campaign expertise and has become the grand dame of the PAC world. In recent elections, it has led all PACs (not just women's PACs) in the amount of money raised. Figure 8.1 shows the growth in the amount of money EMILY's List funneled to endorsed candidates, including both its direct contributions and its bundled money. Indeed, one scholar suggests that Democratic Party efforts to recruit women candidates have become virtually indistinguishable from the candidate recruitment strategies of EMILY's List.[43]

It should also be noted, however, that some commentators have recently questioned the group's ability to elect its endorsed candidates. For example, in an extensive article, Bara Vaida and Jennifer Skalka of the *National Journal* asked, "Can EMILY's List Get Its Mojo Back?"[44] They cited EMILY's List's lackluster success rate in 2006, when only eight of the thirty-one House and Senate challengers it endorsed won (26 percent), in a big Democratic year. EMILY's List achieved a somewhat better 2008 record in the success of the candidates it backed. Twelve of the twenty-six House candidates it endorsed won, for a 46 percent success rate, and the two Senate and two gubernatorial candidates it endorsed were victorious.

Undaunted by challenges to its campaign tactics and muscle, EMILY's List in January 2007 formally endorsed U.S. Senator Hillary Clinton for president, taking women's PAC organizations to a whole new level. EMILY's List not only endorsed Senator Clinton but also became a substantial player in her quest for the Democratic Party nomination, mounting an extensive fund-raising effort and providing an impressive on-the-ground effort targeting and mobilizing voters through its Women Vote! program. Text Box 8.1 details EMILY's List's role in the Clinton campaign.

Opensecrets.org provides a host of campaign finance information on federal elections. Among its data are PAC contributions by interest-group sectors and within sectors by issue emphasis, including women's issues. In 2008, it listed twelve such PACs making contributions to federal-level candidates. Table 8.3 lists these PACs, detailing the amount of money each raised and how much was contributed to candidates from each party. The women's PACs cited earlier are included in this list. Female candidates, and particularly Democratic female candidates, are major beneficiaries of these groups.

Among these PACs is one established by the Feminist Majority Foundation. The group has adopted a strategy of encouraging large numbers of women to run for political office in major party primaries, regardless of the likelihood of their winning nominations and actually getting elected. This strategy contrasts with that of EMILY's List and the WISH List, which are more strategic in their financial aid, endorsing only viable candidates, or those who show evidence of well-organized campaigns with a good chance of winning.

The women's PACs described in this chapter represent groups that give money almost exclusively to women candidates, are run by women, and

---

TEXT BOX 8.1: EMILY's List and the Clinton campaign for the presidency

In the 2008 election, as mentioned in the introduction to this chapter, EMILY's List reached a new political height by endorsing of Hillary Clinton for president on January 20, 2007, and then engaging in extensive fund-raising on her behalf and putting people on the ground in many states to mobilize voters. EMILY's List bundled $855,518 for Clinton (one of the five largest donors to the campaign) and provided more than $1.5 million in independent expenditures. EMILY's List's activities were crucial at certain points in Clinton's campaign.[1] For example, in Ohio and several other states in key March primaries, EMILY's List spent a total of $725,000 on mail aiming to persuade working-class women to support Clinton. "The group targeted 150,000 Ohio women either for mail or personal contacts, particularly non-college educated working women."[2]

The *White House Bulletin* reported on March 18 that "Organizers at Emily's List are touting their on-the-ground efforts to target and mobilize 150,000 women voters in Ohio and Texas as key to Sen. Hillary Clinton's win yesterday in Democratic primaries in both states. Maren Hesla, director of the organization's Women Vote! program[,] said that women went to the polls in far greater numbers than in those states' 2004 primaries. Women made up 59 percent of the electorate in Ohio, a 7 percent increase over four years ago; and were 57 percent of the electorate in Texas, a 4 percent increase. Clinton won women in Ohio by 16 points, and in Texas by 11 points. In a statement released this morning, Emily's List President Ellen Malcolm said that women once again 'made up the backbone of Hillary Clinton's support' and have been the candidate's 'most consistent and committed backers from the beginning.'"[3]

---

[1] Bara Vaida and Jennifer Skalka. June 28, 2008. Can EMILY's List Get Its Mojo Back? *National Journal*, Cover or <http://www.nationaljournal.com/njmagazine/cs_20080628_6871.php> August 5, 2008.

[2] Bill Lambrecht. 2008. CAMPAIGN 2008; Clinton will need support of women to keep hope alive; "Security moms" and working class votes have aided her turnaround. *St. Louis Post-Dispatch*, March 9, A6.

[3] Emily's List Takes Credit for Turnout Boost among Women. March 8, 2008. *White House Bulletin*.

---

have a membership base made up primarily of women. Other groups that have also been considered part of what might be called the women's PAC community do not meet all three of these criteria. Organizations such as the American Nurses Association have mostly female donor bases but contribute to both male and female candidates without insisting that candidates support positions that are necessarily feminist. Other groups, such

TABLE 8.3: Contributions to federal candidates by PACs concerned with women's issues went predominantly to Democrats in 2008

PAC name	Total	Democrats	Republicans
EMILY's List	$161,778	$161,778	$0
Women's Campaign Forum	$100,577	$100,577	$0
Women's Political Committee	$95,000	$95,000	$0
National Organization for Women	$44,381	$44,381	$0
WISH List	$34,761	$0	$34,761
Feminist Majority Foundation	$27,500	$27,500	$0
National Women's Political Caucus	$16,250	$16,250	$0
Minnesota Women's Campaign Fund	$14,500	$14,500	$0
Women under Forty PAC	$14,500	$13,500	$1,000
Women's Action for New Directions	$9,500	$9,500	$0
Women in Leadership	$7,450	$7,450	$0
Value in Electing Women PAC	$2,000	$0	$2,000

Note: Based on data released by the FEC on December 11, 2008.

as the Business and Professional Women's PAC, make funding decisions on the basis of feminist issue positions (similar to NOW).

Sometimes the Susan B. Anthony List, a pro-life women's PAC, is also included in listings of women's PACs. However, the goal of the Susan B. Anthony List is to increase the percentage of pro-life women in Congress and high public office mainly by defeating pro-choice women candidates and women incumbents. Thus, as their Web site describes their goals, the organization "recruits and endorses pro-life women candidates, our primary focus, endorses pro-life men challenging pro-abortion incumbent women, endorses pro-life male incumbents challenged by pro-abortion women candidates, and endorses pro-life male candidates challenging pro-abortion women candidates in open seats." This emphasis on defeating pro-choice women candidates, not just electing pro-life women candidates, makes the Susan B. Anthony List an anomaly in the women's PAC community. In 2008, this PAC contributed $85,000 to nineteen Republican House candidates, including fourteen women candidates. Marilyn Musgrave and Melissa Hart each received more than $20,000.[45] In Arizona's First Congressional District, it endorsed and supported Republican nominee Sydney Hay in an unsuccessful open-seat race against Democrat Anne Kirkpatrick, who had the endorsement and financial support of EMILY's List.[46]

FOSTERING NEW WOMEN POLITICAL LEADERS

Efforts to bring women into the electoral area have expanded downward to encourage young women and girls to become political leaders. A number of universities and organizations around the country have begun developing such programs. The Center for American Women and Politics (CAWP), for instance, since 1991 has run the NEW Leadership summer institute. This intensive residential program educates college women about politics and policy making and encourages them to participate in the political process. In 1999, CAWP expanded this program to colleges and universities across the country (see http://www.cawp .rutgers.edu/education_training/New Leadership). And in 2004, building on the NEW Leadership model, CAWP began collaborating with Girl Scouts of the USA on Pathways to Politics, a two-week program for high school students from across the nation. That program was repeated in 2006 and 2008.

Others have initiated similar efforts to educate younger women and girls about politics. Inaugurated in 2007, Running Start hosts the annual Women's Political Leadership Retreat at American University in Washington, D.C., for high school girls from across the country, with the goal of encouraging them to enter political office. Future Frontrunners, a segment of Lifetime Networks' nonpartisan Every Woman Counts campaign, held a high school and college leadership contest in which contestants submitted written or video essays answering the question, "What would you do if you were president?" The winners attended the Democratic and Republican National Conventions, where they participated in leadership training workshops with women elected officials.

The Girl Scouts of the USA has also developed a Ms. President Patch in cooperation with the White House Project. Whether in their troops or on their own, girls participate in a variety of projects to learn about women in leadership. Such activities can be undertaken locally rather than by attending a national or regional program.

CosmoGirl, working with the White House Project, took another approach with *What's Your Point, Honey?* a film that premiered in 2008. The documentary, created by Amy Sewell and Susan Toffler, tells the stories of seven young women who were leaders on college campuses or local communities and in 2006 participated in Project 2024. The concept of the film is that by 2024 – the year when the magazine's youngest readers will reach the age of thirty-five and be eligible to run for U.S. president – one

"CosmoGirl" from each year of the program will stand on the presidential debate floor as a real candidate.[47]

Organized efforts to increase the numbers of women in public office also reach outward, encouraging women to think of themselves as potential candidates and prepare themselves to run. The Center for American Women and Politics lists a number of these programs, and CAWP itself offers one such model, its Ready to Run campaign training. Held annually, Ready to Run is a bipartisan program for women who want to run for office, work on a campaign, get appointed to office, become community leaders, or learn more about the political system.[48]

Women in South Carolina, the only state with the dubious distinction of having no women in its state senate, created the Southeastern Institute for Women in Politics in early 2008. Its mission is to

> motivate, train, and provide ongoing education and information to women running for elected office at all levels, and to women seeking appointive positions on public policy boards and commissions; to offer women officeholders and appointees access to mentors and other resources that will help them serve ably; and generally to raise public awareness of the unique contributions women make to political discourse and action.

Seventy-five women attended its first training event in February 2008, which was highlighted by an address by Delaware Governor Ruth Ann Minner.

In July 2007, the Women's Campaign Forum launched the She Should Run campaign. By September 2009, the names of more than 1,000 women had been submitted to an online database that lists women who have been identified by friends or colleagues as potential candidates who should run for office. The WCF is working to build on the research finding that women may not put themselves forward as candidates and may need encouragement to consider running.

CONCLUSION

Gone are the days when women candidates won party nominations primarily as sacrificial lambs in districts where a party had little prospect of winning. The parties have found it to their advantage to promote women candidates, and once women become nominees, they are as likely as male candidates to have access to party resources, particularly in highly competitive races in which they can often count on substantial support in the final days of the campaign. Women candidates, particularly those who are pro-choice, also have the advantage of access to women's PACs, which have become formidable players in campaigns. A continuing problem for women candidates, however, is reaching the point of being a competitive candidate, given what research has shown to be women's hesitancy to run for office and the limited opportunity structure for newcomers.

Party organizations no longer control the nomination process in most states. While they are involved in recruiting candidates, few make it a policy to recruit women candidates and promote them over male candidates to increase women's numbers in elective office. Members of Congress and the campaign committees' staffs do appear to encourage some prospective candidates to run. As congressional scholar Paul Herrnson has observed, "Armed with favorable polling figures and the promise of party assistance in the general election they search out local talent. Promising individuals are invited to meet with the members of Congress and party leaders in Washington and to attend campaign seminars."[49]

At this early stage of the campaign process, women's groups are especially valuable. They recruit and train women candidates to make them more viable candidates. They work aggressively in primary elections and provide a substantial resource base, particularly for women candidates who are pro-choice.

In the world of political campaigns, women have come a long way and are now strong players. Several factors have advanced women's prospects: the rise of PACs promoting women's candidacies for public office and funding their campaigns; the lessening of party discrimination against women candidates; and the availability of substantial support from congressional campaign committees in competitive situations. None of these positive factors, however, offsets such negatives as the paucity of women presenting themselves as candidates and the advantages afforded incumbents, most of whom are male, so gender continues to matter in political campaigns.

NOTES

1 The figures are based on the election results, not taking into account subsequent events as some senators leave their Senate positions to take cabinet positions in the Obama administration.

2 Center for American Women and Politics. Facts on Women in State Legislatures. www.cawp.rutgers.edu/fast_facts/levels_of_office/StateLeg-Current Facts.php.

3 Aileen Kraditor. 1965. *Ideas of the Woman Suffrage Movement, 1890–1920.* New York: Columbia University Press.

4 William Chafe. 1972. *The American Woman: Her Changing Social, Economic, and Political Roles, 1920–1970.* New York: Oxford University Press, 25.

5 Kristi Andersen. 1996. *After Suffrage: Women in Partisan and Electoral Politics before the New Deal.* Chicago: University of Chicago Press, 80–1.

6 Anna Harvey. 1998. *Votes without Leverage: Women in American Electoral Politics, 1920–1970.* New York: Cambridge University Press.

7 Ibid., 85.

8 Ibid., 113.

9 Jo Freeman. 1993. Feminism vs. Family Values: Women at the 1992 Democratic and Republican Conventions. *PS: Political Science and Politics* 26 (March): 21–7.

10 Jo Freeman. 2008. *We Will Be Heard.* Lanham, MD: Rowman & Littlefield, 121–32.

11 Allison Stevens. August 24, 2008. This Time, Denver's Political Drama Bows to Women. Women's eNews <www.womensenews.org> September 18, 2008.

12 Patrick Healy. September 4, 2008. Two Conventions with No Shortage of Contrasts. *New York Times*, A22.

13 EMILY's List's Republican counterpart, the WISH List, chose not to host an event at the 2008 Republican National Convention.

14 Ledbetter's story led members of Congress to write the Lilly Ledbetter Fair Pay Act, which had failed in the Senate earlier in 2008 for lack of the sixty votes needed to invoke cloture. The 111th Congress made its passage a high priority, and it became the first piece of legislation President Obama signed into law.

15 Kathleen Parker. September 2, 2008. Palin Animates Conservative Electorate. *San Gabriel Valley Tribune.* Later in the campaign Parker would advocate that Palin drop out as the Republican vice presidential nominee.

16 Jo Freeman. 1987. Whom You Know Versus Whom You Represent: Feminist Influence in the Democratic and Republican Parties. In *The Women's Movements of the United States and Western Europe: Consciousness, Political Opportunity, and Public Policy*, ed. Mary Fainsod Katzenstein and Carol McClurg Mueller. Philadelphia: Temple University Press, 215–44.

17 Austin Scott. 1974. Democratic Women See Gains in 1974. *Washington Post*, March 31.

18 Jo Freeman. 1989. Feminist Activities at the Republican Convention. *PS: Political Science and Politics* 22 (March): 39–47; Bella Abzug. 1984. *The Gender Gap: Bella Abzug's Guide to Political Power for American Women.* Boston: Houghton Mifflin.

19 Ronna Romney and Beppie Harrison. 1988. *Momentum: Women in America Politics Now.* New York: Crown Publishers.

20 Richard Lugar. August 21, 1983. A Plan to Elect More GOP Women. *Washington Post.*

21 Robert Biersack and Paul S. Herrnson. 1994. Political Parties and the Year of the Woman. In *The Year of the Woman: Myths and Realities*, ed. Elizabeth Adell Cook, Sue Thomas, and Clyde Wilcox. Boulder, CO: Westview Press.

22 Paul Herrnson. 1995. *Congressional Elections: Campaigning at Home and in Washington.* Washington, D.C.: CQ Press.

23 Allison Stevens. January 14, 2002. Both Parties Say Women's Wallets Ripe for Tapping. Women's eNews <www.womensenews.org>.

24 Sheryl Gay Stolberg. April 28, 2004. Partisan Loyalties and the Senate Women's Caucus. *New York Times.*

25 Jamie Dettmer. November 12, 2004. Senator Dole Is Eyeing Leadership of Key Senate Committee, GOP Post. *New York Sun.*

26 David Dolan. November 18, 2004. Dole to Lead GOP Senate Efforts; N.C. Senator Will Raise Money for 2006 Campaigns, Recruit Candidates. *Herald-Sun,* Durham, North Carolina.

27 Frederic J. Frommer. November 17, 2004. Republicans Choose Elizabeth Dole to Head 2006 Senate Campaigns. <www.sfgate.com> December 3, 2004.

28 David Espo. December 23, 2006. In Wake of Senate Loss, Republicans Turn Anger on Campaign Committee Led by Elizabeth Dole. Associated Press.

29 Senate Campaign News: Dole Now Facing Criticism over Midterm Losses. December 27, 2006. *The Frontrunner.*

30 Aaron Blake. January 22, 2007. House Republicans Aim for More Recruitment of Women in 2008. *The Hill.*

31 Irwin Gertzog. 1995. *Congressional Women: Their Recruitment, Integration, and Behavior,* 2nd ed. Westport, CT: Greenwood Press.

32 Gail Chaddock. October 19, 2004. The Rise of Women Candidates. *Christian Science Monitor.*

33 Biersack and Herrnson 1994; Barbara Burrell. 1994. *A Woman's Place Is in the House: Campaigning for Congress in the Feminist Era.* Ann Arbor: University of Michigan Press.

34 Barbara Burrell. 2006. Political Parties and Women's Organizations: Bringing Women into the Electoral Arena. In *Gender and Elections,* Susan J. Carroll and Richard L. Fox, eds. New York, NY: Cambridge University Press, 143–68.

35 Barbara Burrell. 2008. Political Parties, Fundraising and Sex. In *Legislative Women,* ed. Beth Reingold. Boulder, CO: Lynne Reinner.

36 Barbara Burrell. 1994. *A Woman's Place Is in the House: Campaigning for Congress in the Feminist Era.* Ann Arbor: University of Michigan Press.

37 Christine L. Day and Charles D. Hadley. 2005. *Women's PACs: Abortion and Elections.* Upper Saddle River, NJ: Pearson Prentice Hall.

38 Candice J. Nelson. 1994. Women's PACs in the Year of the Woman. In *The Year of the Woman: Myths and Realities,* ed. Elizabeth Adell Cook, Sue Thomas, and Clyde Wilcox. Boulder, CO: Westview Press, 181–196. See also Mark Rozell. 2000. Helping Women Run and Win: Feminist Groups, Candidate Recruitment and Training. *Women & Politics* 21(3): 101–16.

39 Jessica Kowal. October 9, 2004. Women Wield Political Power. *Boston Globe.* www.boston.com/news/politics/president/articles/2004.

40 www.opensecrets.org.

41 Center for American Women and Politics. 2005. *Women's PACs and Donor Networks: A Contact List.* New Brunswick, NJ: Eagleton Institute of Politics.

42 Descriptions of these groups and their contact information are available at www.cawp.rutgers.edu.

43 Rosalyn Cooperman. 2001 (September). Party Organizations and the Recruitment of Women Candidates to the U.S. House since the "Year of the Woman." Paper presented at the Annual Meeting of the American Political Science Association, San Francisco.

44 Bara Vaida and Jennifer Skalka. June 28, 2008. Can EMILY's List Get Its Mojo Back? *National Journal.*

45 www.opensecrets.org.

46 An interesting side note is that the Republican establishment worked hard to recruit a candidate other than Hay to run in this district. The DCCC endorsed Kirkpatrick during the primary, an unusual but not unheard-of action for a party organization that publicly tends to refrain from primary endorsement in multicandidate races while maneuvering behind the scenes for the candidate it believes has the best chance of winning the general election, usually one with deep financial pockets.

47 Besa Luci. June 23, 2008. Tweens and Twenties See Future Led by Women. Women's eNews, www.womensenew.org.

48 See www.cawp.rutgers.edu/education_training/ReadytoRun/RtoR_New_Jersey.php.

49 Paul Herrnson. 1998. *Congressional Election: Campaigning at Home and in Washington. Washington,* D.C.: CQ Press.

9   Advertising, Web Sites, and Media Coverage

Gender and Communication along the Campaign Trail

The political career of U.S. Senator Dianne Feinstein, one of five women elected to the U.S. Senate in 1992's so-called Year of the Woman, has been marked by a series of historic firsts. The first female member of the San Francisco Board of Supervisors, Feinstein became the first woman mayor of San Francisco in 1978. In 1992, she won a special election to the U.S. Senate, and she was reelected in 1994, 2000, and 2006. Feinstein was the first woman to serve on the powerful Senate Judiciary Committee and the first woman to chair the Senate Rules Committee and Senate Intelligence Committee. At seventy-six years old in 2009, Feinstein was rumored to be considering a run for governor of the state of California in 2010.

As chair of the Senate Rules Committee in the 110th Congress, Feinstein also became the first woman to chair the Joint Congressional Committee on Inaugural Ceremonies for the January 20, 2009, inauguration of Barack Obama as the first African American president of the United States. On perhaps one of the most visible days of her thirty-nine-year political career, she called the ceremony to order, delivered welcoming remarks, and served as emcee for the event.

Despite her political success and longevity, Feinstein also illustrates the double bind that women politicians face in their media coverage, television advertising, and Web sites in communicating an image that is tough but caring. Like U.S. Senator Hillary Rodham Clinton, who ran for the 2008 Democratic nomination for president, Feinstein was regarded by the media and voters as uncharacteristically – for a woman – tough and spent much of her 1992 U.S. Senate campaign showing her soft and sensitive side. In one of her early 1992 television ads, Feinstein cradled her baby granddaughter, Eileen, in her arms, rocking and bottle-feeding her while talking about such issues as crime, education, the economy, and health

239

care. Feinstein won her 1992 special election with 54 percent of the vote running against a male incumbent.

In 2006, Feinstein again featured her then fourteen-year-old granddaughter, Eileen, in one of her television commercials. Standing and facing each other, the two talked about making California and the nation a better place for the next generation by "reducing global warming... bringing our troops home from Iraq, making our communities safer, and improving our schools." She won her reelection with more than 58 percent of the vote.

Feinstein, considered a moderate in a state known for more liberal Democrats, has played up her independence throughout her political career. Since her 1992 race for the U.S. Senate, her campaign theme has remained "An Independent Voice for California," which is prominently displayed on her Web site. In 2008, she listed on her Web site a blend of "masculine" issues – such as the war in Iraq, crime, and nuclear weapons – along with the more "feminine" issues of education, global warming, and stem cell research.

As one of the more senior of the seventeen women in the U.S. Senate (only Barbara Mikulski of Maryland, who was elected in 1984, has been there longer than Feinstein and Barbara Boxer, also elected in 1992 to represent California), Feinstein was an early and outspoken supporter of Hillary Clinton in her bid for the 2008 Democratic nomination for president. Other more "freshman" women U.S. senators – including Claire McCaskill of Missouri and Amy Klobuchar of Minnesota, both elected for the first time in 2006 – were early supporters of the eventual Democratic Party nominee and president, Senator Barack Obama.

Throughout her career, Feinstein has enjoyed mostly positive media coverage for her independence, leadership, and tough but caring persona. For example, a November 2, 2006, article in the *Los Angeles Times* noted, "She has carved out a niche as a moderate to conservative Democrat that has worked for her. It doesn't always get her loved, but it gets her respect." Her "trademark mix of liberal on environmental and social issues and conservative on fiscal and law-and-order issues has made her arguably the state's most consistently popular politician."[1]

Through her televised political ads, her Web site, and her media coverage, Feinstein has demonstrated how a candidate's communications can create a positive, integrated message that connects with voters. From the time a candidate contemplates her candidacy to the day of the election, she will be engaged in some aspect of communication – including person to person, speeches, interviews with the media, debates, television ads, e-mail, and Web sites. Further complicating the campaign communication process is the recent rise of the Internet and concurrent decline of traditional media sources.

In this chapter, I examine the three major communication channels through which voters see candidates – media coverage, television commercials, and Web sites. In today's political campaign, these three media are powerful and important sources of information, not necessarily because they influence voting behavior, although there is some evidence that they do, but because they draw attention to the candidates and their campaigns. Moreover, candidates, especially for federal and statewide elected office, have found that these media provide efficient ways to reach potential voters, and thus their campaigns use all three channels to get their messages out.

By comparing how female and male political candidates navigate the campaign communication environment, we can see how both are presented to voters and speculate about how differences in media use and coverage might affect their voter support. Ultimately, examining gender differences in candidate communication reveals that both women and men are using television and online communication strategies to define their images and issues – at some times confronting, and at other times capitalizing on, stereotypes held by voters. However, female candidates continue to be covered in gendered and stereotypical ways by the mainstream news media, a phenomenon demonstrated in particular by the media treatment of former U.S. Senator Hillary Clinton's campaign in 2008 for the Democratic nomination for president.

MEDIA COVERAGE OF WOMEN POLITICAL CANDIDATES

Women forging new political ground often struggle to receive media coverage and legitimacy in the eyes of the media and, subsequently, the public. According to some observers, journalists often hold female politicians accountable for the actions of their husbands and children, though they rarely hold male candidates to the same standards. They ask women politicians questions they don't ask men, and they describe them in ways and with words that emphasize their traditional roles and focus on their appearance and behavior.

Back in the 1990s, there were numerous examples of such gendered treatment. For example, in 1992's Year of the Woman campaign, in which record numbers of women ran for and were elected to political office, news stories nonetheless commented on their hairstyles, wardrobes, weight and other physical attributes, children, and the men in their lives. For example, a story in the *Washington Post* described unsuccessful U.S. Senate candidate Lynn Yeakel from Pennsylvania as a "feisty and feminine fifty-year-old with the unmistakable Dorothy Hamill wedge of gray hair ... a congressman's daughter [with] a wardrobe befitting a first lady ... a former full-time mother."[2]

In 1992, the *Chicago Tribune* described Carol Moseley Braun, who was elected to the U.S. Senate from Illinois, as a "den mother with a cheerleader's smile."[3] Six years later, the *Chicago Tribune* was still focusing on Moseley Braun's personality and appearance, as this story from her 1998 reelection campaign shows: "Though she boasts that her legislative record is one of the best in the Senate, it is not her votes that make many of her supporters go weak in the knees. It is her personality, featuring a signature smile that she flips on like a light switch, leaving her admirers aglow."[4]

Also in 1998, the *Arizona Republic* described incumbent gubernatorial candidate Governor Jane Dee Hull as a "grandmotherly redhead dressed in a sensible suit."[5] And, it does not seem to make a difference – in terms of stereotypical media coverage – if two women are running against each other, rather than a male opponent, as these excerpts from stories in the *Seattle Times* covering the 1998 U.S. Senate campaigns of incumbent U.S. Senator Patty Murray and challenger U.S. Representative Linda Smith illustrate: "Murray has been airing soothing television commercials that make her look so motherly and nonthreatening, in her soft pinks and scarves, that voters might mistake her for a schoolteacher." Murray and Smith, the story further noted, are different "in style as well as politics. Even the shades of their blue power suits hinted at the gap between the women. Murray's was powder blue; Smith's royal."[6]

Beginning with the 2000 election, there appears to have been less emphasis on the physical appearance and personality of women political candidates, particularly those running for governor and U.S. Senate. However, examples of such coverage can still be found. For example, the weight, wardrobe, and hairstyles of former first lady Hillary Clinton – who ran successfully for the U.S. Senate in New York in 2000 and 2006 and unsuccessfully for the Democratic nomination for president in 2008 – have been a constant source of media comment. In coverage of her 2000 race, an article in the *Milwaukee Journal Sentinel* declared that Clinton had "whittled her figure down to a fighting size 8" by "touching little more than a lettuce leaf during fundraisers."[7] An article in the *New York Times*, reflecting on her victory, was titled "First Lady's Race for the Ages:

62 Counties and 6 Pantsuits," and referred to retiring U.S. Senator Daniel Patrick Moynihan as walking the newly elected Senator Clinton "down the road to a gauntlet of press like a father giving away the bride."[8]

Media coverage of Lisa Murkowski's 2004 reelection campaign for the U.S. Senate seat from Alaska, to which her father had appointed her in 2002, often focused on the powerful men in her life – her father, longtime U.S. senator and then governor Frank Murkowski, and the state's senior senator, Ted Stevens – rather than on her own accomplishments as an attorney, state legislator, and House majority leader. Thus, she was often described as passive and dependent on her father and Stevens rather than as an independent leader of her own campaign.[9]

Michigan Governor Jennifer Granholm has garnered extensive coverage of her appearance – ranging from praise for her beauty to criticism for her facial moles, minimal makeup, and "frumpy" pantsuits – since she was first elected governor in 2002 and reelected in 2006. For example, an April 24, 2006, article in the *National Review*, titled "Glamour-Girl Gov, Gone?" noted that Granholm is a "smashing combination of Charlize Theron looks and Ivy League brains . . . a former beauty queen who once appeared on *The Dating Game* and thought of becoming an actress before attending college at Berkeley and law school at Harvard."[10] The *Detroit Free Press* columnist Susan Ager later devoted a piece to the "extreme reactions" over Granholm's moles, prompted by online comments posted on the newspaper's Web site following a 2006 gubernatorial debate. Ager noted that comments on Granholm's mole ranged from "I cannot take seriously the candidacy of a woman who lets a festering mole grow unchecked on her own face" to a "distraction from her beauty" and a "trademark, like Marilyn Monroe's beauty mark."[11]

Such examples of the media's attention to the appearance of women political candidates are backed by almost thirty years of research by scholars from political science, journalism, and communication. Even though media coverage has improved, women and men in politics are still treated differently by the media, suggesting that gender stereotypes continue to pose problems for female politicians.

For example, women candidates who ran for election in the 1980s and 1990s were often stereotyped by newspaper coverage that not only emphasized their feminine traits and feminine issues but also questioned their viability – that is, their ability to win the election. In an experiment where fictitious female candidates were given the kind of media coverage usually accorded to male incumbents, respondents rated them equally likely as men to win.[12]

In the mid- to late 1990s, women political candidates began to receive more equitable media coverage, in terms of both quantity and quality, when compared with male candidates. In 1994, for example, women candidates running for the U.S. Senate and governorships received less coverage than their male opponents in open races, more coverage in gubernatorial races, and more neutral coverage than males overall.[13] In 1998, female and male candidates for governor received about the same amount of coverage, but women received less issue-related coverage than men did.[14]

Women running for their party nominations for U.S. senator and governor in the 2000 primary races and general election received more coverage than men, and the quality of their coverage – slant of the story and discussion of their viability, appearance, and personality – was mostly equitable. Still, women candidates in 2000 were much more likely to be discussed in terms of their gender, marital status, and children, which can affect their viability in the eyes of voters.[15]

The media coverage of women political candidates continued to improve in the 2002 and 2004 elections, especially in terms of the number and length of stories written about their campaigns. For example, the newspaper coverage of women and men candidates running against each other for U.S. senator and governor in 2002 was about even in terms of quantity, with 35 percent of the articles focusing on men and 34 percent on women.

However, in 2002, the media paid significantly more attention to the backgrounds of female candidates and to the competence of male candidates. And the media continued to link some issues – particularly those that resonate with voters – with male candidates more often than with female candidates. For example, male candidates were linked significantly more often with taxes in 2002. Perhaps not surprisingly, women candidates continue to be linked more often than men with so-called women's issues, such as reproductive choice, often in a way that is detrimental to their campaigns.

While some stereotyping does exist, the playing field for female candidates is becoming more level, at least for women running for governor and for the U.S. Senate. However, as the 2000 and 2008 campaigns show, women running for the major political parties' nomination for president receive much less equitable coverage than do their male opponents.

For example, Elizabeth Dole received less coverage in terms of quality, and especially quantity, than her male opponents during her eight-month

Figure 9.1: **Obama received more positive television news coverage than Clinton throughout most of the 2008 campaign for the Democratic presidential nomination.**

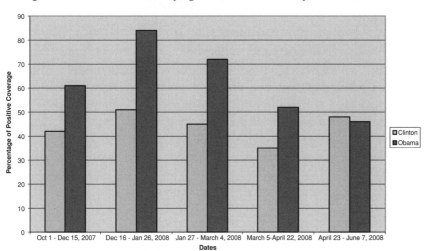

Source: Center for Media and Public Affairs, http://www.cmpa.com/studies_election_08.htm.

run in 1999 for the 2000 Republican nomination for president.[16] Polls consistently showed Dole as a distant runner-up to eventual nominee George W. Bush, but her coverage lagged behind not only that of Bush but also that of Steve Forbes and John McCain, who at the time were behind her in the polls.

Dole received less issue coverage than Bush, Forbes, or McCain. However, Dole's issue coverage was balanced between such stereotypically masculine issues as taxes, foreign policy, and the economy and such stereotypically feminine issues as education, drugs, and gun control. Dole also received more personal coverage than her male opponents, including references to her appearance and, especially, personality.

Perhaps the most dramatic examples of stereotypical media coverage were witnessed in Clinton's eighteen-month bid for the Democratic nomination for president from February 2007 through June 2008. Academic research centers – such as the Center for Media and Public Affairs (CMPA) at George Mason University – and studies by scholars in the areas of political science, communication, and journalism have documented that Clinton's media coverage was different from – and notably, more negative than – that of her male opponents (see Figure 9.1).

For example, the CMPA found that on-air evaluations of Clinton by television news programs on ABC, CBS, NBC, and Fox were mostly negative compared to those of her male opponents from October 2007 through March 2008. Similarly, an October 2007 study by the Project for Excellence in Journalism and the Joan Shorenstein Center on the Press, Politics, and Public Policy of forty-eight different outlets in five media sectors – including newspapers, online news, network television, cable television, and radio – found that Clinton's campaign coverage was 38 percent negative and 27 percent positive compared to Obama's 47 percent positive and 16 percent negative coverage.[17]

The most dramatic difference in television news coverage of Clinton and Obama was seen from December 16, 2007, through January 26, 2008 – the months leading up to the January 3 Iowa caucus, January 8 New Hampshire primary, and February 5 Super Tuesday primaries. During that time, Obama received 84 percent positive coverage compared to Clinton's 51 percent positive coverage (Figure 9.1). Even after Clinton won the New Hampshire primary, despite polls predicting she would lose, her positive coverage dropped to 47 percent while Obama's positive media coverage held steady at 83 percent.[18]

A content analysis of Clinton's newspaper coverage in Iowa and New Hampshire in the months leading up to the Iowa caucus and New Hampshire primary also revealed that Clinton received significantly more negative coverage and significantly less positive coverage than Obama and Edwards.[19] Of the stories focusing on Clinton, 22 percent were coded as negative. Comparatively, just 2 percent of the stories focusing on Obama were considered negative. And none of the stories focusing on Edwards was coded as negative.

Of the stories focusing on Edwards, 61 percent were coded as positive. Of the stories focusing on Obama, 66 percent were considered positive. Clinton, in contrast, received positive coverage in only 33 percent of the stories focusing on her candidacy in Iowa and New Hampshire.

In addition, stories focusing on Clinton were more likely to emphasize her campaign strategies and personal characteristics than issues. For example, only 8 percent of the stories focusing on Clinton emphasized issues, compared to 24 percent of the stories about Obama and 23 percent of those on Edwards. Clinton was linked most often with health care, an issue that she often touted in her television ads and speeches, but also with the war in Iraq, for which her support in the U.S. Senate was seen as a negative with many Democratic voters, especially in Iowa.

Of the stories focusing on Clinton, 27 percent emphasized her campaign strategies compared to 17 percent of the stories on Obama and 16 percent of the stories about Edwards. All three candidates were most likely to get coverage related to their personal characteristics; 47 percent of the stories focusing on Clinton, 44 percent of the stories about Obama, and 42 percent of the stories on Edwards emphasized their personalities, characteristics, and families.

The problem was not just that Clinton received more negative media coverage than her male opponents or that her coverage was more likely to focus on campaign strategies rather than issues. Clinton also drew blatantly sexist coverage of her appearance and personality. Web sites such as Women in Media and News (http://www.wimnonline.org/), The New Agenda (http://thenewagenda.net/), and Media Matters for America (http://mediamatters.org/); blogs; and newspaper articles documented numerous examples of sexist attacks launched against Clinton in the 2008 campaign. Some of the more flagrant and widely discussed examples of Clinton's sexist media coverage are the following:

- In a July 20, 2007, article in the *Washington Post*, fashion writer Robin Givhan criticized Clinton for showing cleavage in an outfit she wore while speaking on the Senate floor on July 18.[20] Other media outlets picked up the story, devoting substantial coverage to Clinton's cleavage as a supposed campaign strategy. According to a report by Media Matters for America, MSNBC devoted almost twenty-four minutes to segments discussing Clinton's cleavage between 9 a.m. and 5 p.m. on July 30.

- Three articles in the September 30, 2007, *New York Times* commented on Clinton's laugh, evoking negative stereotypes about women. Patrick Healy dubbed it the "Clinton cackle,"[21] Frank Rich called her laugh "calculating,"[22] and Maureen Dowd wrote that Clinton was transitioning "from nag to wag."[23] On October 1, ABC's *Good Morning America*, CNN's *Situation Room*, Fox News's *Hannity & Colmes*, and MSNBC's *Hardball with Chris Matthews* all included stories about Clinton's laugh, according to Media Matters for America. One reporter who drew attention to the sexist connotations in the coverage of Clinton's laugh was Joan Vennochi of the *Boston Globe*. "HENS CACKLE. So do witches. And, so does the front-runner in the Democratic presidential contest," she wrote on September 30, 2007, noting that the media's critique of Clinton had moved "from chest to throat, and to a sound associated with female fowl."[24]

- Clinton was referred to as a "white bitch" on MSNBC and CNN; a blood-sucking "vampire" on Fox; the maniac stalker played by Glenn Close in the movie *Fatal Attraction* on CNN, *The McLaughlin Group*, and in the *London Sunday Times*; an "unkillable" zombie moving "relentlessly forward" in the *London Sunday Times*; the "wicked witch of the west" on CNN; and "everyone's first wife standing outside of probate court," a murderous mother trying to "smother infant Obama in his crib," the scheming, manipulative Nurse Ratched in the movie *One Flew over the Cuckoo's Nest*," a "she devil," and the castrating Lorena Bobbitt, all on MSNBC.[25]

After beginning the twenty-first century with six years of mostly equitable media coverage of female and male candidates for governor and U.S. Senate in terms of quantity as well as quality (e.g., assessments of their viability, positive versus negative slant, and mentions of their appearance), Clinton's media coverage, as well as that of the 2008 Republican vice presidential nominee Sarah Palin, then governor of Alaska, certainly can be seen as a setback. (See Carroll and Dittmar, Chapter 2 in this volume, for further discussion of biases in coverage of Palin and Clinton.)

The sexism that Clinton and Palin encountered in media coverage in the 2008 presidential campaign, as well as the differences that persist in the media coverage of female and male candidates for the U.S. Senate and governor, may mesh with gender biases in the electorate to put women candidates in untenable positions. By reinforcing some of the traditional gender stereotypes held by the public, the media affect the outcomes of elections and, thus, how the nation is governed.

TELEVISED POLITICAL ADVERTISING OF WOMEN CANDIDATES

Because women political candidates are often framed in stereotypical terms by the media, television advertising – and the control it affords candidates over campaign messages about their images and issues – may be even more important for female candidates. Over time, researchers have found both differences and similarities in the ways in which female and male candidates use this campaign communication medium.

In the 1980s, female candidates' political ads were more likely to emphasize social issues, such as education and health care, whereas men were more likely to focus on economic issues such as taxes. In highlighting their personal traits, women were more likely to emphasize compassion and men to stress their strength, although sometimes both sexes emphasized stereotypically masculine traits such as competence and leadership. Men were more likely to dress in formal attire, while women preferred "feminized" business suits and office or professional settings.[26]

From the 1990s to the present, as more women ran for political office, my colleagues and I found that female and male candidates were strikingly similar in their uses of verbal, nonverbal, and film or video production techniques, although some differences were discovered.[27] Female and male candidates were similar in the use of negative spots, employing attacks in about 45 percent of their total ads. Female and male candidates were increasingly similar over time in the issues discussed in their ads and, especially, in the image traits emphasized and appeal strategies used.

The similarities and differences that did emerge over the past eighteen years are interesting from a gender perspective. For example, although female and male candidates have used attacks similarly in recent years, they differ in the purpose of the attacks and employ different strategies. Both female and male candidates now use negative ads primarily to attack their opponents on the issues. However, the ads of women candidates are significantly more likely to criticize their opponents' personal character. The ads of male candidates are significantly more likely to attack their opponents' group affiliations or associations and background or qualifications. Women are much more likely to use name-calling to attack their opponents.

Voters may view attacking the opponent's character, rather than issue stances, and calling the opponent names as much more personal. Here, female candidates may be taking advantage of voters' stereotypes, which portray women as more caring and compassionate. Female candidates may have more latitude than male candidates to make personal attacks, because they enter the race with the stereotypical advantage of being considered kinder. Of course, defying stereotypical norms also may backfire for women candidates if they are labeled as too aggressive, rather than assertive, by the media. Male candidates, in contrast, may feel more constrained by expectations that they treat women with some degree of chivalry by refraining from attacks on the personal characteristics of their female opponents. Instead, they may lash out significantly more often at their opponent's group affiliations; guilt by association may be a more acceptable and indirect way to question their opponent's character.

Although female and male candidates are increasingly similar in the issues they discuss, image traits they emphasize, and appeal strategies they use in their ads, the differences that did emerge are interesting from a gender perspective. For example, the top issue in the ads by women candidates running for office between 1990 and 2006 – and one that was discussed significantly more often in females' spots than in the ads for male candidates – was the stereotypically feminine concern for education and schools.

Kathleen Sebelius frequently discussed education in her ads, both in her successful open-seat race for governor of Kansas in 2002 and in her reelection campaign in 2006. In one of her 2002 ads, titled "Dedicated," a male voice-over announces that Sebelius would "lift teacher pay from fortieth in the nation, cut government waste to get more dollars into the classroom, and promote local control so parents and educators decide what's best for their schools." At the conclusion of this ad, Sebelius personally delivers her message, "As governor, I'll always put our children and schools first."

In 2006, Sebelius featured the issue of education – from preschool through college – in several of her ads. One ad, titled "Together," transitions from Sebelius standing in front of a parodied scene of actors posing as Kansas state legislators throwing paper at one another to a classroom with children quietly studying. Sebelius narrates most of the ad, stating: "Yup, this is how things use to be. Politicians in Topeka fighting and foot-dragging over the future of our schools, when this is where their focus should have been all along.... All it took was leadership to bring people together and put our kids and schools ahead of anything else."

In another 2006 ad, titled "Driver's Seat," Sebelius is filmed behind the wheel of a school bus while her grade-school-age passengers cite the governor's accomplishments in strengthening the state's schools. As the door opens to pick up another child, his mother says: "It just took a leader in the driver's seat to put our kids and schools before anything else."

The ads of female candidates between 1990 and 2006 also discussed other issues, such as health care and youth violence, considered feminine because they are more commonly associated with women, significantly more often than did the ads of their male opponents. As with education, female candidates may be conforming to stereotypical expectations that women should be experts on such concerns. However, female candidates were also significantly more likely than male candidates to discuss the economy in general, typically considered a masculine issue.

In her 2004 campaign for reelection, Senator Patty Murray demonstrated how masculine issues, like the economy, could be interwoven with feminine issues, such as education and health care, in the same commercial. In an ad titled "America," Murray is pictured in an orchard behind a cart of red and green apples. She narrates the ad, stating:

> I grew up and raised my family here in Washington State. It's been an honor to serve you in the U.S. Senate. But, today, I'm very concerned about the direction of our country. We need to take care of our own people. Invest in American business. Create American jobs. Improve our own local schools. Lower the cost of heath care right here at home. I'm Patty Murray, and I approved this ad because it's time to change priorities and put America first.

The only issue discussed significantly more often in the ads of male candidates than of female candidates was welfare, which is usually considered a more feminine issue. However, many of the male candidates discussing welfare took a hard-line approach, focusing on limiting the number of families receiving such benefits.

Even fewer differences are evident between female and male candidates in the images they emphasize and appeal strategies they use. However, the traits they choose to emphasize both defy and underscore stereotypical expectations about the roles and behaviors of women and men in today's society. In their ads, women candidates portrayed themselves as successful, action-oriented, aggressive, tough leaders – commonly considered masculine attributes – but also emphasized their honesty, more commonly considered a feminine quality. In their ads, men portrayed themselves as successful, action-oriented, aggressive, tough leaders with experience in politics – all masculine attributes. Among these traits, male candidates were significantly more likely than women to discuss their experience in politics.

Action, leadership, independence, and success were themes emphasized by Maine's U.S. Senator Susan Collins in her successful 2008 reelection campaign. Responding to attacks by her Democratic male opponent for her support of the war in Iraq, Collins emphasized her leadership across party lines on issues such as the economy, home health care, diabetes research, education, and energy independence in a series of commercials. Her ads typically ended with an anonymous male announcer describing Collins as "an independent voice for Maine" or "always working for Maine." In one ad, titled "A Good Senator Knows (1)," Collins closes the ad by telling her audience, "We ought to be able to sit down, negotiate and get the job done."

The appeal strategies used in female and male candidate ads were closely related to the traits they emphasized and are thus interesting from a gender perspective. Both female and male candidates were equally likely to employ all the elements of feminine style, characterized by an inductive structure (moving from specific observations to broader generalizations), personal tone, addressing viewers as peers, use of personal experiences, identifying with the experiences of others, and inviting audience participation. Male candidates did rely on statistics – a masculine strategy – significantly more often than female candidates did, and female candidates were significantly more likely to make gender an issue in their ads, an indication that at least some women are campaigning as female candidates and not political candidates who happen to be women. The fact that both women and men used elements of feminine style in similar proportions may suggest that this style works best for thirty-second spots on television, regardless of candidate gender.

In the nonverbal content of their television ads, female candidates were significantly more likely to dress in businesslike, as opposed to casual, attire and to smile more often than men did. Both of these nonverbal characteristics reflect gender-based norms and stereotypical expectations. The choice of businesslike attire reflects the gender-based norms that society imposes on women as they face the challenge of portraying themselves as serious and legitimate candidates. In their everyday life, smiling is regarded as a nonverbal strategy that women use to gain acceptance. Perhaps women are more likely than men to smile in their ads for the same reason – to gain acceptance from viewers in the traditionally male political environment.

Because society's gender stereotypes more often associate women with families and children, it is interesting to note who is pictured in female and male candidate ads. Interestingly, women candidates distanced themselves from their roles as wives and/or mothers by picturing their families in only 8 percent of their ads, while male candidates showed their families in 18 percent of their ads between 1990 and 2006. In picturing their families or not, both male and female candidates are confronting societal stereotypes. Women candidates may want to show voters that they are more than wives and/or mothers and to dismiss any concerns voters may have over their abilities to serve in political office because of family obligations. Male candidates, in contrast, may want to round out their images beyond business and politics by portraying themselves as loving husbands and/or fathers.

Winning female and male candidates use different strategies from losing female and male candidates. Specifically, female candidates who ultimately won had discussed issues more frequently – taxes, health care, senior citizen issues, and women's issues, in particular – and emphasized being an aggressive fighter more often than other candidates had. Male candidates who won had discussed crime and prison issues more frequently and had emphasized their leadership and experience. Women candidates – both winning and losing – used attacks in almost half of their ads. Losing men were the most negative, and winning men – perhaps because they were running in less competitive races in which they did not need to go on the attack to win – were the least negative of all candidates in their campaigns.

Overall, it is notable that female candidates who won tended to be those who emphasized masculine traits and both feminine and masculine issues (although more feminine than masculine issues). Winning candidates, both female and male, used substantial issue discussion in their advertising, but this was particularly true of the ads of winning female candidates. Winning male candidates, however, incorporated a mix of feminine and masculine strategies to ensure their success. For example, in the first television ad of his successful 2008 reelection campaign against Jill Long Thompson, Indiana Governor Mitch Daniels incorporated many elements of feminine style – such as personal tone, addressing viewers as peers, and the use of personal experiences – and balanced masculine and feminine issues and traits. In an ad titled "Spirit of Optimism," Daniels narrates:

> Traveling the state. Seeing the small towns. Staying in people's houses. That's what we do. That's where we get our marching orders. Where people tell us which problems they want us to go back and tackle. . . . I hope people accept the sincerity of what we are trying to do. And are becoming infected with the spirit of optimism. And they're seeing that change can happen. Budgets can balance. More jobs can happen. People can have their prescription drug costs slashed. Government can actually deliver for people.

In addition to the content of the television ads, it is interesting to look at the effects these appeals have on potential voters. At first, researchers speculated that masculine strategies (aggressive, career) – rather than traditional feminine strategies (nonaggressive, family) – worked best for women candidates in their political ads. However, it now seems that women are most effective when balancing stereotypically masculine and feminine traits, such as being tough and caring. Women are more effective when communicating about stereotypically feminine issues such as women's rights, education, and unemployment than such stereotypically masculine issues as crime and illegal immigration.

On the basis of the research, then, women candidates should be advised to emphasize both stereotypically feminine and masculine images and issues in their television commercials. Voters will perceive a woman candidate as more honest and trustworthy than a man and just as intelligent and able to forge compromise and obtain consensus. However, especially in a climate of international terrorism, homeland security, and the war in Iraq, a woman candidate will need to emphasize her ability to lead the nation during a crisis and to make difficult decisions.

Issue emphasis will vary with the context of the campaign. In the 1990 through 2006 elections, taxes, education, jobs, health care, and senior citizen concerns were the top issues discussed by female and male candidates in their television ads, with women much more likely than men to discuss education, health care, and senior citizens. According to survey research, voters rate female candidates more favorably than male candidates on these issues. However, women candidates are considered less able to handle such issues as law and order, foreign policy, and governmental problems. In elections like those of 2002, 2004, and 2006 – when war and terrorism join other issues among top voter concerns – women candidates must work hard to demonstrate their competence on such issues.

WEB SITES OF WOMEN POLITICAL CANDIDATES

In recent years, the Internet has provided political candidates and office-holders with an important means of communicating with voters and constituents, and researchers with another way to look at the political communication of female and male politicians. Web sites, like television advertising, represent a form of political communication controlled by the politician rather than interpreted by the media.

Recent research shows that female and male politicians present themselves similarly on their Web sites.[28] According to Mary Banwart, who has studied the Web sites of female and male candidates in the 2000, 2002, and 2004 campaigns, both women and men feature feminine issues on their Web sites more than masculine ones.[29] Women are most likely to discuss education, health care, taxes, and senior citizen issues and men to focus on education, the environment, taxes, and health care. In 2004, Banwart found more frequent discussion, as compared to previous election cycles, of homeland security, unemployment, and the economy on both female and male candidates' Web sites.

In her successful U.S. Senate campaign in 2004, incumbent Lisa Murkowski of Alaska emphasized masculine issues such as gas prices, gun rights, Iraq, and Afghanistan along with such feminine issues as quality health care and expanded stem cell research. U.S. Senate candidate Claire McCaskill of Missouri, who ran successfully as a challenger in 2006, emphasized the masculine issues of national security and the economy as well as the feminine issues of education, affordable health care, and retirement security on her Web site.

Overall, female and male candidates discussed mostly the same issues on their Web sites as they did in their television ads, suggesting, once again, that issue emphasis is more related to the context of the particular political campaign than to the sex of the candidates.

Both female and male candidates attempted to establish similar images on their Web sites, highlighting performance and success, experience, leadership, and qualifications – all stereotypically masculine traits. However, in 2004, both were also more likely to emphasize cooperation and honesty – two feminine traits – perhaps in response to media coverage of divisiveness between the political parties. That is, both female and male candidates emphasized that they were willing to cooperate with the other party in the context of the 2004 campaign.

Candidates were also more likely to launch attacks on their Web sites than in their television ads. From 2000 through 2004, more than 60 percent of the Web sites of both women and men employed negative attacks, compared to about 45 percent of their ads. Again, the greater use of attacks on candidates' Web sites, as compared to television ads, underscores the difference between these media. As Web sites are most often accessed by people already supporting the candidate, it is safer to include attacks. Television ads, in contrast, have the potential to reach all voters, who may be turned off by attacks.

As in their political ads, women candidates were most likely to appear in business attire on their Web sites; in fact, they were so dressed in 92 percent of the photographs used. In contrast to their televised advertising, however, male candidates were also more likely to be seen in business attire (71 percent), as opposed to casual attire (39 percent), on their Web sites. Women's dominant use of business attire is characteristic of female candidates' self-presentation; that is, women choose such attire to establish a professional appearance that emphasizes their competence and the seriousness of their candidacy to convince voters of their legitimacy.

However, on a Web site – as opposed to television – male candidates also clearly feel the need to appeal to more traditional political expectations by establishing an image of a serious, viable political candidate.

Most of the photographs on candidates' Web sites showed the candidate with other people, whether the images were located on the candidates' home pages or in their biography sections. Male candidates were slightly more likely (68 percent) than female candidates (54 percent) to include pictures of just themselves in their candidate biography sections, while female candidates were slightly more likely (73 percent) than male candidates (64 percent) to include pictures of themselves with other people, perhaps seeking to illustrate that many are supportive of their campaigns. When others were shown in the photos, female candidates were more likely (88 percent) than male candidates (75 percent) to have men in their photos, and in many instances, these were men in positions of power and prestige, a strategy undoubtedly designed to lend legitimacy to the female candidate's campaign.

For example, in their successful 2006 campaigns for governor, Jennifer Granholm of Michigan included a photo with former president Bill Clinton on her Web site, while Republican Jodi Rell of Connecticut pictured herself with members of the Boston Celtics. Amy Klobuchar, who won an open-seat U.S. Senate race in Minnesota in 2006, featured photos with former president Clinton and former Georgia senator Max Cleland, a disabled Army veteran. Alaska Senator Murkowski included a photo with President George W. Bush on her Web site.

Both female and male candidates featured women in about 80 percent of their Web sites and minorities in about 60 percent. Women (67 percent) were more likely to post photos of senior citizens on their Web sites compared to men (54 percent). Although 61 percent of male candidates' sites included photos of their families, only 44 percent of female candidates' sites included such images. It seems that some female candidates choose not to associate themselves with their families in hopes of not being linked with motherhood and domestic responsibilities, which can diminish their political credibility. For male candidates, however, the presence of family can evoke notions of stability and tradition, suggesting that because they have a family to protect, they will govern in ways that will protect the viewer's family as well.

One advantage that Web sites have over television ads is the potential for interaction with Internet users, allowing the candidates to appear more personal as well as to raise money and recruit volunteers. Female and male candidates seem to be trying to take advantage of the opportunity for interactivity, although in rather limited forms. Female and male candidates in 2004 included more links from their home pages than they had in previous election cycles, although male candidates were more likely to offer more links overall than female candidates. Almost all candidates provided links from their home pages to candidate biography sections, issues sections, contribution sections, "get involved" sections, campaign directories, and news coverage. Male candidates were more likely to link to a calendar of events section, which requires more frequent updates and attention than a well-established biography section, contribution section, or even issues section. So male candidates either are more aware of the need to have their Web sites current and up to date, or they may simply have the financial ability to pay someone to do so.

Overall, the Web sites of candidates running in recent U.S. Senate and gubernatorial mixed-gender races were largely similar. Notably, few gender differences emerged. Thus, it appears that the strategies used in political candidate Web site design are in response to expectations for the medium rather than candidates' sex. The ability to present an unmediated message to potential voters makes the campaign Web site an appealing venue for female candidates in particular.

CONCLUSION

An examination of how female and male candidates are presented in their campaign news coverage, political advertising, and Web sites perhaps suggests more questions than answers. Interpreting the results of more than thirty years of research examining the campaign communication of women running for the U.S. Senate and governor is further complicated by studies of the rarer bids of female presidential and vice presidential candidates, such as Hillary Clinton and Sarah Palin in 2008. In addition, researchers are just starting to examine the impact of the recent emergence of new media – such as online news sites, commercial Web sites, blogs, social networking sites such as MySpace and Facebook, and the popular video-sharing Web site YouTube – on mainstream media coverage and candidate communication.

Nonetheless, several recurring trends help guide our expectations for the future role of gendered campaign communication.

Candidates do not have complete control of how the news media decide to cover their campaigns. In the 1980s and 1990s, especially, female candidates suffered from gendered media coverage that often afforded them less coverage, which focused on their appearance, rather than the issues, and questioned their ability to win. However, in more recent campaign cycles, female candidates for governor and U.S. Senate have achieved sufficient status as candidates to be given equal and sometimes greater coverage in newspapers than their male opponents. In fact, since 2000, female candidates – including presidential candidate Hillary Clinton in 2008 – received as much or more total coverage than did their male opponents.

However, some areas of news coverage remain troublesome for female candidates. The tendency of the media to emphasize candidate sex, appearance, marital status, and masculine issues in news coverage still haunts female candidates. Candidate sex is still mentioned more frequently for women, reporters still comment more often on a female candidate's dress or appearance, and journalists still refer to a female candidate's marital status more frequently. The mostly negative and often sexist coverage of Clinton and Palin in the 2008 presidential race shows that women seeking national executive office face considerable obstacles in their media coverage.

Some of the most negative and sexist comments about Clinton and Palin in 2008 first appeared in the new media and then spilled over into the mainstream media in the coverage of their campaigns. The online universe of political commentary operates outside of traditional media editorial boundaries and is sometimes incisive but often offensive and unsubstantiated. Common themes that originated in the new media – and spilled over into the mainstream media – about Clinton in her 2008 presidential campaign portrayed her as psychotic, a power-hungry stalker, a killer, or a castrator and questioned her sexuality. New media commentary on Palin often exploited her "feminized" sexuality, comparing her to a Barbie doll and Photoshopping her head onto a bikini-clad woman with an automatic weapon.

Although neither male nor female candidates can directly control news coverage, they can have some influence on it. For example, by focusing on a mixture of masculine and feminine issues, a female candidate can achieve a balance that diminishes the likelihood that the media will leave her out of a discussion of masculine issues. Female candidates also can use their controlled communication media – television ads and Web sites – to influence their news coverage. For the past three decades, the news media have increased their coverage of candidate television advertising, so women candidates can influence their news coverage by producing high-quality ads that will attract media attention. It is also likely that, as Web campaigning becomes more popular and more developed, news media will expand their coverage of candidates' Web sites as part of the campaign dialogue.

Television commercials and Web sites also provide female candidates with tremendous opportunities to present themselves directly to voters, without interpretation by the news media. Television advertising is still the dominant form of candidate communication for most major-level races in which female candidates must compete with male opponents. Female candidates are successfully establishing their own competitive styles of political advertising. For example, women candidates have overcome the stereotypical admonition that they must avoid attacks. Even as challengers, they have been able to adopt strategies typical of incumbents to give themselves authority. Female candidates who win also seem to have been successful at achieving a television videostyle that is overall positive, emphasizes personal traits of toughness and strength, and capitalizes on the importance of feminine issues such as education and health care while also discussing masculine issues such as the economy and defense or security. Winning female candidates also top their male opponents by keeping their attire businesslike and their smiles bright.

When it comes to self-presentation in the newest campaign medium, the Internet, research shows fewer differences between male and female candidates. Both men and women candidates' Web sites are characterized by significant amounts of issue information. And, unlike the balance between feminine and masculine issues observed in their television commercials, Web sites for both sexes seem to focus more on feminine issues. Both female and male candidates also focus on past accomplishments on their sites and, especially in 2004, on their ability to cooperate.

Perhaps the newness of this medium has not allowed for sufficient development of different styles for female and male candidates running for the U.S. Senate and governor. Neither sex has taken full advantage of the Web's ability to provide message segmentation for different types of groups. Although the 2004 campaign Web sites provided some additional use of links to solicit contributions and volunteers, both sexes are still lagging behind commercial development trends in providing interactivity and personalization on their Web sites.

The Web may be the best venue for female candidates wanting an equal competition with male candidates, especially in situations where resources are limited. A female candidate can do much more for much less on the Web than through television advertising. Female candidates should develop sophisticated Web sites that provide more specialized messages to specific groups, use innovative types of interactivity, and generate a more personalized presence with voters (e.g., through audio-visual presentations by the candidate and by providing opportunities for citizens to tune in for personal chats and question-and-answer sessions with the candidate or campaign representatives). Web sites also can be used to respond to rumors and attacks generated by the new media.

Despite continuing stereotypes held by voters and the media, women candidates can manage campaign communication tools in ways that improve their chances of success. Women candidates who present themselves successfully in their television ads and on their Web sites may be able to capitalize on these controlled messages to influence their media coverage for a synergistic communication effort.

NOTES

1 Maura Reynolds. November 2, 2006. Post-Election Power Surge Expected for Feinstein. *Los Angeles Times*.
2 Linda Witt, Karen M. Paget, and Glenna Matthews. 1995. *Running as a Woman: Gender and Power in American Politics*. New York: Free Press.
3 Witt, Paget, and Matthews 1995.
4 Michael Dorning. October 22, 1998. Carol Moseley Braun for Senator, Image Is Asset and Curse: Though She Stresses Her Record, the Democrat Finds Her Personality and a Series of Missteps in the Spotlight. *Chicago Tribune*.
5 James Devitt. 1999. Framing Gender on the Campaign Trail: Women's Executive Leadership and the Press. Washington, D.C.: Women's Leadership Fund.
6 Ibid.
7 Jennifer L. Pozner. March 13, 2001. Cosmetic Coverage. <http://www.alternet.org./story/10592> March 1, 2009.
8 Ibid.
9 Kim Fridkin and Miki Kittilson. April 12, 2007. Gender Differences in Media Coverage of Candidates: A Comparative Perspective. <http://www.allacademic.com/meta/p196586_index.html> March 1, 2009.
10 John J. Miller. April 7, 2006. Glamour-Girl Gov, Gone? <http://www.nationalreview.com/issue/miller200604071325.asp> March 1, 2009.
11 Susan Ager. October 17, 2006. Governor's Mole Stirs Extreme Reactions. *Detroit Free Press*.
12 Kim F. Kahn. 1992. Does Being Male Help? An Investigation of the Effects of Candidate Gender and Campaign Coverage on Evaluations of U.S. Senate Candidates. *Journal of Politics* 54: 497–517.
13 Kevin B. Smith. 1998. When All's Fair: Signs of Parity in Media Coverage of Female Candidates. *Political Communication* 14: 71–82.
14 Devitt 1999.
15 Dianne G. Bystrom, Mary C. Banwart, Lynda Lee Kaid, and Terry Robertson. 2004. *Gender and Candidate Communication: VideoStyles, WebStyles, NewsStyles*.

New York: Routledge. Throughout this chapter, references to specific findings and statistics, unless otherwise referenced, are from the research in this book.

16 See Sean Aday and James Devitt. 2001. Style over Substance. Newspaper Coverage of Female Candidates: Spotlight on Elizabeth Dole. Washington, D.C.: Women's Leadership Fund; Dianne Bystrom. 2006. Media Content and Candidate Viability: The Case of Elizabeth Dole. In *Communicating Politics: Engaging the Public in Democratic Life*, ed. Mitchell S. McKinney, Dianne G. Bystrom, Lynda Lee Kaid, and Diana B. Carlin. New York: Peter Lang Publishing; and Caroline Heldman, Susan J. Carroll, and Stephanie Olson. 2005. "She Brought Only a Skirt": Print Media Coverage of Elizabeth Dole's Bid for the Republican Presidential Nomination. *Political Communication* 22: 315–35.

17 Project for Excellence in Journalism. 2007. The Invisible Primary – Invisible No Longer: A First Look at Coverage of the 2008 Presidential Campaign. <http://www.journalism.org/node/8187> March 1, 2009.

18 Donald Rieck. February 1, 2008. Media Boost Obama, Bash 'Billary': NBC Is Toughest on Hillary; FOX has Heaviest Coverage. <http://www.cmpa.com/Studies/Election08/election%20news%202_1_08.htm> March 1, 2009.

19 Dianne Bystrom. August 29, 2008. Gender and U.S. Presidential Politics: Early Newspaper Coverage of Hillary Clinton's Bid for the White House. Paper presented at the annual meeting of the American Political Science Association, Boston, MA.

20 Robin Givhan. July 20, 2007. Hillary Clinton's Tentative Dip into New Neckline Territory. *Washington Post*.

21 Patrick Healy. September 30, 2007. The Clinton Conundrum: What's Behind the Laugh? *New York Times*. <http://www.nytimes.com/2007/09/30/us/politics/30clinton.html> March 1, 2009.

22 Frank Rich. September 30, 2007. Is Hillary Clinton the New Old Al Gore? *New York Times*. <http://www.nytimes.com/2007/09/30/opinion/30rich.html> March 1, 2009.

23 Maureen Dowd. September 30, 2007. The Nepotism Tango. *New York Times*. <http://www.nytimes.com/2007/09/30/opinion/30dowd.html?_r=1&hp> March 1, 2009.

24 Joan Vennochi. September 30, 2007. That Clinton Cackle. *Boston Globe*. <http://www.boston.com/news/globe/editorial_opinion/oped/articles/2007/09/30/that_clinton_cackle/> March 1, 2009.

25 Media Matters for America. Search for articles on Hillary Clinton. <http://mediamatters.org/issues_topics/search_results?qstring=Hillary±Clinton> March 1, 2009.

26 See Anne Johnston and Anne Barton White. 1994. Communication Styles and Female Candidates: A Study of Political Advertisements of Men and Women Candidates for U.S. Senate. *Political Research Quarterly* 46: 481–501; Kim F. Kahn. 1993. Gender Differences in Campaign Messages: The Political Advertisements of Men and Women Candidates for U.S. Senate. *Political Research Quarterly* 46 (3): 481–502; and Judith Trent and Teresa Sabourin.

1993. Sex Still Counts: Women's Use of Televised Advertising during the Decade of the 80s. *Journal of Applied Communication Research* 21 (1): 21–40.

27 Bystrom, Banwart, Kaid, and Robertson 2004. The database of television commercials for female and male gubernatorial and U.S. Senate candidates from 1990 through 2002 used in this book has been updated with ads from similar races in 2004 and 2006 for this chapter. This database now includes 1,550 ads; 782 for women and 768 for men; 810 for Republicans and 740 for Democrats; 956 for U.S. Senate candidates and 594 for gubernatorial candidates.

28 Ibid.

29 Mary Christine Banwart. 2006. Webstyles in 2004: The Gendering of Candidates on Campaign Websites? In *The Internet Election: Perspectives on the Web in Campaign 2004*, ed. Andrew Paul Williams and John C. Tedesco. Lanham, MD: Rowman and Littlefield.

10 State Elections

Why Do Women Fare Differently across States?

The public was transfixed by the historic presidential election of 2008. But below the national level, there were other riveting gender stories.[1] Only one woman sought the presidency, but more than 2,300 women sought state legislative office. A record number of women were elected to state legislatures in 2008. And for the first time in U.S. history, women won a majority of seats in a state legislative chamber: as a result of the election, women constitute a majority of the New Hampshire Senate – thirteen of twenty-four members. After the election, the woman antic-ipated to be the next Senate majority leader, Maggie Hassan, observed: "It feels incredibly exciting, but at the same time, not surprising."[2] The accomplishments of women in the Granite State did not begin in 2008; the state has long been among the nation's leaders in women's represen-tation. Even in the mid-1980s, the legislature was more than 30 percent female. In contrast, as a result of the 2008 election, no women serve in the South Carolina Senate. Unlike New Hampshire, South Carolina has consistently lagged in women's representation. The maximum number of women to ever serve in that state's forty-six-member senate is three.

State elections usually attract less attention than national elections. However, because it is much more common for women to seek state office than federal office, we can learn a great deal about women's candidacies by studying the states. In addition, state legislative or executive office can be a springboard to candidacy for higher office. Therefore, women's gains in the states shape the likelihood that women will reach national office. Indeed, half the members of Congress previously served in the legislatures.[3] For example, in one of the most closely watched races in 2008, a state senator from North Carolina, Kay Hagan, was elected to the U.S. Senate, defeating incumbent Elizabeth Dole.

The presence of women in state offices is also critical to public policy. We know that women legislators are much more likely than men to feel an obligation to represent women as a group and to work on legislation designed to help women, children, and families. Men and women come from different backgrounds, bring different issues to the table, and take different policy positions as well. State policies reach all aspects of daily life, from laws governing family and marriage to voting rights and social policies. Education, health-care, and child-care policies vary dramatically across states. Some states have constitutional amendments guaranteeing women and men equality under the law, while others do not. Access to abortion and contraceptives depends on the state as well.

How did women fare in the 2008 elections in the states? I argue that it was a history-making year for women in some states. Yet this chapter will also show that the total number of women governors remained unchanged and that the presence of women in statewide offices has declined in recent years. We will see that women's opportunities for elective office vary across the states and across the two major political parties. In summary, although there has been significant progress, women remain far from reaching parity with men in elective office. Progress for women has been uneven over time and depends on place. Thus, women's advancement in state politics is not a foregone conclusion.

BACKGROUND: WOMEN IN THE STATE LEGISLATURES

The milestones for women seeking public office are not very well known. Even before the national suffrage fight was won, Clara Cressingham, Carrie C. Holly, and Frances Klock were elected to the Colorado House of Representatives in the 1890s. The first woman to serve in a state senate – Martha Hughes Cannon – lived in Utah. Women's firsts were not limited to the West. In 1924, Cora Belle Reynolds Anderson of Michigan, a Native American, became the first woman of color elected to a legislature. The first African American woman, Minnie Buckingham Harper, was appointed to the West Virginia House of Representatives in 1929.

Women state legislators have become less of a novelty since then. As more women have run for office, voters, parties, donors, and women themselves have become more used to the idea of women as politicians. Whereas women were less than 5 percent of all state legislators in 1971, women are now 24.3 percent of legislators (see Figure 10.1). A total of 1,791 women hold state legislative office in 2009. Women's groups

Figure 10.1: The proportion of women serving in state legislatures reached a record high in 2009.

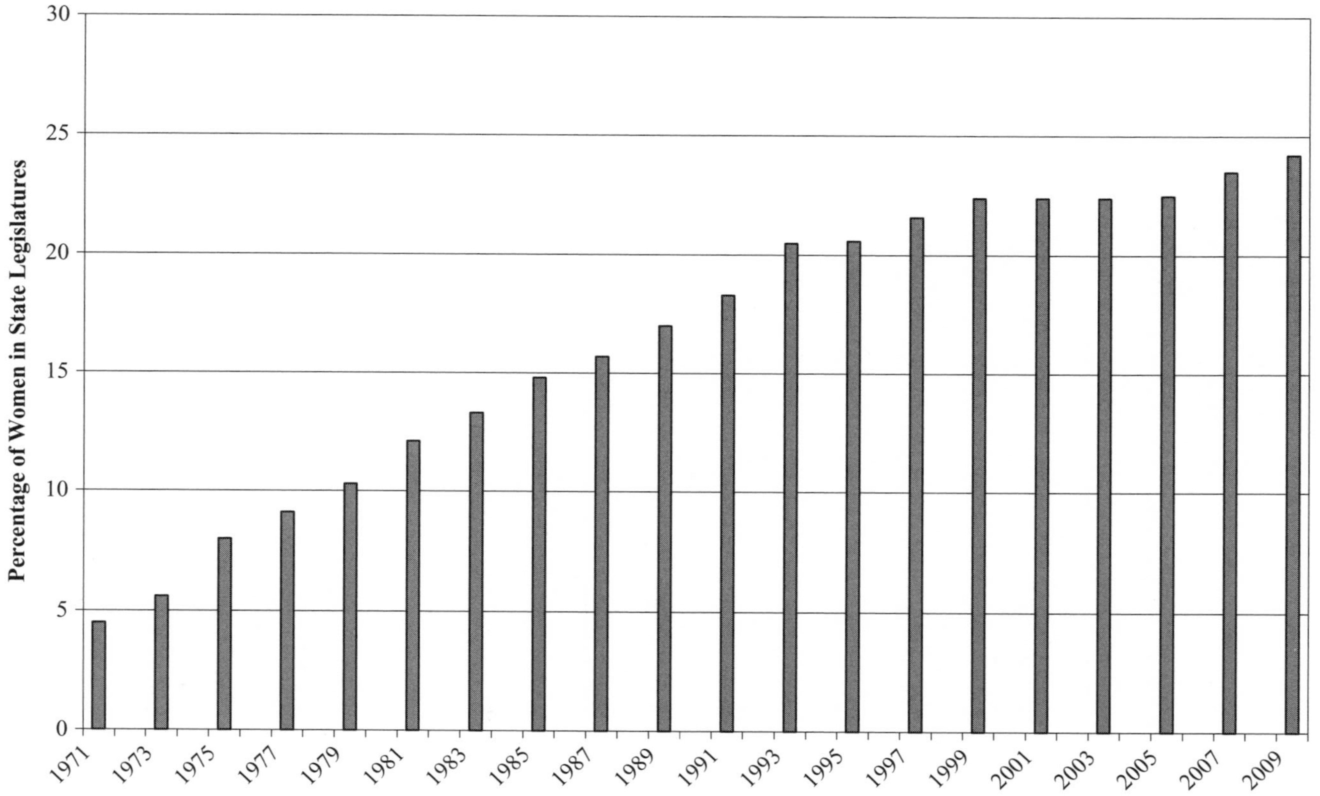

Source: Center for American Women and Politics.

dedicated to electing more women to office have been critical to women's gains.

Women state legislators are increasingly likely to be women of color. In 2009, women of color are 19 percent of all women legislators, compared to about 12 percent in 1988. These numbers include 230 African American women, 72 Latinas, 32 women who are Asian American or Pacific Islanders, and 13 Native American women. Almost all of these legislators of color – 95 percent – are Democrats. One of these women, Karen Bass, is the speaker of the California State Assembly and the first African American woman to ever lead a legislative chamber.

Women's officeholding is also shaped by political party. For most of the twentieth century, the Democratic Party was the majority party and dominated the state legislatures. The Republican Party has become much more competitive in recent decades. In the past two election cycles, though, the Democratic Party fared well; Democrats currently have unified control of twenty-seven state legislatures, while the Republican Party controls fourteen. In eight states, control is divided between the two parties. (And one state, Nebraska, is nonpartisan).[4] Thus, most state legislators today are Democrats. Republican women used to constitute a larger share of all Republican legislators than Democratic women of all Democratic legislators (see Figure 10.2). But now women are much better represented among Democratic legislators. In terms of raw numbers, as well, women state legislators are much more likely to be Democrats than Republicans (see Figure 10.3). In fact, Democratic women are increasingly winning state legislative office, whereas the number of Republican women state legislators has declined since the mid-1990s.

THE 2008 STATE LEGISLATIVE ELECTIONS

A total of 5,824 state legislative seats in forty-four states were up for election in 2008. A total of 2,328 women ran in the general election for these seats, slightly fewer than the number of women running in the most recent comparable election.[5] Women who run for the legislatures do not appear to be at a disadvantage compared to men when other factors are taken into account.[6] A candidate's chances of winning office depend much more on the type of race than on gender. An incumbent seeking reelection is quite likely to win his or her race, while a challenger trying to unseat that incumbent faces long odds. The most competitive races are for open seats, where there is no incumbent seeking reelection. However, the likelihood of winning open seats often depends on the candidate's party

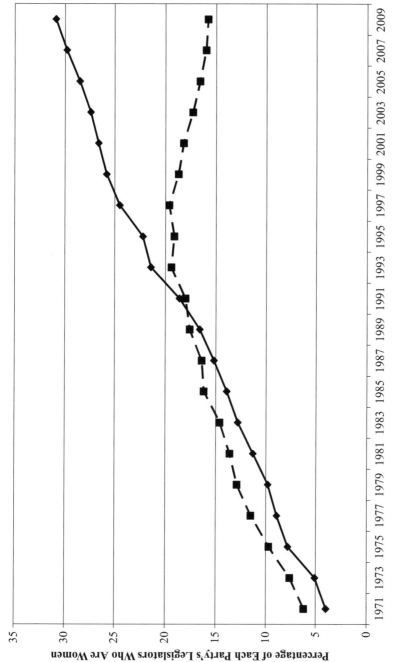

Figure 10.2: **Women are a greater share of Democratic than Republican legislators.**

Source: Center for American Women and Politics.

Figure 10.3: **The number of Republican women in state legislatures has declined.**

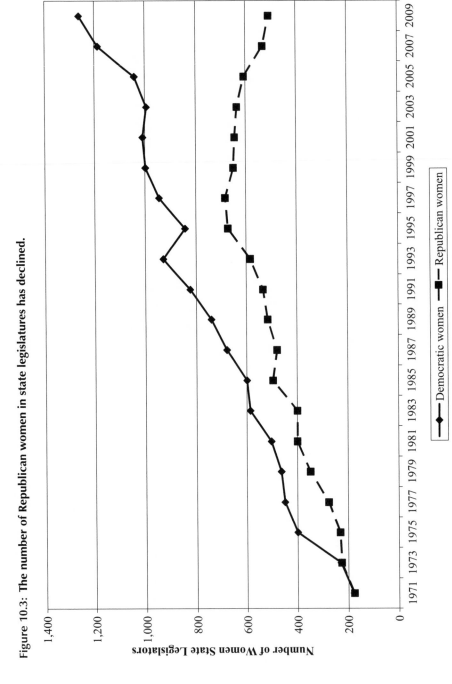

Source: Center for American Women and Politics.

TABLE 10.1: More Democratic women than Republican women sought election to the state legislatures in 2008

	Democrat	Republican
Women candidates		
Open seat	325	186
Challenger	405	240
Incumbent	811	352
Total	**1,541**	**778**
Women winners		
Open seat	189	86
Challenger	47	18
Incumbent	790	326
Total	**1,026**	**430**

Note: Cell entries are numbers of general election candidates and winners by type of race.
Source: Center for American Women and Politics.

affiliation, because most legislative districts are likely to favor one party over the other. When a seat is thought to be safely in one party's column, the other party may not bother to run a candidate; in 2004, for example, 35 percent of all state legislative seats up for election were not contested by one of the major parties.[7]

Like men, women have been much more successful when they run as incumbents than when they run as challengers or for open seats. Of the female major party incumbents running for office, 95 percent won reelection in 2004; similarly, 96 percent won reelection in 2008. Candidates who ran as challengers won only 11 percent of their races in 2004 and 10 percent in 2008 – not atypical statistics, given the difficulties of unseating a sitting legislator. About half of all open-seat candidates were successful in both 2004 and 2008.

As a result of the 2008 elections, twenty-two states saw an increase in women legislators, but twelve states saw a decrease. The largest percentage decreases occurred in Oregon, Wyoming, Delaware, Arizona, and Washington, with the largest increases in Texas, Michigan, Indiana, Connecticut, and Utah. Thus, women's progress is not inevitable, with some elections bringing a decrease in women's officeholding.

Importantly, in both 2004 and 2008, Democratic women candidates outnumbered Republican women about two to one (see Table 10.1). In 2008, for example, 1,541 Democratic women ran in the general election, whereas only 778 Republican women did so. Because most women ran as incumbents, it is not surprising that the party gap continued as a result of the 2008 election. But the gap between the two groups of women grew, in part because Democratic women fared better in the election. In 2008, 97 percent of Democratic women and 93 percent of Republican women won their races when they ran as incumbents, 11.6 percent of Democratic women and 7.5 percent of Republican women won their races as challengers, and about 58 percent of Democratic women open-seat candidates but only about 46 percent of Republican women won.

Because this party gap among women has grown and the Democrats control more chambers, Democratic women are poised to play leadership roles within the legislatures. Indeed, the 2008 elections made possible a number of important milestones for women in leadership roles across the country. For example, for the first time in the history of the state, women lead both the Senate and House in Maine. Senator Elizabeth H. Mitchell was elected Senate president and Hannah Pingree Speaker of the House. Pingree, just thirty-two years old, is only the second woman to serve as Maine's Speaker, the first being Senator Mitchell. Both women are Democrats. Both the Senate president and Speaker of the House in New Hampshire are women as well, which is the second time in New Hampshire's history this has occurred. Meanwhile, Rhode Island elected its first female Senate president, M. Teresa Paiva-Weed. Thus, women state legislators are achieving important positions within their institutions and setting new records, state by state.

CROSS-STATE VARIATION IN WOMEN'S LEGISLATIVE OFFICEHOLDING

Because men and women tend to win their races at similar rates, the crux of the problem of women's underrepresentation lies in the dearth of women state legislative candidates. Despite significant advances, women remain much less likely than men to become candidates. In recent years, for example, women have been only about one-quarter of state legislative candidates. Making sense of the patterns of women's state legislative officeholding calls our attention to the paucity of women candidates and the need to understand the environments in which women decide to run for office.

The scarcity of women candidates can partially be explained by incumbency. Because most state legislators who are incumbents win reelection, and most incumbent legislators are men, women are more likely to increase their presence in office by running for open seats where there is no incumbent in the race rather than as challengers trying to unseat incumbents. Incumbency is an institutional constraint on the pace at which any new group of officeholders, including women, can increase their presence.

Even in races for open seats, though, women remain much less likely than men to run. Among the pool of potential candidates with the informal qualifications for office, studies have shown that women are less likely to think about becoming candidates.[8] For example, women potential candidates with backgrounds in law, business, and education are much less likely than men to have considered running for political office.

The problem of the scarcity of women candidates is easy to observe in states that limit the number of years individuals can serve in the legislature. These term limits, in effect in fifteen states, were expected to open doors for women and yield a dramatic increase in women officeholders by creating open seats. Yet that has not been the result. Term limits create openings, but women have not necessarily taken advantage of these open seats.[9] Meanwhile, all incumbents – men and women – are prevented from seeking reelection after they have served the designated number of terms. New women may achieve office via open seats, but incumbent women must depart. Term limits also mean that women who have worked hard to achieve leadership positions can lose their positions as a result. For example, Representative Dianne Byrum might have become Michigan's Speaker of the House had she not been barred from running for reelection in 2006 because of that state's term limits. She served in both chambers from 1991 to 2007. As the state's first female Democratic minority leader, she helped the Democrats win the house in 2006: "We ended up winning 11 seats over two cycles and took control of the House, which no one thought was possible."[10] She noted: "I was the first woman in Michigan's history to ever lead a caucus, and not only lead that caucus, but take it to its best performance in 70 years. And I had to walk out the door."[11]

Although women constitute about one of every five legislators nationwide, women are not equally likely to seek state legislative office across states.[12] In South Carolina, Oklahoma, and Alabama, women are only 10–13 percent of the legislature (see Table 10.2). Low numbers are not limited to the South, though, as Pennsylvania and Wyoming are also among the lowest-ranked states for women's representation. Meanwhile, Colorado, New Hampshire, and Vermont rank highest.

TABLE 10.2: The presence of women legislators varies considerably by state

More than 30%	25%–30%	20%–24%	15%–19%	Less than 15%
Colorado	Arizona	New York	Georgia	Pennsylvania
New Hampshire	Maine	Idaho	South Dakota	Kentucky
Vermont	New Jersey	Florida	Tennessee	Mississippi
Minnesota	Kansas	Michigan	Wyoming	Alabama
Hawaii	California	Texas	Virginia	Oklahoma
Washington	Illinois	Arkansas	West Virginia	South Carolina
Nevada	Oregon	Iowa	North Dakota	
Connecticut	Massachusetts	Rhode Island	Louisiana	
Maryland	Montana	Utah		
New Mexico	North Carolina	Indiana		
	Delaware	Wisconsin		
		Missouri		
		Ohio		
		Nebraska		
		Alaska		

Source: Center for American Women and Politics, 2009 Fact Sheets. States are listed from high to low in each column.

Why do women fare better in some states than others? The pattern across states is not random. Instead, a number of factors partially explain why women are much more likely to run for office in some states than others. Women find more favorable environments in some states than others, which means that the challenges and opportunities that women face depend on place.

One factor is ideology: in states where the public holds more liberal views, women tend to be much more likely to seek and hold state legislative office.[13] Voters are more accepting of women in nontraditional roles, women are more likely to think of themselves as candidates, and political parties are more likely to see women as viable candidates as well. Thus, it is not surprising that women are least well represented in the South, given the greater conservatism in that region.

The presence of women in the social eligibility pool also matters. Most state legislators do not have prior officeholding experience.[14] But it is common for voters to have expectations about the qualifications and backgrounds of state legislators, or what are known as informal requirements for the office, in addition to the state's formal requirements for holding office, such as residency or age requirements. Legislators often have backgrounds in law, for example. Thus, more women serve in state legislatures where there is a larger pool of women with the informal qualifications expected of state legislative candidates – for example, where more women are in the labor force and more women are lawyers.

The type of legislature is yet another factor related to the presence of women. In about one-fifth of all states, being a state legislator is essentially a full-time job resembling service in Congress – as in Pennsylvania, where legislators earn about $76,000 annually and meet year-round, or California, where the pay is $116,000. These types of legislatures are considered to be full-time or professional. New Hampshire, where legislators earn just $100 per year, offers a stark contrast. In such states, legislators often pride themselves on being citizen-legislators who serve on a part-time basis.[15]

Women tend to be less well represented in the more professional legislatures. It may be more difficult for women in these states because potential candidates are keenly interested in running, putting women, the relative newcomers in electoral politics, at a disadvantage. Alternatively, parties may need to recruit more where the office is less desirable, and they may turn to new groups of candidates, including women, for these roles. Regardless, women tend to be more likely to hold office where service in the legislature is less than full-time. Of the top states for women legislators – Colorado, New Hampshire, Vermont, Minnesota, Hawaii, Washington, and Nevada – none has a full-time, professionalized legislature.[16]

In states with multimember rather than single-member districts, women are more likely to serve. In most states, only one legislator is elected per legislative district. But some states, such as Arizona, Maryland, and Washington, have multimember districts. A woman may be more likely to put herself forward to run for office when she is one candidate among many. Or perhaps when voters are able to elect more than one representative from the district, voters seek a gender balance in who represents them.

CANDIDATES AND RECRUITMENT FOR THE LEGISLATURE

Thus, the pattern of women's representation across states is not random; it can be systematically explained by both cultural and institutional factors. But informal recruitment processes within states matter as well. Recruitment is a critical component of women's election to office. The role of political parties in candidate recruitment helps explain why women remain less likely than men to run for open state legislative seats.[17] Gender differences in social networks mean that women are not typically thought of as candidates. Despite dramatic changes in the role of women in society, social networks remain quite segregated by gender. Among officeholders and political activists alike, talk of an old-boys network is not uncommon in some states. Party leaders and legislators who recruit candidates tend to look to those they know – people they do business with, people they play golf with, and so on.

Meanwhile, some party leaders have doubts about the abilities of women and their electability, which can reduce the likelihood that women will be tapped to run for office. The phrase "when women run, women win" is a popular slogan, reflecting the fact that women are as likely as men to win their races when the type of race is taken into account. But not all party leaders are in agreement about women and winning. Because party leaders want to win elections, women are not likely to be drafted for important races if party leaders think women are going to lose. Party leader attitudes are important predictors of where women hold office and can pose an obstacle to increasing women's representation.[18]

The combination of networks segregated by gender and doubts about women's capacity for politics means that women are typically worse off where parties are more influential in choosing the party nominee. Indeed, states with stronger party organizations typically have fewer women in their legislatures, and where the process is more open, women are better represented.[19] Thus, how candidates are recruited for office and whether parties are more actively involved as gatekeepers to the nomination help explain why women are more likely to seek office in some states than others.

Women candidates may have strong party support in some cases, though. Most parties recruit candidates and help them win election to maintain or increase their party's share of seats in the legislature. Parties are often selective about the candidates they recruit and support.[20] Although strong parties tend to be negatively related to women's representation, parties do sometimes select women candidates for important races.

Although being a woman can be a disadvantage in some states, it is sometimes seen as an electoral advantage, increasing the likelihood that women will be recruited to run for office. Voters perceive women as more honest and compassionate and better on education and women's issues, for example. However, other stereotypes put women at a disadvantage; men are perceived as better leaders and better able to handle issues such as foreign policy and crime. Although some voters would like to see an increase in women's representation, other voters have doubts about women's ability and would prefer to vote for male candidates.[21] In Massachusetts, where the public is fairly liberal, the viability of women state legislative candidates is not an issue, whereas in other states, such as Mississippi, voters are much less familiar with women in leadership roles.

Women sometimes talk themselves out of running, fearing they do not have the right qualifications. Thus, it is not enough for women to possess the right qualifications for office; women must also perceive themselves as qualified. Indeed, studies have shown that women are much more likely to run for the legislature after having been recruited to run; meanwhile, men are more likely to run because they are "self-starters" – arriving at the decision to become a candidate without external encouragement.[22] For example, a recent study of state legislators conducted by the Center for American Women and Politics found that about half of women legislators reported that they first sought elective office because someone else suggested it, while more than 40 percent of male legislators reported that running was entirely their idea.

The status of women in Ohio, which ranks thirty-fourth in the nation for women's representation in the legislature, illustrates the importance of recruitment. Most women candidates in Ohio think that men are more encouraged to run for the legislature than women.[23] Part of the reason that the presence of women in the legislature has declined is the departure of Ohio's first female Speaker of the House, Jo Ann Davidson. While she was minority leader and speaker, Davidson was credited with recruiting Republican women, but she was forced from the legislature in 2000 by term limits. Only six Republican women serve in the Ohio House in 2009, down from fourteen in the 1990s. Only one Republican woman, Karen Gillmor, serves in the Senate.

Because of the gender gap in who runs for office, recruitment by parties and women's organizations remains critical. The reason that women fare better in some states than others has much to do with recruitment, the presence of women in leadership roles, and the types of networks that women have at their disposal. Women have formed networks and political action committees (PACs) to elect more women. State versions of the influential national PAC EMILY's List help elect pro-choice Democratic women to the legislature in such states as Ohio, North Carolina, and

Colorado. Republican women have also organized in some cases, such as a group of Republican women legislators in North Carolina. Other groups, such as Iowa's Women in Public Policy, which recruits and trains women for the Iowa legislature, are bipartisan. Jo Ann Davidson, who founded a leadership institute for Republican women, continues to train women in Ohio. She noted, "We have a growing cadre of women. It is a slow process, but we are making progress."[24] In South Carolina, the only state without a woman in the Senate, a new organization called the Southeastern Institute for Women in Politics is seeking to recruit and train more women to enter politics.

WOMEN GOVERNORS

Statewide elective executive offices, such as governor or secretary of state, are more visible than state legislative offices. Indeed, one woman governor grabbed headlines in 2008: Governor Sarah Palin of Alaska was tapped by Senator John McCain to join the Republican presidential ticket. It is not unusual for statewide office to be a stepping-stone to national office. Palin, a former city councilwoman and mayor, won election to the governor's office by defeating the incumbent governor in her party's primary. She claimed to have taken on the "good old boys" in Alaska and promised to do the same for Washington during her vice presidential campaign.

It is much more common for women to run for school board or state legislature than governor, and studies show that voters may be more comfortable with women in legislative positions than executive positions.[25] Because executive office vests power within one individual, candidates for these offices must persuade voters that they have the requisite leadership skills and can command authority. Running for statewide office typically means more competitive races and higher campaign expenditures than running for the legislature.

On the one hand, that women statewide candidates and officeholders frequently make national news attests to the challenges women face. Jane Swift of Massachusetts, a Republican and former state senator, campaigned for lieutenant governor while pregnant with her first child. She was expecting twins when she ascended to the governor's office several years later to fill a vacancy. When Democratic male politicians criticized her for attempting to govern while hospitalized after her delivery, women from both parties were quick to come to her defense. In contrast, whether men can juggle governing and fatherhood is not usually a public concern.

TABLE 10.3: Only six women served as governors in 2009

Governor	State	Party	Date first held office
Linda Lingle	Hawaii	Republican	2002
Jennifer M. Granholm	Michigan	Democrat	2003
M. Jodi Rell	Connecticut	Republican	2004
Christine Gregoire	Washington	Democrat	2004
Beverly M. Perdue	North Carolina	Democrat	2009
Jan Brewer	Arizona	Republican	2009

Source: Center for American Women and Politics, 2009 Fact Sheets.

On the other hand, women can generate positive headlines and excitement when they set new records. For example, Arizona made history in 1998 by electing five women to hold the top executive offices in the state: governor, attorney general, secretary of state, treasurer, and superintendent of public instruction. In that year, women were 37 percent of the legislature, making the state the second in the nation for women's representation.

As the federal government continues to devolve more responsibilities to the states, state executive officeholders become increasingly important. Governors are positioned to play major roles in policymaking. In 2009, a total of six women serve as governors, including three Democrats and three Republicans (see Table 10.3). The maximum number of women governors to serve simultaneously in the United States is nine, which occurred in 2004 and 2007. Across the country, a total of only thirty-one women have ever held the office of governor, and only twenty-three states have ever had women governors.

Some of the first women to hold statewide offices did so in the footsteps of their husbands. One example is Nellie Tayloe Ross of Wyoming, the nation's first woman governor, who was selected to succeed her deceased husband in 1925.[26] It would be fifty years before Ella Grasso of Connecticut became the first woman elected governor in her own right, without a family connection. In another milestone, Janet Napolitano's election as governor of Arizona in 2002 meant that a woman succeeded another woman as governor for the first time in history.[27]

The American public is very familiar with Governor Sarah Palin, who was serving as governor of Alaska when she became the first woman to ever run on the Republican presidential ticket. But the other women governors are also trailblazers. Take Jennifer M. Granholm, governor of Michigan. Granholm, born in Canada, was first elected in 2002 and won reelection in 2006. In 1998, she had won election to the office of attorney general, the first woman to do so in the state. Although often discussed as presidential material, she is not eligible to serve as president because she was born in Canada.

Like Granholm, Governor Christine Gregoire had previously served as Washington's attorney general – the first woman to ever hold that position in the state. Gregoire's first race for governor in 2004 was so close that a statewide recount was needed. In the end, she won by just 133 votes out of 2.8 million cast. Gregoire won reelection in 2008.

WOMEN IN OTHER STATEWIDE OFFICES

All fifty states elect governors and almost all states also elect a lieutenant governor and an attorney general. The offices of secretary of state and treasurer are elected positions in thirty-five states. Depending on the state, other elective positions include auditor, comptroller, chief agriculture official, and chief education official. Of these statewide offices, women have been more likely to seek offices that are consistent with voters' gender stereotypes. They have been less likely to run for what could be considered masculine offices and more likely to run for feminine offices. For example, a state's superintendent of education position could be considered a feminine office because education is a policy domain where voters have traditionally believed that women are more competent than men.[28] This relationship between office type and stereotypes may occur because women are more likely to come forward to run for those positions consistent with voter stereotypes. Alternatively, party leaders may be particularly interested in recruiting women for these offices.

Women hold at least one statewide elective executive office in about three-quarters of all states today. Women tend to hold the highest statewide offices in those states where women are a greater proportion of legislators and where women have been successful in winning statewide office in the past. In Connecticut, for example, four of five top statewide offices are currently held by women, including the governor's office, and the state ranks eighth for women's state legislative representation. Given the relationship between the presence of women in the pool and the presence of women in higher office, it is perhaps not surprising that there is a relationship between the overall level of women in state legislatures and women in statewide office.[29]

In 1971, only twenty-four women held statewide offices (including governor), 7 percent of the total. In contrast, a total of seventy-five women currently serve, holding 23.8 percent of all statewide offices. Figure 10.4 demonstrates that the presence of women in statewide office more than doubled between 1983 and 1995, but that women's presence has leveled off since then.[30] Women of color have also increased their presence in statewide office, but they remain very few in number. A total of five women of color currently hold statewide office, including Denise Juneau, the superintendent of public instruction in Montana and the first Native American woman elected to statewide executive office. No woman of color has ever served as governor, which speaks to the challenges posed by the intersection of race and gender.

Women have achieved more success as lieutenant governors than as governors. Forty-three states elect lieutenant governors. Balancing the gubernatorial ticket by gender seems to be an attractive electoral strategy – particularly for the Republican Party, which tends to fare better with men voters than women voters.[31] Yet the number of women serving as lieutenant governors has declined in recent years. A high of nineteen women served as lieutenant governors in 2000. As of 2009, though, there are only eight women lieutenant governors – six Democrats and two Republicans. The position of lieutenant governor can be a stepping-stone to the governor's office. In fact, five of the thirty-one women who have ever held the office of governor were lieutenant governors who became governor after the sitting governor resigned.

THE 2008 STATEWIDE ELECTIONS

Thirty-six women were general election candidates for statewide office in 2008. Election years for many statewide offices do not typically coincide with presidential election years. In the non-presidential-election year 2002, for example, there were thirty-six gubernatorial races; in the presidential election year of 2008, there were only eleven. Four women ran in the general election for the eleven gubernatorial races. Although the first woman governor served in 1925, it remains unusual for women to run for or hold the office of governor. There was only one newly elected woman governor in 2008: Beverly Perdue, the first woman to be elected governor of North Carolina.

The 2008 election was not particularly noteworthy overall for women in statewide office. Women continue to be more likely to seek some statewide offices than others. For example, although there were eleven

Figure 10.4: The proportion of women elected to statewide office has declined in recent years.

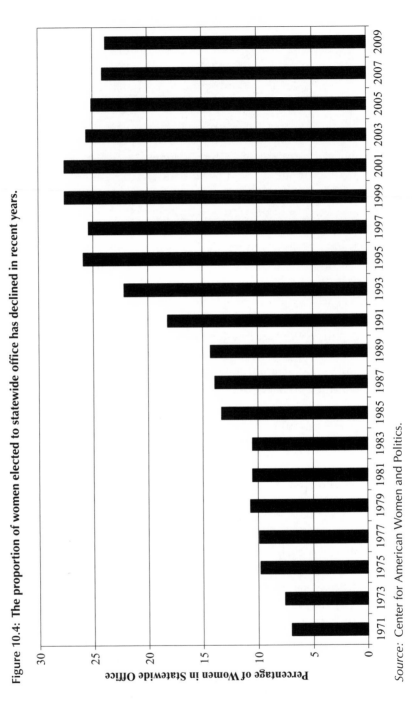

Source: Center for American Women and Politics.

280

TABLE 10.4: The presence of women varies by type of statewide office

Office	Percentage of offices held by women in 2009
Governor	12
Lieutenant governor	19
Attorney general	9
Secretary of state	34
State treasurer	26

Note: Selected statewide executive elective positions.
Source: Center for American Women and Politics.

races for attorney general in 2008, only two women ran in the general election for those seats, and neither of them won election. In contrast, six women ran in secretary-of-state contests and all six won, including three incumbents. Today, women constitute a greater share of all secretaries of state and treasurers than attorneys general or governors (see Table 10.4).

Because state legislative office can be a credential for statewide office, the party gap among women state legislators shapes the status of women at the statewide level. Democratic women outnumber Republican women in statewide executive elective office overall. At twenty-two, the number of Republican women in statewide office is its lowest since 1992. In contrast, a record high of Democratic women – fifty – currently hold statewide office. Thus, at both the legislative and the executive level, the numbers of Republican women serving are declining. The current number of Republican women legislators is at its lowest in twenty years.

Yet 2008 was record breaking in some respects. Despite an overall decline in statewide executive officeholding in 2008, women won six of North Carolina's ten statewide executive offices, also known as the Council of State (see Table 10.5). In some respects, it might seem surprising that women accomplished this feat in North Carolina, given that women are least well represented in the South. However, women have been making inroads in that state. Today, women are 26 percent of the legislature, making North Carolina twentieth in the country for women's legislative representation. And the six women elected to the Council of State are not new to politics; four of the six served in the legislature prior to running statewide, including Governor Perdue, who first won election to the North Carolina House of Representatives in 1986. At that time, she faced skepticism that a woman could win a seat in the legislature from her part

TABLE 10.5: Women won six of North Carolina's ten statewide elected positions in 2008

Office	Woman winner
Governor	Beverly Perdue (D)
Secretary of state	Elaine Marshall (D)
State treasurer	Janet Cowell (D)
State auditor	Beth Wood (D)
Superintendent of public instruction	June Atkinson (D)
Labor commissioner	Cherie Berry (R)

Source: Center for American Women and Politics.

of the state. Perdue went on to cochair the powerful Senate Appropriations Committee and developed a reputation for recruiting more women to the legislature. She was also the state's first female lieutenant governor. Perdue's story demonstrates that opportunities abound for women to set new records in their states and that the women who have set these records typically have long track records in elective office.

GENDER AND CANDIDACY IN THE FUTURE

The states are increasingly important arenas of policy making, and they continue to be training grounds for higher office. Compared to past decades, women have made tremendous progress in both state legislative and statewide executive office. Yet men remain much more likely to run for office than women, and so the recruitment of women candidates continues to be critical.

The 2008 elections largely saw a continuation of the preelection patterns for women in office. In some states, women gained state legislative seats. Elsewhere, however, women lost seats. Democratic women legislators and statewide officeholders outpace their Republican counterparts – a trend that continued with the 2008 election.

Not all electoral environments are created equal with regard to women candidates; some states provide more favorable environments for women candidates than others. For example, women are more likely to hold office in liberal states, states with less professionalized legislatures, and states with a greater share of women in the pool of eligible candidates. Meanwhile, the presence of women in the pipeline of lower offices has implications for where women have been able to achieve statewide office: women fare better statewide where more women serve in the legislature.

While women have made impressive gains across the country, there are many firsts that women have yet to achieve. In most states, women leaders are missing from the highest levels of public office. Women of color, in particular, have yet to win more than a handful of statewide races.

In the coming years, women are poised to seek election to the governor's mansion in several states. For example, Senator Kay Bailey Hutchison, the first woman to represent her state in the U.S. Senate, will run for governor of Texas in 2010. Prior to winning her Senate seat, Hutchison, a Republican, had served in the Texas House of Representatives and had been elected Texas state treasurer. Hutchison will be challenging an incumbent of her own party, Governor Rick Perry. In New Jersey, Governor Jon Corzine picked a woman, State Senator Loretta Weinberg, to serve as his 2009 running mate for lieutenant governor, a newly created office in the state. Corzine's Republican competitor, Chris Christie, named his female running mate first: Monmouth County Sheriff Kim Guadagno.

As more women run for state legislative and statewide office, voters become more accustomed to women candidates. With generational change and increases in women's officeholding, we are now seeing mother-daughter political legacies. As Chellie Pingree is seated in Congress as a newly elected representative from Maine, her daughter Hannah will preside over Maine's House. Although Dianne Byrum of Michigan no longer serves in the Michigan House because of term limits, her twenty-eight-year-old daughter, Barb Byrum, won the 2006 race to replace her.

Progress for women is occurring at an uneven pace across the country. The comparison of New Hampshire with South Carolina is a reminder of the vast differences women face across states. The dearth of women candidates continues to be a vexing problem for those who would like to see the number of women in office rise – particularly on the Republican side. Whether future elections will see an increase or decrease in women's representation in the states will depend on whether women put themselves forward as candidates for public office, and whether they are recruited.

NOTES

1 All data on women officeholders and candidates are from the Center for American Women and Politics (CAWP), Eagleton Institute of Politics, Rutgers University. The author is grateful to Gilda Morales and Kelly Dittmar for their assistance.
2 Eric Moskowitz. November 12, 2008. Gamely, Women Gain Grip on the Granite State. *Boston Globe.*

3 National Conference of State Legislatures. 2008. Movin' on Up: Half of Congress from Statehouses. <http://ncsl.typepad.com/the_thicket/2008/11/movin-on-up-half-of-congress-from-statehouses.html> December 27, 2008.

4 National Conference of State Legislatures. 2008. 2008–09 (Post-Election) Partisan Composition of State Legislatures. <http://www.ncsl.org/statevote/partycomptable2009.htm> December 27, 2008.

5 National Conference of State Legislatures. 2008. Seats Up in 2008. <http://www.ncsl.org/magazine/articles/2008/08slsep08_perils.htm> December 27, 2008; Center for American Women and Politics. October 6, 2008. Election 2008: Women Candidate Numbers Down from Recent Records. Press release. New Brunswick, NJ: Center for American Women and Politics, Eagleton Institute of Politics, Rutgers University.

6 R. Darcy, Susan Welch, and Janet Clark. 1994. *Women, Elections, and Representation*, 2nd ed. Lincoln: University of Nebraska Press; Richard A. Seltzer, Jody Newman, and Melissa Vorhees Leighton. 1997. *Sex as a Political Variable: Women as Candidates and Voters in U.S. Elections.* Boulder, CO: Lynne Rienner.

7 National Conference of State Legislatures. 2004. Uncontested State Legislative Seats, 2004. <http://www.ncsl.org/programs/press/2004/unopposed_2004.htm> December 15, 2004.

8 Richard L. Fox and Jennifer L. Lawless. 2004. Entering the Arena? Gender and the Decision to Run for Office. *American Journal of Political Science* 48: 264–80.

9 Susan J. Carroll and Krista Jenkins. 2001. Unrealized Opportunity? Term Limits and the Representation of Women in State Legislatures. *Women & Politics* 23: 1–30.

10 Ivy Hughes. February 16, 2008. The Byrum Brand. *Dome Magazine.* <http://www.domemagazine.com/features/feb08/cover_feb08.html> February 7, 2009.

11 Peter Slevin. April 22, 2007. After Adopting Term Limits, States Lose Female Legislators. *Washington Post.*

12 The number of 2008 women general election candidates is highly correlated with the number of women legislators serving in 2008 ($r = .96$, $p < .001$).

13 Kira Sanbonmatsu. 2006. State Elections: Where Do Women Run? Where Do Women Win? In *Gender and Elections: Shaping the Future of Gender and American Politics*, ed. Susan Carroll and Richard Fox. New York: Cambridge University Press 189–214. See also Barbara Norrander and Clyde Wilcox. 1998. The Geography of Gender Power: Women in State Legislatures. In *Women and Elective Office: Past, Present, and Future*, ed. Sue Thomas and Clyde Wilcox. New York: Oxford University Press 103–117; Kevin Arceneaux. 2001. The 'Gender Gap' in State Legislative Representation: New Data to Tackle an Old Question. *Political Research Quarterly* 54: 143–60.

14 Pew Center on the States. 2003. The Pew Center on the States State Legislators Survey: A Report on the Findings. Princeton Survey Research Associates.

15 National Conference of State Legislatures. 2008. Full-and Part-Time Legislatures. <http://www.ncsl.org/programs/press/2004/backgrounder_fullandpart.htm> December 27, 2008.

16 National Conference of State Legislatures. 2008. Full-and Part-Time Legislatures. <http://www.ncsl.org/programs/press/2004/backgrounder_fullandpart.htm> December 27, 2008.

17 I conducted interviews with party leaders, state legislators, and political activists across several states in 2001 and 2002. Kira Sanbonmatsu. 2006. *Where Women Run: Gender and Party in the American States.* Ann Arbor: University of Michigan Press.

18 Ibid.

19 Albert Nelson. 1991. *The Emerging Influentials in State Legislatures: Women, Blacks, and Hispanics.* Westport, CT: Praeger; Kira Sanbonmatsu. 2002. Political Parties and the Recruitment of Women to State Legislatures. *Journal of Politics* 64: 791–809; Kira Sanbonmatsu. 2006. *Where Women Run: Gender and Party in the American States.* Ann Arbor: University of Michigan Press.

20 Kira Sanbonmatsu. 2006. *Where Women Run: Gender and Party in the American States.* Ann Arbor: University of Michigan Press.

21 Leonie Huddy and Nayda Terkildsen. 1993. Gender Stereotypes and the Perception of Male and Female Candidates. *American Journal of Political Science* 37: 119–47; Barbara C. Burrell. 1994. *A Woman's Place Is in the House: Campaigning for Congress in the Feminist Era.* Ann Arbor: University of Michigan Press; Kira Sanbonmatsu. 2002. Gender Stereotypes and Vote Choice. *American Journal of Political Science* 46: 20–34.

22 Gary F. Moncrief, Peverill Squire, and Malcolm E. Jewell. 2001. *Who Runs for the Legislature?* Upper Saddle River, NJ: Prentice Hall.

23 Sanbonmatsu 2006.

24 Dennis J. Willard. February 17, 2008. State Is Regressing in Electing Women at One Time, Ohio Ranked 15th in Nation for Females in Legislature. *Akron Beacon Journal.*

25 Leonie Huddy and Nayda Terkildsen. 1993. The Consequences of Gender Stereotypes for Women Candidates at Different Levels and Types of Office. *Political Research Quarterly* 46: 503–25.

26 Susan J. Carroll. 2004. Women in State Government: Historical Overview and Current Trends. *Book of the States 2004.* Lexington, KY: Council of State Governments.

27 Center for American Women and Politics. 2009. Statewide Elective Executive Women 2009. New Brunswick, NJ: Center for American Women and Politics, Eagleton Institute of Politics, Rutgers University.

28 Richard L. Fox and Zoe M. Oxley. 2003. Gender Stereotyping in State Executive Elections: Candidate Selection and Success. *Journal of Politics* 65: 833–50.

29 Carroll 2004.

30 Carroll 2004.

31 Richard L. Fox and Zoe M. Oxley. 2005. Does Running with a Woman Help? Evidence from U.S. Gubernatorial Elections. *Politics & Gender* 1: 525–46.

Index